The TRS-80
MODEL 100
PORTABLE COMPUTER

A Complete Step-by-Step Learner's Manual

by DAVID A. LIEN

COMPUSOFT® PUBLISHING

A DIVISION OF COMPUSOFT, INC., SAN DIEGO

Copyright© 1983 by CompuSoft Publishing, A Division of CompuSoft, Inc., San Diego, CA 92119

All rights reserved. No part of this publication may be reproduced, stored in a retrieval system, or transmitted, in any form or by any means, electronic, mechanical, photocopying, recording or otherwise, without the prior written permission of the publisher. No patent liability is assumed with respect to the use of the information contained herein. While every precaution has been taken in the preparation of this book, the publisher assumes no responsibility for errors or omissions. Neither is any liability assumed for damages resulting from the use of the information contained herein. Portions of the material contained herein were originally created by the author for Radio Shack in support of the TRS-80 computer.

CompuSoft® is a registered trademark of CompuSoft, Inc.

This book contains official CompuSoft® software.

TRS-80 is an registered trademark of Radio Shack, a Division of Tandy Corporation.

International Standard Book Number: #0-932760-17-1

Library of Congress Catalog Card Number: #83-72487

10 9 8 7 6 5 4 3 2 1

Printed in the United States of America.

A Personal Note From DAVID A. LIEN Author

The Model 100 is the most exciting computer I have seen since the old Model I, and preparing this book to make it usable has been a real delight.

In 1976-1977 I participated in development of the original Model I TRS-80 -- and wrote the original book for it. Translated into many foreign languages, it probably remains the world's best selling full length computer book. The old Model I TRS-80 opened the computer frontier to countless millions, and it was fun to be there at the very beginning.

But a lot has changed. One single portable computer with all the features of the Model 100 was not 'even a wild dream in 1976. The technology simply did not exist until now.

I wrote this book for the average person who has no computer experience. The style is light and non-threatening. You will be using your Model 100 effectively and profitably in less than an hour!

It's not necessary to learn everything in this thick book, unless you want to. It's written so you can learn only those features which correspond with your needs and interests.

Busy executives will learn to use the NOTEBOOK and SCHEDULING features. Those who travel will learn how to SEND and RECEIVE memos, orders and contracts over the telephone. Programmers learn to write programs in the BASIC computer language, and anyone with anything to write will use the built-in WORD PROCESSOR. Beginners of all ages can use the Model 100 and this book to gain computer literacy and learn BASIC programming.

Enjoy your new computer! With this book, it can become the best investment you've made in a long time.

Dr. David A. Lien
San Diego -- 1983

Acknowledgements

The following played key roles in the creation of this book:

Technical Director: Dave Waterman
Technical Researchers:
    Maria Melendrez
    Morgan Davis
    Linh Nguyen
    Steve Frostrom
    Mark Schaffroth
Editorial Director: Gary Williams
Production Coordinator: Janice Scanlan
Cartoons and Illustrations: Bob Stevens

and Margie McMurray, Personnel Manager, and Jackie Bohan, Associate Marketing Director, who use Model 100s daily at CompuSoft.

Introduction

This manual is actually two books in one. Book One introduces you to the Model 100 and all its remarkable built-in capabilities.

Book Two is a complete course in BASIC programming, Model 100 style.

While the first two parts of Book One are required reading for everybody, the rest of the Manual is divided into Parts from which you can pick and choose as you have the desire or need.

Here is the "Curriculum":

BOOK ONE

    Part 1 -- **Set Up** (Required of all readers)
    Teaches how to set up the Model 100, set the realtime clock and calendar, and understand the different ways to use the keyboard.

    Part 2 -- **Word Processing** (Required of all readers)
    Teaches how to use the Word Processor and its many features to create and edit memos, letters, contracts, BASIC programs and special "notes" to transmit and receive over a telephone line.

    Part 3 -- **The Little Black Book** (Optional)
    Teaches the use of the Model 100's "information manager" in keeping track of schedules, addresses, notes and other personalized reminders, and its "Find" capabilities for instant access to this information.

    Part 4 -- **A Message to Garcia** (Optional)
    Teaches how to use the Model 100 to communicate with other computers, both inside the office and over a telephone line.

BOOK TWO

Book Two teaches how to write programs in the BASIC language in 50 fun-filled Chapters. At the end of many Chapters are Exercises to test your knowledge and exercise your creativity.

Appendices

Include all the necessary charts and tables as well as Answers to Exercises. Interesting and practical User's Programs are ready to type right in and use. Some are for business, some for education, and some just for fun.

We hope you have as much fun learning with this book as we did preparing it.

Table of Contents

T.M. EMPKIE MD

A Personal Note from the Author	iii
Acknowledgements	v
Introduction	vii

BOOK ONE: THE MODEL 100's BUILT-IN CAPABILITIES

Part 1: Set Up — xv

1	Insert Tab A into Slot B	1
2	The Keyboard	6
3	Tecktalk	15

Part 2: Word Processing — 21

4	Beginning Word Processing	23
5	Intermediate Word Processing	29
6	More Cut and Paste	36

Part 3: The Little Black Book — 41

7	The Scheduled Life	43
8	The Black Book	51

Part 4: A Message to Garcia — 57

9	Why Telcom?	59
10	The Other Connection	67
11	Reading the Mail	77
12	A Letter to the Office	83
13	Talking Computer to Computer	89

BOOK TWO: LEARNING MODEL 100 BASIC

Part 1. BASIC's Basics — 101

1	Getting Ready	103
2	Expanded Program	108
3	Using the EDITor	116
4	The Soft Keys	122

Part 2. Speak to Me, Oh Great Computer — 127

5	Math Operators	129
6	Scientific Notation	138
7	Using ( ) and the Order of Operations	141
8	Relational Operators	146
9	It Also Talks and Listens	152
10	Calculator or Immediate Mode	157
11	Saving and Loading BASIC Programs	163
12	FOR-NEXT Looping	170
13	Son of FOR-NEXT	180
14	Formatting with TAB	188
15	Grandson of FOR-NEXT	193
16	The INTeger Function	199
17	More Branching Statements	209
18	RaNDom Numbers	218
19	READing DATA	226

Part 3. Strings — 233

20	Intermediate BASIC	235
21	The ASCII Set	246
22	Strings in General	251
23	Measuring Strings	256
24	VAL and STR$(N)	264
25	Having a Ball with Strings	268

Part 4. Variable Precision and Math — 281

26	What Price Precision?	283
27	Intrinsic Math Functions	292
28	The Trigonometric Functions	300

Part 5. Graphics and Display Formatting — 307

29	Video Display Formatting	309
30	Intermediate Graphics	319
31	Display Formatting with PRINT@	330
32	Graphing Trig Functions	335
33	INKEY$	340
34	PRINT USING	347
35	PRINT USING - Round 2	356
36	Using a Printer	365

Part 6. Arrays　　　　　　　　　　　　　　　　　　　　　　　　　　　　373

37	Arrays	375
38	Search & Sort	387
39	Multi-Dimension Arrays	395
40	Advanced Graphics	405
41	Graphic INKEY$	416

Part 7. Sound　　　　　　　　　　　　　　　　　　　　　　　　　　　　　423

42	A Cheap Buzz	425

Part 8. Miscellaneous　　　　　　　　　　　　　　　　　　　　　　　　　433

43	PEEK and POKE	435
44	Logical Operators	442
45	Advanced Saving and Merging of BASIC Programs	452
46	File Handling	459
47	A Study of Obscurities	467

Part 9. Program Control　　　　　　　　　　　　　　　　　　　　　　　　481

48	Flowcharting	483
49	Debugging Programs	489
50	Chasing the ERRORs	500

Appendices　　　　　　　　　　　　　　　　　　　　　　　　　　　　　　509

Appendix A -- ASCII Chart	511
Appendix B -- Control Codes	519
Appendix C -- Reserved Words	521
Appendix D -- Communication Parameters	522
Appendix E -- Error Report Codes	523
Appendix F -- Hex-to-Decimal Conversion Chart	525
Appendix G -- Answers to Exercises	526
Appendix H -- User Programs	543

Index　　　　　　　　　　　　　　　　　　　　　　　　　　　　　　　　　549

Book 1

The Model 100's Built-In Capabilities

"Keys F1 thru F8 are called *Function* or *'Soft Keys'*. They can be changed to do different things under different circumstances."

Part 1

Set Up

Chapter 1

Insert Tab A into Slot B...

Out of the box it comes.

Just one little thing. Did you buy batteries?

Batteries?

Yes. 4 size AA Alkaline cells are needed unless you bought the TRS-80 AC Adapter (Cat. No. 26-3804).

All Set?

Now we can proceed.

    1. Install the 4 batteries as shown in Figure 1.

    2. Flip the MEMORY POWER switch (located on the bottom) to ON, and never switch if off.

    3. If you have AC power supply (26-3804) plug it into the wall, and the Computer as shown in Figure 2.

    4. Switch your new Computer ON (switch located on the right edge).

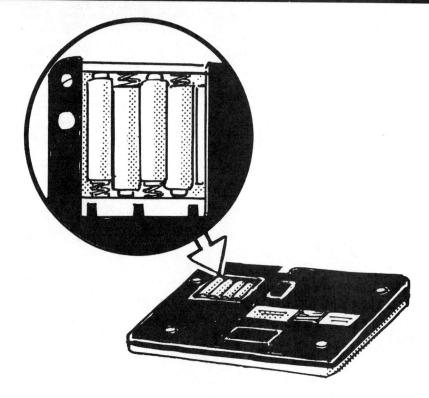

Figure 1

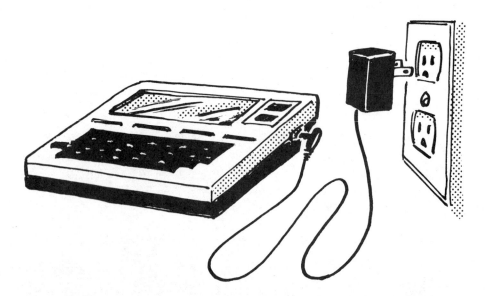

Figure 2

> If the Computer display doesn't light right up, let it sit for 5 minutes and try again. It takes an overnight charge of the internal Nickel Cadmium storage cell to bring the Computer up to full capacity. The internal rechargeable cell is charged from either the AA batteries or the AC power supply.

5. Adjust the display using the DISP knob located next to the Power Switch until it is the easiest to read. The LIQUID CRYSTAL DISPLAY (LCD) has a narrow range of visibility, so this adjustment needs to be made each time the Computer is moved very far.

We are now up and running!

Setting the Clock

We have to set the clock and calendar only once, like right now.

If the shaded (reversed) block isn't over the word BASIC it means you've been fiddling with the keys. If so, turn the Computer OFF, then ON again.

```
Sep 16,1983 Fri  10:54:29    (C)Microsoft
 BASIC       TEXT        TELCOM      ADDRSS
 SCHEDL      -.-         -.-         -.-
 -.-         -.-         -.-         -.-
 -.-         -.-         -.-         -.-
 -.-         -.-         -.-         -.-
 -.-         -.-         -.-         -.-
Select: ▓                    29638 Bytes free
  ⸺1  ⸺2  ⸺3  ⸺4  ⸺5  ⸺6  ⸺7  ⸺8
```

Now press the **ENTER** key.

Altho we don't want to learn the BASIC Computer language at this instant, we are now in what is called its BASIC INTERPRETER. Nearly all commands to do special things with the Computer are given from the Model 100's BASIC INTERPRETER.

Carefully and slowly type:

    `DATE$="06/30/84"`   **ENTER**   (using today's date)

> Be sure to place the / exactly as shown above.

then

      `TIME$="14:35:00"`   **ENTER**   (if the time is 2:35:00 PM)

The standard 24 hour clock is used instead of AM and PM.

then

      `DAY$="THU"`   **ENTER**   (if today is Thursday)

Use only the first 3 letters of the day.

Press key **F8**. It is always used to return us from whatever we were doing back to the safe harbor, otherwise known as the *MAIN MENU*.

The top line of the MENU should now display the same DATE, DAY and TIME we just entered, and the clock should be running. If it's not correct, go back into BASIC and simply retype the DATE, TIME or DAY that is wrong.

See -- there's nothing to this Computer business!

Memories

Look at the lower right hand corner of the display. It tells how many "Bytes" are free. For our purposes, a Byte is roughly the amount of memory space required to remember 1 single keystroke. Depending on how much memory you purchased, the number of Free Bytes should be about:

    8K version = 5062
  16K version = 13252
  24K version = 21447
  32K version = 29638

Differences in amount of memory do not affect the operation of the Model 100. Different versions just remember different amounts of information, and more memory can be easily added at the candy store should the need arise.

Having savored a bit of success, let's move onward to our next little victory over fear of Computers, hi-tech, and those other intimidating buzz words.

Chapter 2

The Keyboard

The keyboard isn't nearly as difficult as it appears. Let's take a part at a time, leaving detailed explanations for later when they will make more sense.

If you get lost during this session, press key **F8** to return to the menu. If that doesn't work, press and release the RESET button in the back as shown in Figure 3. RESET is our ultimate PANIC button, and should be used only in case of emergency.

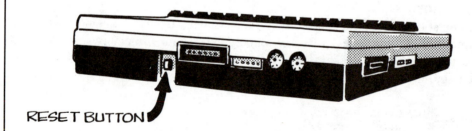

Figure 3

The Shadow Knows

Four keys control movement of the Shadow, or CURSOR.

Play with the cursor controls to see how the arrows move the shaded cursor to different screen locations.

The Keyboard

To be able to fiddle with the rest of the keys we must convert the Computer into a typewriter. Move the cursor over the word TEXT, and press **ENTER**.

The Computer answers our message by saying:

`File to edit?`

and blinks a different cursor at us. A blinking cursor always means "it's your turn." Our Model 100 knows we want to type something, but insists that we tell it a name, first. It will hold our typing in a FILE. Think of it like being a FILE folder, or a FILE drawer. The Computer insists we give that FILE a name.

Since we are all learning, everybody answer by typing:

`learn`   **ENTER**

It seems satisfied, but the cursor is still blinking at us. Don't panic. Let it wait. This is as good a time as any to let the Computer know that it waits on our pleasure, not the other way around. No blinking cursor is going to intimidate us!

If we leave the Computer waiting too long, about 10 minutes, it automatically shuts down to conserve battery power. If that happens, simply flip the power switch OFF then back ON again.

Minor Caution
The ESCape key

should not be pressed at this time as it will send us back to the MENU. If that should happen, just find your way back the same way we got here. When the question:

    `File to edit?`

is asked, answer again with:

    `learn`   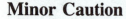

The Main Keyboard
The middle part of the keyboard is just like an ordinary typewriter. Letters and numbers are usually in the same place on all typewriters, but the punctuation moves around from brand to brand.

Go ahead and press keys within the box above. Hold one down and see how they automatically repeat, a great feature for underlining.

Locking Caps
Press the `CAPS LOCK` key and do it again.

The key locks down, so press it again to unlock when done.

Numeric Keypad
By pressing the `NUM` key

these keys become a NUMERIC KEYPAD. Go ahead and press them. Bookkeepers and others who work a lot with numbers really appreciate this feature.

When done playing, press the `NUM` key again, to unlock it.

DEL/BKSP
No messy bottles of erasing paint here.

Press the `DEL/BKSP` key a few times. Then hold it down and erase everything typed in so far. Great for erasing long mistakes.

10   Chapter 2

Sprecken Sie Deutsch?
Some keys can display special foreign language variations.   Press the **CODE** key down

with one hand, and type each letter, number and punctuation key with the other:

Now try holding down the **SHIFT** and **CODE** keys and pressing the numbers, letters and punctuation marks.

A complete set showing which key does what is provided in Appendix A.

Graphics
The last trick involves graphics -- the kind used both in video games and graphing financial or other data. Press the **GRPH** key with one hand:

and again type each letter, number and punctuation character key.

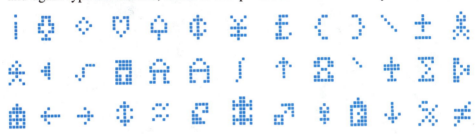

WOW! 39 graphics characters. Did you find the cents sign above the **6**? Try pressing **SHIFT** **GRPH** and see 33 more! This is the sort of thing creativity thrives on. Don't bother writing them down as all are shown in Appendix A.

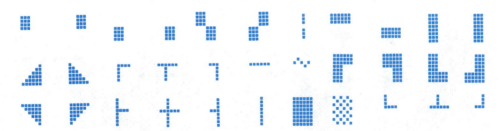

If you want to delve more into the graphics world, hang on. We'll cover it in more detail with BASIC!

On the other hand, if you have no interest in graphics, that's alright. The Model 100 contains far more capability than the average user will ever need or use. There's something for everyone.

Soft Keys

Keys **F1** thru **F8** are called *Function* or *"Soft Keys"*. They can be changed to do different things under different circumstances.

In a sense, most of the other keys are "soft keys" too, but they do have a primary use labeled on them. True soft keys can be changed by the user by making a change in the Computer software. We will learn to do it later, in BASIC.

Meanwhile, press the **LABEL** key

and look at the bottom line. Every key but **F4** has been assigned a specific purpose.

Press **F8**, as before, and we return to the MENU.

14   Chapter 2

Command Keys
The remaining 4 keys

will be discussed in more detail as we need them. In general however, the **PASTE** key is used in the "cut and paste" part of the word processing program. **LABEL** turns the soft keys labels on and off to show what they are used for under different circumstances. **PRINT** is used to send information to a printer, and **BREAK/PAUSE** stops execution of Computer programs or video displays so we can take a closer look.

One Last Look
Look at the display. Do you see any additional entries to the MENU?

Thats right. LEARN.DO was added. The "junk" we typed while learning about the keyboard has been saved in a FILE named LEARN.DO. But, we named it just LEARN?

Yes, but the Computer added the suffix ".DO" to indicate it's something we typed, not a file or program that came with the Computer. Different suffixes are added for different reasons, as we will see.

In this Chapter we entered and exited the TEXT or WORD PROCESSING program. The keyboard, not Word Processing, was the subject of this Chapter, but only files created in the Word Processor add a .DO to their names.

Press on.

Chapter 3

Tecktalk

There are a few technical features of the Model 100 which you must learn and understand. Even if you couldn't care less about the "technicals", please study this short Chapter very carefully.

The Computer memory is powered by a "permanent" built-in Nickel-Cadmium rechargeable battery. This battery is continually recharging from 4 type AA Alkaline batteries which need to be changed frequently. How often depends on usage, and the amount of memory installed.

When the Computer is in the office or at home where 120V AC is available, a converter may be used instead of the AA batteries. The converter keeps recharging the built-in battery and provides power to operate the Computer. One way or the other, the internal battery must be *continually* recharged.

When the Red **LOW BATTERY** light comes ON (front panel below the label), the irreversible demise of what you have created and saved is imminent! The factory says you have only about 15 minutes to turn it OFF, or your files buy the farm.

Turn the Computer OFF almost immediately to conserve the remaining electricity.

In the OFF position, the fully charged internal battery should last from about 8 days with 32K of memory, up to about 30 days with only 8K. If this battery discharges, power to the memory is lost.

Then, exercise one or more of these options:

1) Replace the 4 AA Alkaline cells.

2) Plug the Computer into a 120V AC power supply.

3) Record the contents onto cassette tape so they may be reloaded into the Computer when fresh batteries are available. (Requires carrying a portable recorder or dictating machine with an AUX jack, and special cassette cable #26-1207.)

4) Plug into a printer and make a "hard copy" of everything. (Requires carrying printer cable (26-1409), and being close to a compatible printer.)

5) Do nothing, but don't turn it back ON until the batteries have been changed, or it's hooked up to an AC converter.

Based on extensive global travel experience with the Model 100, we *strongly* recommend carrying a set of premium quality AA Alkaline batteries in the same briefcase, and *two* sets on any trip of several days or more. The red light seems to come on at the most inconvenient time, requiring immediate shutdown to save critical and non-duplicateable information. Just one loss of memory due to battery failure can be devastating, possibly necessitating a great expenditure of time and money to reconstruct.

In the interest of preserving relatively expensive battery power, we recommend buying 3 AC power supplies (26-3804). They are very inexpensive, and can be left permanently plugged in at the office and home, with the third one in the briefcase.

If you plan to store your Model 100 for a long time, it's a good idea to turn the memory switch on the bottom OFF. This should prevent the rechargeable battery from completely discharging. **Do not** turn this switch OFF until you have saved the files on cassette, to another Computer, or have made a hard copy with a printer. Once the memory switch is turned OFF, all files and programs that don't come with the Computer are lost forever.

When travelling with the Computer, it is best to bring along the following:

1. A plastic case or protective cover

2. Extra AA Alkaline cells (8)

3. An AC Power Supply

4. A small cube tap

"PASTING, BLOCKING and COPYING isn't as complicated as it may seem, and is very powerful. When you've done it a few times, its use will become natural and automatic."

Part 2

Word Processing

Chapter 4

Beginning Word Processing

Our TRS-80 Model 100 has a built in Word Processor.

Swell. What's a word processor?

Very hard to describe since it requires knowledge of things unseen by most new users. Sort of like trying to describe *Return of the Jedi* to someone who didn't see *Star Wars*. It's much easier to just go through a lesson or two, and let it speak for itself.

I'm writing this deathless prose on a Computer which has a powerful word processing program (Model III TRS-80). Each Chapter is changed literally dozens of times, trying desperately to get the right words in the right places.

Many years ago I avoided word processing, finding all manner of excuse to ignore it. Having now become a fanatic on the subject, I could not write another book if it meant using a typewriter and all the grief that goes with endless editing, retypes, etc. Wanna buy a good used Selectric?

So much for the testimonial. Let's get YOU using one.

Office Memo
Power up the Computer to its MENU, and see how many Bytes of memory space are free. Write that number down.

The name of our Word Processing Program is TEXT, so position the cursor over TEXT and **ENTER**. Answer:

`File to edit?` with `OFFICE`   **ENTER**

The file name can be up to 6 characters long.

Double check the **NUM** and **CAPS LOCK** keys to ensure they are up, and start typing. Do *not* press **ENTER** at the end of each LINE, only at the end of each PARAGRAPH. Type in the following short letter but be sure to make mistakes. Mistakes are necessary to the success of this lesson. We get to come back and correct them.

```
Dear Joe,ENTER
ENTER
You're not going to believe this, but
I'm using a computer with a word
processor.  I'm not really sure what
it's supposed to do, or how it's
different from a typewriter, but people
sure talk a lot about them.ENTER
ENTER
They say you never have to use an eraser
or white paint, and can move words,
sentences or whole paragraphs around
without retyping them.  When the letter
or memo is in final form, a push of the
SHIFT key and PRINT button dumps the
whole thing out to a printer.  It all
seems pretty amazing to me, and I'm
still somewhat skeptical.ENTER
ENTER
I have to go now.  We're supposed to take
this letter and perform all sorts
of magic on it.  I'll let you know how
it comes out.ENTER
```

First, some observations:

1) Look carefully at the cursor, wherever it's located. The shadow flashes over the character it's covering, alternately displaying it "regular", then "in reverse".

2) Look at the mark which follows each paragraph and separates them. It's a triangle pointing left.

3) Note that there are no special markings at the end of a sentence. Just a period.

Controlling the Cursor
Slow Speed: Ignore the typing errors and practice moving the cursor around.

Move the display "window" up and down the full height of the text. Move the cursor back and forth, learning how to make it go wherever you want.

Medium Speed: Do it all over again, this time holding the `SHIFT` key down.

Do you see that vertically it bounces alternately between the top and bottom of the window? Horizontally, each press of the cursor arrow moves it to the first letter of the next word?

Fast Speed: Do it all over again, this time holding the `CTRL` key down.

Vertically, the cursor goes to either the top or bottom of the text. Horizontally, it goes to either the far right or left of the window.

Good Cursor control is the key to fast word processing.

Now let's learn some more so we can correct the errors.

Inserting
We'll begin by INSERTING some new text. Let's say we want to send the letter to both JANE and JOE.

1) Position the cursor just before the `J` in `Joe`.

2) Type `Jane and` (leave a space after `and`).

That's all there is to INSERTING. It's automatic on the Model 100. The entire balance of the text moved down to accommodate the insertion.

Deleting
Let's change our mind and send it just to Jane, deleting Joe. There are 2 ways to do it.

Forward

1) Position the cursor just after the `e` in `Jane`.

2) Hold down **SHIFT** and press the **DEL** key once for each character to be deleted. On long DELetions, just hold the keys down and it shifts into hi-speed.

Backward (Type `and Joe` back in)

1) Position the cursor on the `e` in `Joe`.

2) Press **DEL** once for each character to be DELeted. To remove the final character, the `e` just after `Jane`, it's necessary to switch to the **Forward** technique above, using **SHIFT** **DEL**.

Summary

The **Forward** mode of DELetion requires 2 keys, but deletes the character the cursor is sitting on. It's usually the simplest way.

The **Backward** mode only requires 1 key, but deletes the character just before the cursor.

Okay, that's a good introduction. You have now learned enough to correct the mistakes in your typing. Finish cleaning up the letter by a process of deleting and inserting.

Closing the File

When you're satisfied the letter is correct, press **F8** and go back to the MENU. It's always a good idea to turn the Computer OFF with the cursor positioned on the MAIN MENU, rather than when in the word processor or in any other program it may be running.

Look now at the number of Bytes free. Subtract the number from the one we wrote down at the beginning of this Chapter. I get a difference of about 18919 - 18235 = 684. If our typing was identical, so should the amount of memory space used. A hand count of the number of keystrokes should be very close.

The Printer

You need access to a printer. There is no satisfactory way around this requirement. Word processing without producing PRINTED words some place along the line is very rare.

The Model 100 hooks easily to any Radio Shack printer, or any other printer that is "Epson" or "Centronics parallel" compatible, including virtually all of the Epson "look-alike" printers. Price bears some relationship to print quality, but compatibility is critical.

More Than You Wanted to Know

From my word processor I will "dump" this text we're reading to an Epson MX-100 dot matrix printer for review and editing. The Model 100 is hooked to an Epson MX-80 for "wringing out" purposes.

Back at the office, another Model III with word processor will feed the final manuscript to a NEC 7730 letter quality printer for final editing. The Model 100 feeds all the above printers just fine, too.

Finally, another Model III with word processor will feed the finished manuscript into a Mergenthaler typesetting machine, the output from which you are now reading. (The Model 100 can also feed the typeset machine, without any modification whatsoever. Just hop right off the plane and plug it right into a printer or typeset machine!)

Assignment: With the Computer and printer OFF, hook interconnecting cable 26-1409 between them. Turn the printer on first, then the Computer.

"Bring up" the file named OFFICE. Press:

SHIFT PRINT

and answer the WIDTH: question with: 40 **ENTER**. Watch the finished letter appear on paper.

Chapter 5

Intermediate Word Processing

We'll continue our study of word processing using the letter to the OFFICE from the last Chapter. Set the cursor to the beginning of the letter.

If you turned the Computer off since we left the last Chapter, place the cursor over `TEXT` `ENTER` to enter the TEXT mode, then `OFFICE` `ENTER` to load in the file named OFFICE. A "short-cut" way to do the same thing is simply place the cursor over `OFFICE.DO` and press `ENTER`.

Search and Destroy

The Model 100 has a helpful feature called FIND. Press the **LABEL** command key and see the bottom display line read:

Function key #1 lets us FIND anything contained in the text. Press it, and see:

`String:`

The question may not seem clear, but its asking us what it should look for, and FIND. Let's have it find the word "amazing".

Type the word `amazing` and press `ENTER`.

Where is the cursor located now? *Amazing,* isn't it?

This time, press **F1** again and see:

<pre style="color:blue">   String:amazing</pre>

It remembered what we looked for last time and is ready to do it again. Press **ENTER**. It looked again, from the present cursor position, and found:

<pre style="color:blue">   No match</pre>

There aren't any more *amazings* in this letter.

Next time we want to FIND a letter, word or part of a word, just position the cursor (usually at the beginning), press **F1** and type in the word sought.

Try it yourself. Pick out at least 3 different words in the letter and FIND them. Use parts of the word and also try using upper and lower case letters. The Computer will find the letters in either case. FIND is especially valuable in finding words in very long letters.

Safety Backup

There are 2 ways to protect our profound scribbling from potential loss, 1 inside the machine, and the other outside it. Let's learn both.

Inside: We frequently want to make a number of changes in a letter, but want to keep the original intact. The easiest way is to make a COPY, as seen above **F5**.

To make a COPY we first "define" what is called a "block". A block is just a part (or all) of the letter we wish to COPY. To copy the letter we:

1) Press **F7**. The Computer will *not* acknowledge this action.

2) Press **CTRL** ↓. The entire text will appear in reverse image, indicating it is defined as a block.

3) Press **F5** to COPY the block into what's called the "PASTE buffer". A buffer is a temporary parking place in memory for pieces of data. We can PASTE blocks of words into either the original letter, or, as in this case, the entire letter into a new safety file. The original letter is totally unchanged.

4) Press **F8** and return to the MENU.

5) Return to the TEXT mode and create a new file we'll call:

SAFETY   ENTER

6) Press the **PASTE** key and see our letter named OFFICE appear in the new file under the name SAFETY.

PASTING, BLOCKING AND COPYING isn't as complicated as it may seem, and is very powerful. When you've done it a few times, its use will become natural and automatic.

Since we are simply COPYing, not cutting or erasing anything, the BLOCK we have in the PASTE buffer remains there until **F7** *and* either **F5** *or* **F6** are pressed in the future.

Press **F8** and return to the Menu. It should look like this:

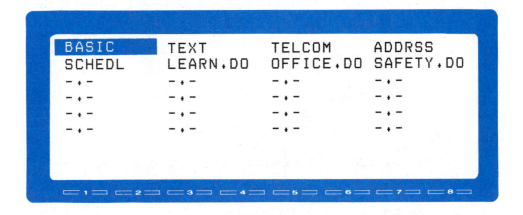

Cassette Storage

The only way to achieve a higher degree of file safety is to make copies *outside* the Computer itself. We already know how to use a printer to make "hard copy".

So called "soft copy" can be made by recording the file onto cassette tape. The process is very simple.

1. Obtain a Recorder (CCR-81 #26-1208), Interconnecting Cable (26-1207) and cassette tape (26-302).

2. Connect the cable between the CASSETTE jack on the back of the Model 100 and the Tape Recorder as shown on next page:

Chapter 5

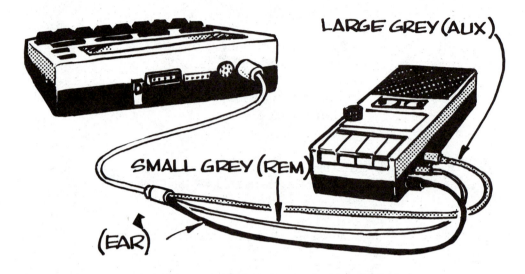

Figure 4

A. The small gray plug goes into the REM jack.

B. The large gray plug goes into the AUX jack.

C. The black plug goes into the EAR jack.

3. Press the PLAY and RECORD buttons *at the same time* until they lock.

4. Press **F3**, and after the Computer displays

    Save to:

"DUMP" the program to tape by typing

    LETTER   ENTER

The motor on the Recorder will start and stop several times while recording the file in 256 keystroke chunks onto the tape.

When the flashing cursor returns and the motor stops, the file is SAVEd on tape. It is also in the Computer's memory having only been "copied" out.

Do it again, for safety, under a different name.

> Any name with 6 or less characters can be used. The first character must be a letter.

LOADing

Reversing the process and loading (copying) the program from tape into the Computer is just as easy.

1. Be sure the tape is fully rewound and the plugs are all in place.

2. Push down the PLAY button until it locks. Set the Volume control to about 5.

> **Important:** Too little or too much volume will cause a bad "LOAD".

3. Clear the display by pressing **F7** and **CTRL** ▼ (or ▲) and then **F6**. If the existing display is not removed, the new LOAD will be appended to its bottom.

4. Press **F2**, and after the Computer displays

    Load from:

type:

    LETTER   **ENTER**

and the data flows from the tape into the Computer.

When the Computer finds the file, it displays

    Found:LETTER

As it accepts the data, the internal speaker lets us listen to the data. *Digital data sounds terrible! You were expecting maybe Lawrence Welk?*

Intermediate Word Processing   35

When the flashing cursor returns, the motor stops and the LOAD is complete. The file also remains on the tape.

> If the recorder does not stop, press **SHIFT BREAK** or the RESET button. This will take the Computer out of the LOAD or SAVE mode and return control to the keyboard.

5. Look the letter over to see that the data transfer was successful. In the event that it was not, repeat the above steps, being sure that all cables are properly connected, *the volume is set to 5* and the tape recorder heads are clean.

When traveling, this optional method of recording information will keep the weight of our luggage to a minimum:

1. Small hand-held dictating machine w/ AUX jack.

2. Cassette cable.

3. Several Computer grade cassettes.

Housekeeping

After all this FILE work, we have more files in the Computer than are really needed. Let's "kill off" the unnecessary ones. First, write down the number of Bytes free.

From MENU, call up BASIC and type the following:

```
kill"LETTER.DO"          ENTER
```

kill any other .DO files except OFFICE.DO and SAFETY.DO.

Press **F8** and check the MENU. See how it cleaned things up and made more memory space available?

Chapter 6

More Cut and Paste

In the last two Chapters we got a brief taste of the EDITing capabilities of this word processor. While the TEXT program is a very elementary sort of processor, it is quite adequate for our portable computer, and even if we don't do much typing, it's important to learn the remaining few advanced features. Readers who continue into the BASIC programming section also need to know these features since they are used when EDITing BASIC programs.

Short Blocks
Select `SAFETY.DO` from the Main Menu. We'll experiment with this copy of our letter and leave `OFFICE.DO` intact for later use.

```
Dear Joe, ENTER
ENTER
You're not going to believe this, but
I'm using a Computer with a word
processor. I'm not really sure what
it's supposed to do, or how it's
different from a typewriter, but people
sure talk a lot about them. ENTER
ENTER
They say you never have to use an eraser
or white paint, and can move words,
sentences or whole paragraphs around
without retyping them. When the letter
```

```
or memo is in final form, a push of the
SHIFT key and PRINT button dumps the
whole thing out to a printer. It all
seems pretty amazing to me, and I'm
still somewhat skeptical.ENTER
ENTER
I have to go now. We're supposed to take
this letter and perform all sorts
of magic on it. I'll let you know how
it comes out.ENTER
```

Press the **LABEL** key to display the soft key functions. In this section we'll get a chance to use the Copy, Cut and Sel keys to edit our letter.

Place the cursor over the letter Y in the word You're in the first paragraph. Now press the **F7** key (Select) and then press SHIFT ↓. Press ↓ (without the SHIFT key) again until the entire first paragraph is shaded. We may end up with a strange looking letter when this is finished, but we're learning Editing, not grammar.

Press **F5** (Copy) and watch the shading disappear. The Computer placed the entire shaded text into the Paste Buffer while leaving the original text intact. In the last Chapter we placed the entire letter in the buffer to make this backup copy. We just replaced it with a single paragraph. Drop to the bottom of the letter by pressing CTRL ↓ and press the **PASTE** key. We PASTEd a copy of the first paragraph to the end of the letter.

Practice using the SHIFT key with the ←, ↓ and ↑ keys to copy other portions of this letter.

Cutting
Since we now have two identical paragraphs in the same letter, let's Cut out the first one. Place the cursor over the letter Y in the word You're in the first paragraph again. Press **F7** and use SHIFT ↓ to shade in the entire first paragraph. When it is shaded again, press **F6** (Cut). The paragraph has once again been placed in the Paste Buffer except this time the shaded area was Cut out of the letter.

Clearing the Paste Buffer
In the last Chapter we "blocked" out the entire letter, then SAVEd it by PASTEing into another file. There is one peril in doing that. The PASTE buffer borrows memory space from our total, and it's possible to tie up so much space with one

long letter and it's safety file and the same letter temporarily stored in the paste buffer that there's no room left for anything else. Here's an easy way to clear out the paste buffer and free up that memory space.

Press the **F7** key (Select) and then press **F5** (Copy). Since we didn't designate (shade) any text to be placed in the buffer, the Computer cleared the buffer and placed nothing back into it.

The paste buffer retains only what it last stored.

"If you can remember even a portion of an entry, it will be found and displayed or printed. So will all other entries which contain the same characters."

Part 3

The Little Black Book

Chapter 7

The Scheduled Life

The SCHEDULE program is a fairly powerful one, with some very interesting possibilities. It allows us to store notes and appointments and schedule-type things -- then quickly retrieve whatever we want.

To use SCHEDULE, we must first create a file named NOTE. The NOTE file contains all our facts. The SCHEDULE program searches the NOTE file for meetings, trips, appointments and other information we have put there, and places it on the display.

Enter the TEXT program and create a file named NOTE. (It must be named NOTE for SCHEDULE to recognize it, and no other file may be named NOTE.)

Let's put this information in the NOTE file. Carefully type the following 3 Lines:

>   ABC   **ENTER**
>   123   **ENTER**
>   3bc   **ENTER**

Return to the Menu (as always) by pressing **F8**.

Position the cursor over SCHEDL and press **ENTER**.

The SCHEDULE program lets us search the NOTE file, looking for whatever we want. Press **F1**:

and have it FIND a 3

The number 3 is found in two lines, and those 2 lines are printed out in their entirety.

```
123
3bc
```

Press **F1** again, this time FINDing a lower case b.

The letter b is found in two lines:

```
ABC
3bc
```

and they are both displayed. But the SCHEDULE program ignored our request for only lower case B's. It cannot make the Upper/Lower case distinction.

Only 3 function keys are used:

F1 for searching.
F5 for printing the FIND on paper.
F8 for the usual return to MENU.

Everybody back to the MENU!

Now let's return to the NOTE file and edit out what we put there. We'll replace it with an example that is more typical and meaningful.

Who, What & When

To illustrate the SCHEDULE program's information handling capabilities, let's assume you're a Manufacturing Director, and you need to schedule and track three products through three departments, and depend on three outside suppliers for parts.

We'll invent a product (which we'll call a Gooseflesh Eradicator) and write a schedule for its manufacture.

Our responsibility for this product involves these departments:

Engineering
Tooling
Production

Supplies will come from:

    Fred's Plastics
    Martha's Metal Fabricators
    Bernie's Boxes

In typing in the schedule it will be helpful if we give each entry the prefix GE, for Gooseflesh Eradicator.

```
GOOSEFLESH ERADICATOR
GE ENGINEERING in 2/15--out 2/28
GE Order plastic from Fred's 2/28
GE Order knobs from Martha's Metal 4/01
GE TOOLING in 4/05--out 5/01
GE Plastic due from Fred's 4/08
GE Boxes due from Bernie's 4/13
GE PRODUCTION in 4/12--out 4/26
GE SHIP DATE 5/01
```

Now, just to make things more interesting, (and realistic) let's throw in the schedules for a couple more current products -- the OMELETTE INVERSION MODULE, and the DIGITAL TOOTHBRUSH. Again, OI stands for Omelette Inversion Module, and DT stands for Digital Toothbrush.

```
OMELETTE INVERSION MODULE
OI ENGINEERING in 3/21--out 4/01
OI Order plastic from Fred's 3/24
OI TOOLING in 4/26--out 5/01
OI Plastic due from Fred's 5/01
OI PRODUCTION in 5/02--out 5/15
OI SHIP DATE 5/18


DIGITAL TOOTHBRUSH
DT Design meeting with Fred's Plastics--4/03
DT ENGINEERING in 4/08--out 4/22
DT Order plastic from Fred's 4/26
DT TOOLING in 5/20--out 5/30
DT Plastic due from Fred's 5/17
DT PRODUCTION in 6/02--out 6/15
DT SHIP DATE 6/18
```

That's quite a lot to keep track of, but nothing a few 3x5 cards couldn't handle.

But, short of reading every card in our file, how do we look up things like:

- What plastic does our supplier Fred owe us, and when?

- When is the Engineering Department going to have some slack time?

- What's going on the day of the golf tournament (5/15)? Can we get away?

- What's going on today?

The answers to these and dozens of other questions is as simple as pushing the **F1** button.

> We entered these schedules in the NOTE file, but, remember, to use them, we have to be in SCHEDULE. So, **F8** to MENU, then cursor over to SCHEDL and **ENTER**.

Suppose we get a message to call Fred's Plastics. Before we call him, we want to have at our fingertips a list of everything he's working on for us, so we can talk somewhat intelligently.

Press **F1**.

```
Schd:   Find Fred           ENTER
```

There before us is every entry in all our schedules that mentions Fred:

```
GE Order Plastic from Fred's 2/28
GE Plastic due from Fred's 4/08
OI Order plastic from Fred's 3/24
OI Plastic due from Fred's 5/01
DT Design meeting with Fred's Plastics--4/03
DT Order plastic from Fred's 4/26

       More   Quit
```

The `More   Quit` at the bottom means that there's *more* than the display can hold. Press **F3** and see one more line.

> Now you see why we stuck those prefixes on the front of every entry -- good to know which job we're supposed to be ordering plastic for on 3/24.

Let's see...we also want to know when there will be some slack time in Engineering...**F1**

    Schd: Find Engineering   **ENTER**

Suddenly we know everything the Engineering department has to do for the next couple of months:

```
GE ENGINEERING in 2/15--out 2/28
OI ENGINEERING in 3/21--out 4/01
DT ENGINEERING in 4/08--out 4/22
```

Looks like we might be able to squeeze in another project in early March.

Finally, and most important, the golf tournament. We can check any date -- today's, the date somebody wants to make an appointment, or the date of something vital, like a golf tournament: **F1**

    Schd: Find 5/15   **ENTER**

```
OI PRODUCTION in 5/02--out 5/15
```

Oops! The Omelette Inversion Module is due out of Production the day of the tournament.

Well, what about the tennis tournament on 5/05?   **F1**

```
Schd: Find 5/05         ENTER

Schd:
```

Nothing. There wasn't anything in NOTE to find, so the Computer just says "Schd:" which means "next request?"

Looks like we play tennis.

But I'm Not a Manufacturing Manager

You may not track projects as part of your day-to-day responsibilities, but it won't take long to come up with some good uses for this instant-access capability.

How about customer names instead of product names? Or territories, or expenses? Think of the possibilities for a research project: enter information in random order, as you find it, and the Computer will sort it out.

The Model 100 can retrieve any character, number, graphic, word, or sentence we put in the NOTE file. Just ask for enough to identify it -- the first word or two, or even the first couple of characters.

Traveling on business? Need to keep track of expenses as they occur? Just place a $ somewhere in the entry, and back at the office, ask the Computer to Find $. Up comes a list of everything you put in with a $ in it, and it doesn't matter how many other reports, schedules, jokes or golf scores you have put in between all those expenses. The Computer will find them all, and line them up neatly, ready for printing out.

Executive Notepad

Do you find yourself jotting down notes on yellow pads? What happens to those pieces of paper? Did your notes from the last two meetings and Joe Smith's phone number and the contact reports from the last three stops and your flight number (not to mention departure time) and the racquetball game you promised Ed and the name of that house painter Shirley recommended all sort of get absorbed into your desk/pockets/briefcase/floor somewhere?

Enter them into the magic NOTEpad any time, anywhere, as they come up.

Even if you're in the middle of inputting a big schedule, or the contents of the wine cellar, stick them right in. Later, to find out when the racquetball game with Ed is supposed to be, `Find Ed`, or if you can't even remember who, `Find Racquetball`, or game, or if you can only remember that there was something on Thursday night, `Find Thursday`.

Develop a set of codes. For instance, an * in a note might mean "important, don't forget". Every day, or several times a day, `Find *`.

Anything important will come to the surface no matter how buried in the pad it may be.

If, during the day or on the plane, you make a note to place a phone call, include the little "fone" graphic `GRPH F` in the note. When you're ready to make phone calls, `Find GRPH F`, and you'll have a list of all your calls.

Don't forget to "clean house" once in a while. We can Find entries in the SCHEDULE, but we have to go back to the NOTE file to change, add or delete them.

The major difference between Find in NOTE and SCHEDL is that in NOTE we Find them only one at a time.

Found in a CompuSoft Computer

The above are admittedly hypothetical examples. To see how this thing is really used, let's look at a NOTE file found in the computer of a notorious CompuSoft executive:

```
6/18 National Widget Conference
2/1-9 New Zealand Bass fishing
12/15 Taxes due on Avocado Ranch
10:00 Tuesday - Another fool Budget meeting
10/08-10 Wyoming antelope hunt
3:30 Today - Phone Mad King Ludwig
7/21 Meet with Broker
7/22 Meet with Swiss Banker
7/23 Meet with IRS
7/24 Pick up tickets to Brazil
```

Chapter 8

The Black Book

The ADDRSS program is virtually identical to the SCHEDL program. Only its application intent is different. It allows us to find names, addresses, phone numbers and other special information we previously stored in a TEXT file named ADRS.DO. Actually, we can store any information we want in the ADRS file, but for the sake of a simple example, we'll learn how it's done using names and addresses.

Begin from Main Menu by placing the cursor over TEXT and **ENTER**

as when creating any other Word Processor program. Name the file ADRS, then enter the names, addresses and telephone numbers of several friends, clients or those who make up your own special hit list. Be sure to include the following, so we can all have a common example:

```
CompuSoft Publishing, 535 Broadway, El
   Cajon, CA 92021  619 588-0996
```

Press **F8** as usual to return to the MENU, then move the cursor over the ADDRSS program and press **ENTER**.

```
Adrs:
```

appears, asking "what address shall I find"?

Notice that the labels at the bottom of the display indicate that only 3 soft keys are used. **F1** searches and displays. **F5** searches and prints on a printer, and of course **F8** returns to MENU. It's the same as SCHEDL. Press **F1**.

Answer `Adrs:` with:

```
CompuSoft          ENTER
```

and see the entire CompuSoft Publishing entry appear.

Press **F1** again and answer with:

```
535          ENTER
```

Same results.

That's really about all there is to it. If you can remember even a portion of an entry, it will be found and displayed or printed. So will all other entries which contain the same characters. Try searching for a single letter and see what happens.

For a complete display of the ADRS.DO file contents, answer **F1** with a simple **ENTER**. If it fills more than one screen, keep pressing **F3** until you've found what you want.

The Yellow Pages

By now you probably have the hang of this finding business, but we don't want to overlook any of the possibilities.

We know that the ADDRESS program will find CompuSoft, or 535 or any other part of the address, but don't forget that it will also find *Publishing*. Furthermore, it will give us a list of all the Publishing companies in the file.

What that means is that we can get a list of all the companies that do a given thing, as long as we have included the type of business in the listing. If Publishing had not been in the company name, we would have to add it when we put the address in the list:

```
CompuSoft Inc. (Publishing), 535 Broadway,
El Cajon, CA 92021   619-588-0996
```

The Model 100 will even do things the Yellow Pages won't. It will allow us to use our own personalized categories:

```
Joan Johnson (Steering Committee) 1234 B St.
Fred Wannamaker (Class of '63) 4567 C St.
Bob Williams (Sales Rep) 8910 D St.
```

FINDing '63 will produce a list of the whole class, (assuming we've listed them all and included '63 in each entry).

Some entries may be on more than one list and therefore automatically cross-referenced:

```
Joe Collins (Class of '63) (Sales Rep)
1112 E. St.
```

Fred's address will show up when we search for all the Reps, and again when we want a list of the Class of '63.

Remember, no changes can be made in the ADRS.DO file from ADDRSS, which is strictly a "read" program. Additions, deletions and changes can be made only by reentering the ADRS.DO file and working it over with the word processor.

"Listen for the dialing relay and watch the numbers appear on the display."

Part 4

A Message to Garcia

Chapter 9

Why TELCOM

TELephone COMmunications between computers is not new, but is always exciting. With this little Computer we can sit in the comfort of our home or office, dial up a Computer that is equipped to talk to us and send or receive messages, memos, telexes, contracts, financial reports, stock market quotations, weather forecasts, make airline reservations and do just about anything else that can be reduced to writing.

That's the good news. The bad news is that we have a problem. Despite these glowing promises it's seldom mentioned that *two* computers are required in order to wallow in this ecstasy. One to send the message, and another to receive it. Our Computer makes 1, and then there's, ah, um, ... you see the problem. Since our teaching style requires *doing* things, not just talking about them, we have to solve this problem of finding a second computer.

Let's assume we can solve the 2-computer problem (since we can), and perform the preliminaries necessary to set up *our* Computer. Hereinafter, the 2 computers will be referred to as *ours* and the *other* one.

A Little Theory

A computer TERMINAL is connected to a COMPUTER via 2 wires. If the physical distance between the TERMINAL and the COMPUTER is great, they will be hooked together by a telephone line.

A TERMINAL can either be "dumb", that is be completely slaved to the OTHER computer, or be "smart", having independent capabilities of its own. Dumb terminals are typically found in business and educational environments where a very large central computer does all the thinking, and many terminals are scattered about, providing the means for many users to talk to it.

More elaborate TELeCOM setups involve a remote COMPUTER talking to the central (or anOTHER) computer. The remote computer, since it can do special things we will soon learn, is a *smart* or *intelligent* TERMINAL. Our Model 100 can work as either a "dumb" or "smart" terminal, or be a complete stand-alone computer which can talk to other terminals or computers.

In order for computers to talk to each other, or to a terminal, arrangements must be made to transmit the digital signals over wires. Altho ordinary telephone lines were not designed to carry digital data, they can do so reliably as long as we don't try to send it too fast. Our normal speed is 300 bits of data per second -- about 360 Words Per Minute. That's several times the speed of a top typist.

We've all heard what computer data sounds like when loading in TEXT files from cassette tape. It's not at all like the human voice. To make all this work, that data has to pass thru converters called *MODEMs* at both ends of the phone line. MODEM stands for MODulator/DEModulator. The Model 100 has a built-in Modem.

There is a lot we are NOT going to learn about the very large field of Telecommunications. The theory of MODulation and DEModulation is one of them. We ARE going to learn HOW to use our Model 100 as both a "dumb" and "smart" terminal.

Setting It Up
Locate the PHONE jack at the back of the Computer. This is where we plug the telephone line into the built-in MODEM. It is necessary to purchase Radio Shack Cable assembly (26-1410) to make the connection. If your phone does not plug into the wall via a U.S. Standard modular jack (as with a multiple line system, at a pay telephone, or in an overseas hotel room) there are other ways to hook the Computer into the phone system. They are covered later in this Chapter.

The Fine Print
Before making any DIRECT electrical connection to a U.S. telephone line, you are required to contact the telephone company and provide them with the following information. (Don't be surprised if they don't understand why you are calling. If they do, don't be surprised if they try to raise your rates -- a lot!):

Manufactured by Radio Shack
Model No: TRS-80 Model 100 Computer with built-in Modem 26-3801
FCC ID No: AWQ9SB26-3801
FCC Registration No: AWQ9SB-70372-DT-R
Ringer Equivalence Number (REN): 0.0B

The Direct Connection

Locate yourself near a modular jack, or a telephone that is plugged into one. See Figure 5.

Figure 5

The Radio Shack cable assembly is really a bit elegant and more than needed for a minimum hookup. It is very nice however, for a semi-permanent installation in the office or home where the Computer is frequently plugged and unplugged, and a telephone must use the same phone jack. Figure 6 shows the connection in its simplest form.

Notice that the phone cable #26-1410 has two cords attached to one round plug, and a round jack is hung on with a plastic strap. Insert the round plug into the jack marked PHONE on the back of the Computer.

If you're plugging into an extension phone jack and don't need that phone for regular phone use, unplug the entire phone and cable from the wall and set it aside. Insert the modular plug on the TAN cable into the wall jack. Let everything else just hang.

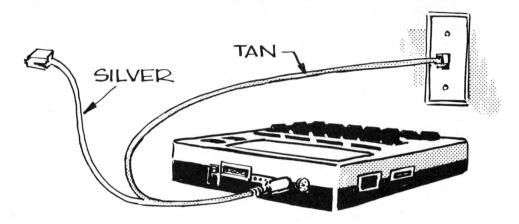

Figure 6

If the phone must also be used for regular voice communications, insert the modular plug on the SILVER cord into the phone. Whenever the Computer is unplugged from the cable assembly, insert the round plug into the shorting jack (hanging on the cord). This reconnects the phone to the wall outlet.

> If the wall outlet is hidden or too hard to reach, the original telephone cord can be used as an extension. Disconnect it from the telephone at the PHONE end (shown in Figure 7) and connect the SILVER cable to the phone. Plug the original phone cord and the TAN cable into the inline adapter.

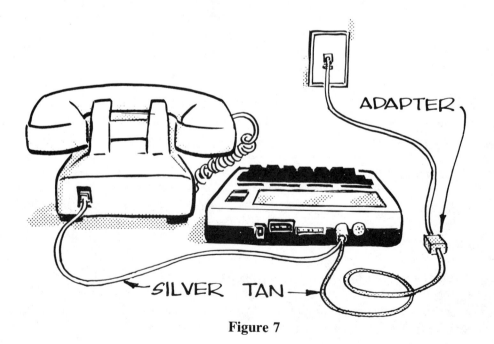

Figure 7

The Indirect Connection
It is impossible to make a simple DIRECT connection to many phones, especially pay phones. The easy way out is to use the *Acoustic* Coupler for the Model 100, Radio Shack 39-3805. These rubber covered muffs slip over the ear and mouth piece of a standard telephone handset. Their use will be covered in the next Chapter, after we finish setting up the Computer.

If you made the connection above without difficulty, or will be using the Acoustical Coupler on a standard handset, skip this rest of the Chapter until such time as you may find need for it in the future.

The Overseas Connection
It is often impossible to find a phone with a modular jack, and the rubber cups on the *Accoutical* Coupler won't fit many fancy phones in this country or others.

Disclaimer
The following information is furnished for discussion purposes only. If you get into trouble with the phone company (or foreign governments) for using it, don't contact us. Likewise, just because I may have used these techniques in the U.S. and numerous Foreign Countries in no way guarantees its accuracy, safety or applicability to your particular situation.

Anyway
If your Computer installation is to be a permanent one, it's best to call the phone company and have a modular jack installed. Second best is to buy a modular jack and install it yourself. They are available at Radio Shack and telephone specialty stores.

Many modern hotel rooms have modular telephones with jacks to match and the techniques described at the beginning of the Chapter apply. Travelers may wish to carry the following kit for connecting to those phone systems not yet equipped with modular jacks.

MODEL 100 TRAVEL KIT
TELECOM OPTION - DIRECT CONNECT KIT

1. Special 3' computer to modular plug.

2. Special 3' computer to alligator clips (Figure 8).

3. Inline adapter -- Modular to Modular.

4. Duplex Jack -- Modular to Double Modular.

5. Tool Kit:

1) Screwdrivers - wall, inside jack, phone base, inside phone.

2) Pliers, needle and diagonal cut.

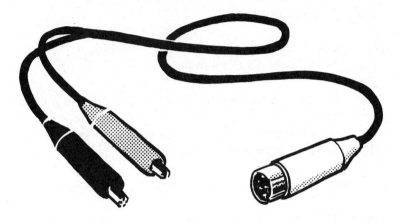

Figure 8

Screwdriver, Alligator Clips...

In the U.S., there is an older type telephone plug which is easy to clip onto. Merely pull the plug out of the wall as far as possible without breaking the connections, then hook the alligator clips on as shown below. It usually doesn't matter which color clip goes to which:

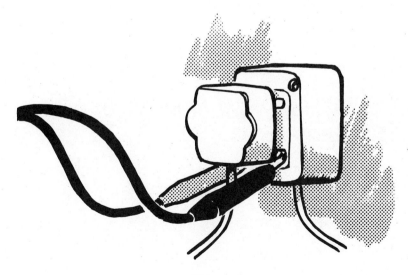

Figure 9

In Europe, 3 and 5 prong plugs are very common. Use the same technique.

If no modular system is used, it's necessary to open up either the wall jack or the phone itself -- usually easy jobs.

1) Remove the wall plate. Only the GREEN and RED wires are needed. Ignore the rest.

2) Clip one lead onto a terminal to which the GREEN wire is attached, and the other onto the RED's terminal.

3) If the wall plate is too hard to get at, or (as in Holland) it's easier to locate the wires by removing a plate from the bottom of the phone, do so. Be sure to use the RED and GREEN wires coming from the wall, not those used for wiring inside the phone.

4) Proceed with communications as covered in subsequent Chapters.

5) When done, "button up" the system as you found it.

Chapter 10

The Other Connection

Even tho we haven't found that elusive OTHER computer yet, we must learn how to make the phone call to make the connection.

There are 3 ways to dial the phone. The most obvious is to simply lift the receiver and dial it with the rotary dialer or push-buttons. This way works just fine if the phone is still plugged in after hooking up the Computer. In fact, since the Computer can only dial using the "pulsing" method, in order to access the new lower-cost forwarding services such as MCI™ which *require* touch tone, use of a touch tone phone is critical. The Computer's "pulsing" system will dial regular "touch tone" systems just fine for all other applications.

The second way to dial is to simply type the numbers on the Computer. The rest is automatic.

The third and most exotic way is to store the phone number (or many different numbers) in our ADRS.DO file (see Chapter 8). The TELCOM program looks up the number(s) and dials them automatically, like an automatic phone dialer. All things considered, except in those special cases where touch tone is absolutely required, automatic dialing is usually preferable.

If you skipped Chapter 8, return there now and learn how to use ADRS.

The Second Way
Turn on the Computer and select:

TELCOM   ENTER

Turn the Model 100 into a TERM by pressing **F4**.

What happened? That scratching sound is the dial tone. It may not sound like a dial tone, but we have hooked the Computer up to the telephone line. Now what do we do? Better learn some more about all this before we get into trouble.

Press **SHIFT BREAK** to Disconnect and return to:

```
Telcom:
```

This time, let's CALL a number and see what happens. If there is a second phone line in the office or house, use its number. If not, use the same number the Computer is hooked to.

Press **F2**, which means CALL. Follow up by typing the number of your choice, using this format:

```
123-4567<>        ENTER
```

The <> is necessary to indicate the end of the number, and prevent automatic hang-up when dialing is complete.

Listen for the dialing relay and watch the numbers appear on the display. When done, you will hear either the other phone ringing, or a busy signal sound scratching in the speaker.

To abort the call, hold down **SHIFT BREAK** for several seconds.

So much for the keyboard method of dialing a number. Let's move right on to automatic dialing so we can forget these preliminaries and get to the good stuff.

The Little Black Book (Revisited)
F8 back to the MENU and select:

```
TEXT        ENTER.
```

Answer the `File to edit?` question with:

```
ADRS
```

> If you *didn't* skip Chapter 8, you already have an ADRS file. In that case, put the cursor over `ADRS.DO` instead of `TEXT` and **ENTER**.

Enter your same phone number in the ADRS.DO file using the following format.

```
TEST:123-4567<>
```

To allow the dialer to call a phone number AND an extension, we would use this format:

```
TEST:123-4567   EXT. 8 <>
```

Press **F8** to store the file, then select:

```
TELCOM         ENTER.
```

The display will show something like:

```
M7I1E.10 PPS
Telcom:




Find Call Stat Term            Menu
 1   2   3   4   5   6   7   8
```

The top line shows the Computer's present STATUS as regards its talking with other computers. We'll look at STATUS in more detail in a minute.

The second line indicates that we are in the Telcom mode.

The bottom line gives us 5 soft key options. Let's start by FINDing the TEST phone number. Press **F1** and:

Find

```
TEST         ENTER
```

As we expect, the TEST phone number is displayed:

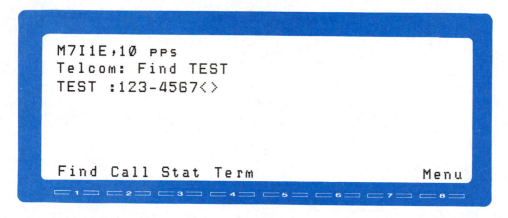

Notice the difference between this FIND and those we saw earlier in TEXT, SCHEDL and ADRS. This listing displays everything up thru the <> symbol. The colon (:) tells the Computer that a phone number immediately follows, and it is ready to perform an auto-dial. The <> marks the end of the number.

Look again at the bottom line. When the Computer found our listing, it reprogrammed the **F2**, **F3** and **F4** keys to read:

Let's go ahead and make our call. Press **F2**, (or simply **ENTER**).

See the **F** keys reprogrammed again to their prior Functions, and each number is displayed as it is dialed.

    Calling TEST:1234567

After the entire phone number is dialed, the Computer makes a grinding sound. This is actually the ringing signal being processed by the Computer and fed to the internal speaker.

We aren't ready to talk to a computer yet, so hold down **SHIFT BREAK** and again bail out of this situation.

The CompuServe Connection

When you purchased the Model 100 Cable #26-1410, it came in a package along with a CompuServe™ Information Service User's Guide and other information and propaganda. If you can understand ANY of it you're not a beginner.

The most important part of that package is a sealed envelope with your **SECRET PASSWORD** and admonitions about keeping the **SECRET PASSWORD**, ah, er secret. Since we only get 1 hour free time on the OTHER computer, unless you sign up for more, it's OK to whisper the password to the dog. It can be changed later, or you may sign up with another service, or have your own OTHER computer. There are lots of possibilities.

In a frenzy of excitement, *rip open the envelope!*

What is this, another credit card application? Ignore all the fine print and look on the bottom for the:

User Identification Number *and* Secret Password

(Isn't this exciting?) My fortune cookie reads:

70076,174 *and* KNIGHT/SLEPT

(And that's how Camelot was lost?)

On the plains of the horizon bleach the bones of countless thousands who, at the dawn of victory paused to rest, and resting, died! (Apologies to Rudyard Kipling, but this password strikes me as very funny.)

Your ID# and PASSWORD will hopefully be different, but for learning purposes we'll use mine to tiptoe through this process. You substitute yours as necessary.

Don't swallow the paper containing the **SECRET PASSWORD**.

Locate the sheet that's titled: CompuServe Information Service Access Numbers. Find the telephone number that's closest to your location. If there isn't one close and you don't want to spring for an hour's worth of Long Distance time, they have a supplemental network system where service is available at a lower toll charge. For that number, call CompuServe Customer Service at (800) 848-8990 or (614) 457-8650.

The Other Computer
F8 back to the MENU, and select:

    ADRS.DO

Add the CompuServe Information Service name and phone number using the same format. This example uses the number for the San Diego area.

    CIS:283-6021<>

F8, back into TELCOM and the familiar:

What is your Status?
Press **F3** **ENTER** for a computer to computer Interfacing STATUS report:

If it doesn't read:

    M7I1E,10 PPS   (don't worry about the details, yet)

simply press **F3** and type the above, then press **ENTER**.

Doublecheck the status to be sure it was changed, by typing **F3 ENTER** again.

The Whole Enchilada
We have one final check to make before we get down to business and make our first real call to the OTHER computer. Look at the 2 slide switches on the left-hand edge of the Model 100. The one toward the back of the Computer can be set to DIR or ACP. Select DIR for a DIRect phone connection, or ACP if using the portable acoustical coupler cups.

Acoustically Coupled

Acoustic coupler cups #26-3806 are specifically made for the Model 100 and do not require an external power supply, thus are ideal for making calls from any pay phone.

Figure 10

The disadvantage of using an acoustical coupler is that the Computer cannot dial the phone. Everything else works as stated.

Who's Going to Answer

For two computers to communicate, one modem must act as the ORIGinator, while the other ANSwers. This has nothing to do with who dials the phone or who answers, it simply establishes which tone each will use to send and receive the data. In most cases the *host* computer (CompuServe in our case) is set to ANSwer. Our Computer must therefore be set to ORIGinate (check switch on left side). If we were to call someone with another Model 100, one or the other must set this switch to ANSwer in order for the two computers to communicate.

The DIR/ACP and ANS/ORIG switches have no effect when using the RS-232C connector on the back (studied later). They are only a concern when using the internal modem.

At Last

With these many preliminaries taken care of, let's **F8** back to the MENU and make our first real call to the OTHER computer, taking it from the top.

    1) Select TELCOM from the main menu.

    2) Press **F1** **ENTER**.   Find CIS. The display now shows:

Chapter 10

```
M7I1E,10 pps
Telcom: Find CIS
CIS:283-6021<>




        Call More Quit
```

3) Press **F2** `ENTER` or just `ENTER` to auto-dial the number.

4) When you hear the tone and the bottom line on the display changes so it reads:

```
M7I1E,10 pps
Telcom: Find
CIS :283-6021<>
Calling CIS :2836021



Prev Down  Up  Full              Bye
```

the connection has been made and the OTHER computer is waiting for us to "Log In."

5) Press `CTRL` and `C` keys.

Note: if `ENTER` is accidently pressed before pressing `CTRL` `C`, the system may ask for the "Host Name". If this should happen, answer with `CIS` `ENTER`. It just tells the OTHER computer that we are using CompuServe Information Service. The normal procedure is to simply use `CTRL` `C`.

6) The system asks:

`User ID:   70076,174` `ENTER` (Enter your own 8 digit ID number)

`Password: KNIGHT/SLEPT` `ENTER` (Enter your own password)

Note: Most OTHER computers do not "echo back" the Password so someone looking over your shoulder can't read it. Of course, we can't read it either, so don't make a mistake typing the Password. This system will accept the Password in either upper or lower case.

7) CompuServe sends the local time and date and allows us the opportunity to change the CompuServe system configuration to match ours. The CompuServe computer will talk to our Model 100 in its normal configuration so simply press **ENTER** and move on.

8) CompuServe sends a welcome message and a long commercial, advising how to sign up as a regular paying customer. Press **ENTER** at each check point until it finally pops the big question by way of a 2-choice menu:

```
1   SIGN UP FOR CONTINUED SERVICE
2   GO TO MENU OF SERVICES
```

Select item 2. They'll take the money anytime.

9) A list of new CompuServe features is displayed. Those that look interesting will be viewed on a later pass.

10) Press **ENTER** at the next check point. CompuServe's Main Menu is then listed. This menu is too long to fit on our display so here is a complete listing:

```
COMPUSERVE                    PAGE CIS-1
COMPUSERVE INFORMATION SERVICE

1 HOME SERVICES
2 BUSINESS & FINANCIAL
3 PERSONAL COMPUTING
4 SERVICES FOR PROFESSIONALS
5 USER INFORMATION
6 INDEX

ENTER YOUR SELECTION NUMBER,
OR H FOR MORE INFORMATION.
```

Let's hurry right on to the next Chapter and explore a few of them.

Chapter 11

Reading the Mail

There is a lot of information flowing between the OTHER computer and our Model 100, much of it faster than we can read. The CompuServe Main Menu is a good example of how there are more items to select than we can hold on the display at one time.

Press **F1**. The Model 100 displays the Previous 8 lines. They are stored in memory at all times for recall and review. The OTHER computer has no idea this is happening, and really doesn't care. It has its own set of problems.

Press **ENTER** (or any other key) and the latest set of 8 lines is displayed. How then do we recall the previous 8 lines?

2 options are available.

   1) Reread the previous CompuServe menu by typing M (for MENU), or

   2) Store the information inside the Model 100 for "off-line" reviewing at a later time.

Option 2 is often the best solution since it allows us to review the information at our leisure. As long as we remain hooked to anOTHER computer, its meter is ticking away, and perhaps long distance charges as well.

Down Loading
Accepting information from anOTHER computer and storing it for later retrieval

is called DOWNLOADING. Its opposite, sending a message from our Computer to the OTHER one is called UPLOADING. We will learn to UPLOAD in the next Chapter.

Let's review CompuServe's Menu item 5, USER INFORMATION. Since we may want to study this later let's first open the Model 100 memory for a DOWNLOAD to store it. Press **F2** then answer the `File to Download` question by typing:

> USER   **ENTER**

...a descriptive name for the file which will hold what we are saving.

Notice the shading around the word Down on the display. As long as Down is shaded, all information entering the Model 100 is being stored in memory. Storage will continue until we either press **F2** again to stop the DOWNLOAD (it does not stop the data from entering the Computer), or until the Model 100 runs out of memory. All isn't lost if the Model 100 runs out of memory. It simply drops out of the DOWNLOAD mode, saving all data received to that point. Select option:

> 5   **ENTER**

What's this, another Menu? Yes. CompuServe is designed around many menus in a "tree structure". Select a topic that looks interesting and read the information as it is downloaded. Continue selecting other menu items and pressing **ENTER** at the various checkpoints.

When you have seen enough, press **F2** to close the Model 100 file named USER. The shading disappears, indicating the Download has ended. If we want to save more incoming information, we can press **F2** and give it another file name. Be sure to select a new file name. If we used the same file name again, all data previously stored under that name would be erased. But for now, let's disconnect from this OTHER computer and review what we have already received.

Press **CTRL** and **C** keys to tell the OTHER computer that we want to quit. After it sends a ! symbol, type:

> BYE   **ENTER**

CompuServe will bid a fond adieu and report the amount of time you were hooked to their computers. Record it to keep track of how much time was used.

Press **F8** (Bye) and answer:

      `Disconnect?` with a Y   **ENTER**

Press **F8** to return to the Main Menu and select the USER file.

Observe how everything received during the DOWNLOAD and everything that was typed in on our keyboard when the memory was open is in the text? We are free to EDIT the text and make a hard copy, just as we would with any other TEXT file.

It's generally a good idea to use the Download feature whenever accepting a message from anOTHER computer. Superfluous information can always be deleted later.

We don't want to waste any more of our "free hour" at this time, so read the rest of this Chapter, then we'll learn how to UPLOAD in the next one.

Your Own Other Computer

If you feel a little flustered and frustrated by our experience on the OTHER computer, don't feel alone. These services tend not to be written for casual users, and are often downright hostile. It's easy to get lost in their extensive branching system and not know what else to do but hang up. There's not much that can be done about it, except own your own OTHER computer.

That idea is not at all farfetched. CompuSoft Publishing has had their own HOST or OTHER microcomputer for over 5 years. There are many options available, but CompuSoft's HOST consists of a plain old vanilla Apple II computer with HOST software (produced by Southwestern Data Systems), further customized and simplified by CompuSoft staff and yours truly. There are better choices available today than there were then, so this should not be construed as an endorsement.

The CompuSoft In-House system is much easier to use than the one we just exercised and is used on a 24 hour 7-day week basis. Writers, researchers, sales staff and sub-contractors use it to pick-up and send their "mail" when convenient, rather than be disturbed at other times. As long as the phone connection is good, it works just great!

On a recent trip to Europe I used a Model 100 to maintain contact with the CompuSoft HOST from Amsterdam and Deventer Holland, Uppsala Sweden, plus Oslo, Stavanger and Bergen Norway. Later, from Hong Kong and Tokyo. Others access it on a daily basis from pay telephones and hotel rooms around the country. No problem!

Your HOST might have the same "Closed Computer" rules. Since CompuSoft's is for business, the phone number is unlisted, users have their own ID#'s and PASSWORDS, and guests are not welcome. Greeting messages at Sign-On time have been deleted and it doesn't waste either phone or staff time exchanging niceties. As a business tool it's powerful and pays for itself quickly.

Other OTHER Systems

There are literally hundreds of OTHER host computers run by computer clubs and hobbyists and which are open to the public. Since they are available to use without charge, the sponsors have no obligation to serve anyone's specific needs, but if you wish more experience with OTHER computers it's suggested that you give them a try.

These public hosts are typically known as BULLETIN BOARDS, PUBLIC MESSAGE SYSTEMS, NET-WORKS and by a score of other names and acronyms. They are found in virtually every medium-to-large city in America and in many foreign countries.

Space doesn't permit listing the systems active today, and such a list would become quickly dated. If, however, you are interested in pursuing this alternative, CompuSoft has agreed to mail a 10 page listing at its cost. Send $5.00 to cover compilation, printing, postage and handling to:

   CompuSoft Publishing
   ATTN: Public Computers
   Box 19669
   San Diego, CA 92119

Sorry, we can't give additional consulting in this area except to point you in the right direction, as above.

Chapter 12

A Letter to the Office

The CompuServe computer does not allow first time users to leave messages. The UPLOADING feature is not available in the first "free" hour. We can still practice UPLOADING however, even though the message will not be stored there. Sort of like Demosthenes practicing orating to the waves.

The purists among us ask the good question "If we can't upload to CompuServe, why spend computer time hooking up to it?"

Answer: We need the "handshaking" which it offers in order to put our Model 100 in an UPLOAD mode. Without the "tone" from the OTHER end, the soft keys will not be reprogrammed and the UPLOAD feature will not be available. OK?

Preparing the Message
The message we send can consist of anything. If you still have the letter we wrote and practiced on in the TEXT Chapters, it will do fine. Its name was OFFICE. (If you don't have it, write another short letter OFFICE).

Select TELCOM and Log-on CompuServe again using the procedures we learned in Chapter 10.

Press **ENTER** in response to the configuration question and at each check point. When the 2-choice menu is displayed,

```
1   SIGN UP FOR CONTINUED SERVICE
2   GO TO MENU OF SERVICES
```

again select item 2.

Press the **F3** (Upload) key after the Menu is displayed, and answer the:

    `File to Upload?`

question with:

    `OFFICE`   `ENTER`

The Model 100 responds with a question:

    `Width:`

...the same question asked as when PRINTing to paper.

Most HOSTS are limited to the number of characters they can accept before receiving an end-of-line indicator, such as an `ENTER`. The Model 100 handles this requirement by letting us specify how many characters we want to send before declaring an "end-of-line". To keep our message compatible with the Model 100's 40 character display width, answer the question with:

    `40`   `ENTER`

As soon as we specify the width, a shadow is cast over the Up indicator. At this point the OFFICE file is sent to the OTHER computer, a character at a time. The shadow remains while the message is being sent. When the shadow leaves, the message has been sent. If the message is sent to anOTHER computer that does not echo the text back for our viewing, we have to rely on the shadow to tell us when the message has been sent since we won't see it as it leaves the Model 100.

The Model 100 doesn't understand the reception it's getting from the OTHER computer so it buzzes that something strange is going on. What is being displayed is a series of responses from the OTHER computer. It can't figure out what we are trying to tell it to do.

Anything typed on the keyboard at this point will be added to our message. If we were actually sending this message to a computer that was paying attention, this would be a good time to add a P.S.

Anyway, that's how UPLOADING works.

By now we have the OTHER computer so confused it's best to simply bail out by hanging up the phone.

Press **F8**.

Answer

    `Disconnect?`

by typing `Y`   **ENTER**

The Model 100 hung up the phone, and the OTHER will recognize that we have left, and will disconnect itself.

Advanced Features (Optional)
The average user can use TELCOM just fine with what we have learned so far, and what we will learn in the next Chapter. In the interest of completeness however, these advanced dialing and logging features are explained.

Speed Dialing
Select `TELCOM`   **ENTER**

Before we make our call, press **F3**. Enter this new Status:

    `M7I1E,20`

This change makes the Model 100 dial the phone at twice the rate we used in prior dial-ups. Give it a try. If it can't handle the faster dialing rate, change the configuration back to:

    `M7I1E,10`

Auto Log-On
Press **F8** then select `ADRS.DO`. Change the entry to read:

    `CIS :283-6021<`   (use your number)

then add this line:

```
=^C?D70076,174^M?dKNIGHT/SLEPT^M>
```
Insert your ID# and Password)

When the Model 100 reads the < sign following the phone number, it enters the "auto-log-on" mode. It continues sending the information after the < until it finds a >. Now let's analyze that second line.

Auto-Log Codes

When the Computer enters the auto-log-on mode, it uses 4 special characters to control the auto-log-on message. They are:

= Pause 2 seconds.
^ Send the following character as a "control" character.
? Wait for a specified character from the HOST.
! Send the next character, including any of these 4.

Our new line starts right off with =. This tells our Model 100 to pause 2 seconds before sending the next character. We can use more than one question mark here since each one gives us an additional 2 seconds delay. One is adequate time for this particular HOST to get set to receive our ID#.

When the CompuServe HOST answers the phone, we have to press **CTRL** **C** before it will ask for our ID#. Looking at the ASCII chart in Appendix A, we find ASCII code #3 is the same as Control C. The ^ symbol before the letter C tells the Model 100 to treat the following letter (in this case "C") as a control character.

If there was a need to send two or more consecutive **CTRL** codes, each code must be preceded by a ^. For example:

```
^C^XM
```

would tell the Model 100 to send a Control C, followed by a Control X, followed by the letter M.

?D tells the Model 100 to wait until it receives the letter D back from the HOST. Once it sees the D in ID: it continues the auto-log-on sequence by sending the 7 digit ID number.

The ID number is followed by ^M. By sending a Control M (ASCII 13), the

computer has sent the same code that is sent by pressing the **ENTER** key. (Check the ASCII chart if you're confused). We're simply letting the Model 100 do it for us.

At this point we could have told our Computer to wait a few seconds for the CompuServe HOST to respond with the Password question. But, since we're not sure how many seconds delay this may take, we used the ? command followed by the letter d. This tells the Model 100 to wait until it receives the first d (in the word Password) before continuing the log-on sequence.

> The Computer will only recogize a lower-case d. If the HOST were to send a capital letter D, it would be ignored and the pause would continue until a d was received.

When the d in Password is received, the Model 100 sends our personal Password. We could have selected any letter in Password, but it's best to select one near the end to avoid sending our answer before the system is ready to receive it.

After our password is sent, another **CTRL** **M** is sent to tell the HOST to **ENTER** our password into the system.

What would happen if we wanted to send a question mark after our Password?

```
=^C?D70076,174^M?dKNIGHT/SLEPT?^M>
```
(use your ID# and Password)

The ? is a legitimate character that could be used as part of the Password. However, the Model 100 would see the ? as a code to wait for the following character (^) before continuing through the sequence. By placing our fourth log-in command (!) before the question mark, the log-on routine sends ? as if it were any other character.

```
=^C?D70076,174^M?dKNIGHT/SLEPT!?^M<
```

Check your completed log-on message to make sure it looks like this sample:

```
CIS :283-6021<
    =^C?D70076,174^M?dKNIGHT/SLEPT^M>
```
(use your ID# and Password)

Then press **F8** to return to the Main Menu.

Putting Auto-Log-On to Work
Select TELCOM and press **F1** **ENTER**. The display will show:

```
CIS :283-6021<>
```

Notice that our log-on message does not display all the automatic and private information we placed between the <> signs. The entire log-on message is purposely left off the display to protect its confidentiality.

Go For It
When you press **ENTER** the next time, things happen fast, so watch the display carefully.

When the dialing sequence is completed, the Computer buzzes as the phone rings and when the tone is received from the remote modem. If you hear a pulsing type clicking sound, the line is busy. Press **SHIFT** **BREAK**, wait a few minutes and start the sequence over by pressing **F1**.

Once the connection is made, the auto-log-on sequence begins. No sooner are the questions received from the CompuServe Computer, than they are answered by our Model 100.

When you feel comfortable with what we've learned in these last 3 Chapters, use up the remaining time to explore different areas in the CompuServe Menus.

Chapter 13

Talking Computer to Computer

The Computer Handshake

In order for any two computers to converse they must speak the same language and be able to coordinate who speaks when. Only one can talk at a time. Most computers, terminals and printers are equipped with standard connections and conversational instructions known as the RS-232C Serial Interface.

Even though the connections and voltage levels used are standard, there are many different "protocols" that can be selected by the communications software. Both systems must have their STATUS configured the same way so they have what is known in the biz as a proper "handshake". Handshaking means both systems have agreed on a mutual set of communications formats which allow them to talk to each other.

Establishing a Common Language

The Model 100 is capable of changing its software configuration to match that of just about any other RS-232C system. All that is needed is to determine what the other system is using. For this example we will hook our Model 100 to a TRS-80 Model III or Model 4 (in the Model III mode) with the Radio Shack Videotex software (#26-1588). If you are using any other computer or communications software, refer to its operation manual for its RS-232C parameters and software protocols.

Turn on the Model 100 in TELCOM. Using **F3**, change the status to:

   38N1D   **ENTER**

Looking at the Communications Parameter Chart in Appendix D, we can see what these letters and numbers represent.

3   Tells the Model 100 to send the data direct through the regular (not phone) RS-232C connector in the back.

8   Send each character using 8 bits of data.

N   No error checking bit (parity) to be used.

1   Send 1 pulse (bit) at the end of each character to indicate the end.

D   Disable remote control of data output.

The dialing rate is not specified since we will not be dialing a telephone.

A special back-to-back ("null modem") adapter (#26-1496) must be used when connecting the standard RS-232 cable (#26-1408) between the Model 100 and the Model III. We found that it's easier to use the standard cable (#26-1408) and simply reverse the leads on pins 2 and 3 on either connector. This way only one cable (and no adapter) is needed to connect the Model 100 to the Model III. Make the connections as shown in Figure 11.

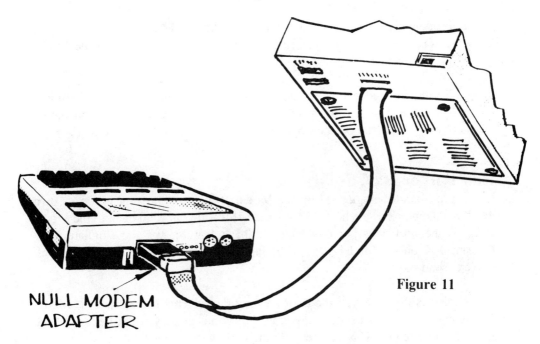

NULL MODEM ADAPTER

Figure 11

The Model III will be the HOST.

Once you have the host OTHER computer in its Terminal mode, its communication configuration should be set to:

> Baud Rate = 300
> Word Length = 8
> Parity = none
> Stop Bit = 1

The Videotex Communication Software boots up in this configuration. It can communicate with the Model 100 as-is. If you are using a different software package or computer, check its configuration and change it as necessary. We want to make sure we are all looking at the same configuration before we make any changes to the Model 100. If you're not sure how to make the changes on your host computer, you can leave it as-is. Once you learn how to do it on the Model 100, you can set it to match the other guy.

Press **F3** `ENTER`

The Model 100 should now show:

> `38N1D,10 pps`
>
> `Telcom: [ ]`

If you accidentally enter a code that the Model 100 can't accept, it will let you know by sending its error beep. In fact, most any wrong move in the Model 100 TELCOM results in a beep.

With the computers connected to each other and both computers in the Terminal mode (**F4** on the Model 100), type a few words on each keyboard. You should see the typing displayed on the opposite computers. It's pretty exciting!

Half Full or Half Empty?

If the information being typed on the Model 100 is not showing up on its own display, this indicates the host computer is not feeding an echo back to the Model 100. If the host does not have this feedback feature, we can simulate it by pressing **F4** on the Model 100. Pressing **F4** toggles between "Half and Full duplex" send mode.

Full duplex is the preferred mode of sending data. This means that the Model 100 is not listening to itself. Anything sent is not displayed until echoed back from the other end. This ensures that the data was received as we sent it.

Half duplex is used when the data is not echoed back. By selecting Half, the Model 100 displays each character as it is sent as well as each character received. Its value lies solely in letting us know where we are in the message being sent, not in ensuring its accuracy of reception.

Direct Uploading

When satisfied that both computers are talking to each other, and both are listening, press **F3** (Up) on the Model 100. When the display shows:

```
File to Upload?[]
```

enter the file name `OFFICE` **ENTER**. If you have removed that file, the Model 100 responds with:

```
No file
Upload aborted
```

If this is the message you received, better go back and reenter the letter or another name you have it stored under.

If this worked properly, the message:

```
Width:[]
```

appears. To see the effect of this question, type:

```
20        ENTER.
```

The shadow over Up indicates it is Uploading. Watch the screen on the HOST. The Model 100 is sending a Carriage Return after each line is 20 characters long.

When the shadow goes out and the flashing cursor returns, the letter has been sent.

Try Uploading the message using different Width values. If **ENTER** is pressed without entering a Width value, the Model 100 sends the data, entering Carriage Returns only as they actually appear in the text.

Direct Down-Loading

Reverse the procedure by pressing **F2** (Down) on the Model 100. Answer the `File to Download?` question by typing:

    `DATAIN`   **ENTER**

The shadow over Down indicates the Model 100 is storing all data that enters.

After you have typed in some data from the host computer press **F2**, turning Download off. The DATAIN file can now be selected from the Main Menu to see what was received.

High Speed Data Transfer

Depending on the capabilities of the host computer, the data transfer rate can be greatly increased.

Following the instructions in your host computer's communications software manual, set its transmission speed to 1200 Baud.

Press **F8** on the Model 100. The display shows:

    `Disconnect? []`

Answer by typing Y   **ENTER**

and after `Telcom: []` returns, press **F3** and enter this new Status:

    `58N1D`

The only parameter changed is the first one. The 5 tells the Model 100 to send the data at 1200 Baud through the RS-232C port as before.

Repeat the Upload and Download steps above and watch the difference in transmission speed. Higher transfer speeds are limited largely by the length of cable between computers. 1200 baud is very fast, and more than adaquate to quickly fill the memory of a Model 100.

Between Model 100's

By using the special "null modem" cable arrangement described earlier, we can interface the Model 100 to another through their RS-232C Ports.

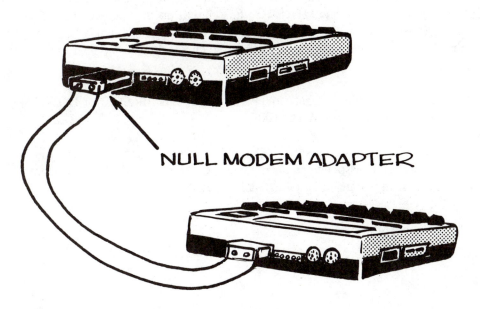

Figure 12

In order for 2 computers to communicate properly, they must both be set to the same configuration. The configuration itself is not important, as long as they are the same. For example, the STAT in both could be set to:

    Stat: 58N1D

One computer must be set to ANSwer and the other to ORIGinate with the switch on the left-hand side of the case. Now, press **F4** to enter the TERM mode. Press **F4** again to switch from sending in Full Duplex mode to Half Duplex. This allows the character to be echoed on the display as it is being typed.

Type this message:

    TESTING 1 2 3   ENTER

If all went well, we should have the words "TESTING 1 2 3" on the display at both computers. If this is not the case, then check to make sure both computers have the same communication configuration (including HALF duplex), and try the test again.

Notice that the Model 100 does not send a line-feed after we press a carriage return **ENTER**. It assumes that the OTHER computer will do the line-feeding. By typing **CTRL J** before or after pressing **ENTER** the Model 100 sends a line-feed function. Do it a couple of times and watch the cursor drop to the next line on both computers.

At this point, we are able to "chat" in TERM mode, and UPLOAD or DOWN-LOAD files between the two Model 100s.

Now go out and talk to somebody -- CompuServe, the office computer, your friend next door, or an associate on the other side of the world. For you, Telcom may be the most important thing the Model 100 does.

Book 2

Learning Model 100 BASIC

Introduction to Book Two

Model 100 BASIC incorporates many of the best features of Radio Shack's original *Level I* and *Level II BASICs* with a few additional ones. This book is written for the beginning programmer who has no computer experience. The style is light and non-threatening since we have no anxieties or insecurities to pass along. Learning to program should be fun, not intimidating,...

And why shouldn't learning be fun...?

Sit back, relax, read slowly as though savoring a good novel, and above all, let your imagination wander. I'll supply all the routine facts and techniques we need. The real enjoyment begins when *your* imagination starts the creative juices flowing and the Computer becomes a tool in *your own* hands. *You* become its master -- not the other way around. At that time it evolves from just a box of parts into an extension of your own personality.

Enjoy.

"From the moment we turn it on, our Model 100 follows a well-defined set of rules for coping with us..."

Part 1

BASIC's Basics

Chapter 1

Getting Ready

From the moment we turn it on, our Model 100 follows a well-defined set of rules for coping with us, the "master." This makes it an exceptionally easy Computer to use.

So far, we have learned to use TEXT, SCHEDL, ADDRSS and TELCOM, programs written by others. We can also write our own programs, opening up unlimited possibilities for meeting specific needs. Doing so is called COMPUTER PROGRAMMING. The 50 Chapters in Book Two will teach you how to write "custom" programs in the BASIC computer language.

Turn the Model 100 ON, place the cursor over `BASIC`, press **ENTER** and watch it say:

```
TRS-80 Model 100 Software
Copr. 1983 Microsoft
21190 Bytes free
Ok
▓ (flashing prompt)
```

The number of Bytes free will vary with the amount of memory installed and the space required by other programs and files being stored at the time.

What Is A Computer Program?

There are many "computer languages" in which we can write programs. BASIC is an easy one to learn, and is by far the most popular. Our BASIC INTERPRETER is, itself, a very complex program written by others, but its very name tells us how easy it is to use.

Let's write a simple one-Line program to let the Model 100 introduce itself. Be sure the last line on the screen shows a prompt.

Type in the the following Line, *exactly* as shown:

```
10 PRINT "I ARE A COMPUTER PROGRAMMER."
```

Do not hit the `ENTER` key yet!

Since all BASIC Statements and Commands are upper case, we may just as well press the `CAPS` `LOCK` key and leave it down for the duration, even though the Computer converts the words to upper case automatically. There's plenty to learn without confusing upper and lower case at this time.

If you made a typing error, don't worry. Just use the `DEL` `BKSP` key as with the word processor. (After pressing the `ENTER` key, editing becomes more complex.)

Study very carefully what we have typed:

1. Did you enclose everything after the word PRINT in quotation marks?

2. Are there any extra quotation marks?

If everything's okay, press `ENTER`. The ▓ prompt reappears, telling us *"Fine -- what's next?"*

> If we press `ENTER` again, the screen will read:
> ▓
> As long as the bottom item on the screen is the flashing prompt, we know it's "our turn."

If It's Too Late

If you found an error *after* the `ENTER` key was pressed, the `DEL` `BKSP` key cannot correct it. The best way to change it is by retyping the *entire* Line, correctly. When the `ENTER` key is pressed, the new Line will replace the old one

since they both share the same starting number (in this case, 10). In several Chapters we'll learn how to "EDIT" out errors instead of retyping entire Lines.

"Allow Me To Introduce Myself"
Let's tell the Computer to "execute" or RUN our program. Type:

```
RUN
```

and press **ENTER**.

If you made no mistakes, the display will read:

```
I ARE A COMPUTER PROGRAMMER.
```

If it doesn't work, try typing RUN again. If RUN still doesn't produce the greeting, there's something wrong in the program. Type NEW **ENTER** to clear it out, then type it in and RUN again.

If it did work -- let out a yell!

"I are now a REAL computer programmer!"

This is very important, because now that you've tasted success with computer programming, it may be the last you are heard from in some time.

In Summary
Note that the word PRINT is not displayed, nor are the Line Number or the quotation marks. They are part of the program's *instructions* and we didn't intend for them to be printed. Everything inside the quote marks is printed, including blank spaces and the period.

Type the word RUN again and hit **ENTER**

Type RUN **ENTER** to your heart's content, watching the magic machine do as it's told. When you feel you've got the hang of all this, get up and stretch, walk around the room, look out the window -- the whole act. You'll soon be hooked on programming and won't have time for such things.

Learned in Chapter 1

Commands	**Statements**	**Miscellaneous**
`ENTER`	PRINT	▓ prompt/cursor
NEW		"" quotation marks
RUN		

Whether typing in a program, or giving direct commands like RUN, we have to hit `ENTER` to tell the Computer to look at what we typed, and act accordingly. *Commands* (like RUN) are executed as soon as we type them in and press `ENTER`.

Statements (like PRINT) are put into programs and are executed only after we type the RUN `ENTER` command.

It is possible during programming to "lose control" of the Computer so it won't give an OK message when you press `ENTER`. To regain control, just press `CTRL` and `C` simultaneously (it looks like ^C on the display). If that doesn't work, push the RESET button (in the back). If *that* doesn't work, turn the Computer OFF for 10 seconds, then turn it back ON.

We'll put a review summary like this at the end of each Chapter. Use it as a checkpoint to make sure you didn't miss anything.

Chapter 2

Expanded Program

We now have a program in the Computer. It's only a one-Liner, but let's expand it by adding a second Line. In BASIC, every Line in the program *must* be numbered, and the instructions are executed in order from the lowest Line number to the largest. Type:

```
20 PRINT "YOU HAVE A COMMAND, MASTER?"
```

ENTER

Check it carefully -- especially the quote marks, then:

```
RUN      ENTER
```

Have you noticed that we use 0 for the number zero -- so we can distinguish between the letter O and number 0. The Video Display does it this way -- and it's standard throughout Computerdom.

If all was correct, the display will read:

```
I ARE A COMPUTER PROGRAMMER,
YOU HAVE A COMMAND, MASTER?
```

If it ran OK, answer the question by typing:

    YES   ENTER

Oh -- sorry about that! It "bombed", didn't it? The display said:

    ?SN Error

We deliberately "set you up" to demonstrate the Computer's ERROR troubleshooter. The Computer is smart enough to know when we've made a mistake in telling it what to do, and it prints a clue as to the nature of the error.

In this case, the ? tells us that it doesn't understand what we are saying. SN stands for the word "syntax" (an obscure word that refers to the pattern of words in a language). ERROR means we have made one. The Computer is expecting a new program Line or a BASIC command. A bit later we'll learn how to make the Computer accept a "YES" or "NO" and respond accordingly.

There are many possible errors we can make, and in good time we will learn to understand the built in "ERROR CODES."

    A complete listing of ERROR CODES is provided in Appendix E.

Meanwhile, there is one other important ERROR situation which we should be able to recognize to pry ourselves out of accidental trouble. Let's retype Line 20 and deliberately make a spelling error:

    20 PRIMT "YOU HAVE A COMMAND, MASTER?"

and RUN   ENTER

We get the same ERROR message:

    ?SN Error in 20

We have misspelled PRINT, a specific BASIC word. Computers are extremely fussy about these things. They cannot stand ambiguity. Retype Line 20 to correct the misspelling in PRIMT before continuing on.

And The Program Grows

It is customary, traditional (and all that) to space the Lines in a program 10 numbers apart. Note that our 2-Line program has the Line Numbers 10 and 20. The reason...it's much easier to modify a program if we leave room to insert new Lines in between the old ones. There is no benefit to numbering the Lines more closely (like 1,2,3,4). *Don't do it.*

RUN again and look at the display. What if we'd rather not have the two Lines printed so close together, but would like some space between them? Type in the new Line:

    `15 PRINT`   **ENTER**

Then:

    `RUN`   **ENTER**

It should now read:

    `I ARE A COMPUTER PROGRAMMER,`

    `YOU HAVE A COMMAND, MASTER?`

> Note: To make this book easier to read, we are using more space between all our program Lines than you actually see on the display.

Looks neater, doesn't it? But what about Line 15? It says `PRINT`. PRINT What? Well -- print *nothing*. That's what followed `PRINT`, and that's just what it printed. But in the process of printing nothing it automatically inserted a space between the PRINTing ordered in Lines 10 and 20. So *that's* how we space between Lines.

> Didn't that room between Lines 10 and 20 come in handy?

Another important program statement is REM, which stands for REMark. It is often convenient to insert REMarks into a program.

Why? So you or someone else can refer to them later, to help remember complicated programming details, or even what the program's for and how to use it. It's like having a scratch-pad or notebook built into the program. When we tell the Computer to execute the program by typing RUN `ENTER`, it skips right over any numbered Line which begins with a REM. *A REM statement has no effect whatsoever on the program.* Insert the following:

```
5 REM THIS IS MY FIRST COMPUTER PROGRAM
ENTER
```

Then:

```
RUN      ENTER
```

The display reads just like the last one, totally unaffected by the presence of Line 5. Did it work that way for you?

Well, this programming business is getting complicated and I've already forgotten what is in our "big" program. How can we get a listing of what our program now contains? Easy. A new BASIC command. Type:

```
LIST     ENTER
```

The display should read:

```
5 REM THIS IS MY FIRST COMPUTER PROGRAM
10 PRINT "I ARE A COMPUTER PROGRAMMER."
15 PRINT
20 PRINT "YOU HAVE A COMMAND, MASTER?"
```

We can LIST the program any time the prompt appears on the display.

Where Is The End Of The Program?

The end of a program is, quite naturally, the last statement we want the Computer to execute. Many Computers require placing a program Line containing the word END at this point, so the Computer will know when to stop. With our Model 100, an END statement is optional -- we can put it in or leave it out. Remember though, if we want to RUN our BASIC programs on fussier Computers, we'll probably need the END statement.

> When we get into more complex programs, we'll use END statements to FORCE the Computer to stop at specified points -- so actually, END comes in very handy even with the Model 100.

Let's take a close look at END. By the rules governing its use, most dialects of BASIC which require END insist that it be the last statement in a program, telling the Computer "That's all, folks." By tradition, it is given the number 99, or 999, or 9999 (or larger), depending on the largest number the specific Computer will accept. Our Model 100 accepts Line numbers up to 65529.

Let's add an END statement:

Type:

    `99 END`   **ENTER**

Then:

    `RUN`   **ENTER**

The sample run should read:

    `I ARE A COMPUTER PROGRAMMER.`

    `YOU HAVE A COMMAND, MASTER?`

"Why didn't the word END print?" **Answer:** Because nothing is printed unless it is the "object" of a PRINT statement. So, how could we make the Computer print `THE END` at the end of the program execution? Think for a minute before reading on, and typing the next Line.

    `98 PRINT "THE END."`

and `RUN`   **ENTER**

> This assumes that Line 98 is the last PRINT statement in the program. We now have an END statement (Line 99) and a "THE END" PRINT statement (Line 98). 98 says it; 99 does it.

Erasing Without Replacing

Just for fun, let's move the END statement from Line 99 to the largest usable Line number our Model 100 will accept, 65529. It requires two separate steps.

The first is to erase Line 99. Note that we're not just making a change or correcting an error in Line 99 -- we want to completely eliminate it from the program. Easier done than said:

Type:

    `99`   **ENTER**

The line is erased. How can we be sure? Think about this now. Got it? Sure -- "pull" a LISTing of the entire program by typing:

    `LIST`   **ENTER**

The display should show the program with Lines 5, 10, 15, 20, and 98. 99 should be gone. Any entire Line can be erased the same way.

The second step is just as easy. Type:

    `65529 END`   **ENTER**

...and the new Line is entered. Pull a listing of the program to see if it was. Was it? Now RUN the program to see if moving the END statement changed anything. Did it? It shouldn't have.

Other Uses For End

Move END from #65529 to Line #17, then RUN.

What happened? It ENDed the RUN after printing Line 10 and a space. RUN it several times.

Now move END to Line 13 and RUN. Then to Line 8 and RUN.

Do you see the effect END has, depending where it is placed (even temporarily) in a program? Feel like you are really gaining control over the machine? You ain't seen nothing yet!

Learned in Chapter 2

Commands   **Statements**   **Miscellaneous**

LIST   PRINT (Space)   Error Messages
                   REM   Line Numbering
                   END

Chapter 3

Using The EDITor

A valuable capability of our BASIC INTERPRETER is its EDITor. Its purpose is as simple as its name and it is quite similar to the TEXT EDITOR. It lets us make changes in a program without retyping an entire Line.

Clear out the current program with NEW **ENTER**. Then type in this Line (errors and all):

    10 PRINT "THIS CONFUSER ARE GRATE!"

...and RUN.

It should RUN just fine, and if that's the way you usually talk you may wonder what there is to EDIT. If, on the other hand, you wish to change the sentence to something like:

    THIS COMPUTER IS GREAT!

then we have a good excuse to do some EDITing.

In the first 2 Chapters we eliminated errors by just retyping the entire Line, hoping we didn't make more mistakes than we eliminated. This particular example needs so many changes it might be just as easy to retype it, but our purpose is to "exercise" the EDITor, so type:

    EDIT 10   **ENTER**

and see what happens.

Hokay...we get:

    `[1]0 PRINT "THIS CONFUSER ARE GRATE!"`

a good sign it's in the EDITor mode.

> Being in EDITor Mode isn't like being in BASIC. The EDITor is *not* part of the BASIC language. It's a special "sub-program" we call up from BASIC using the word EDIT. To EXIT the EDITor when done and return to BASIC we will hit **F8**. Then, from BASIC, if we hit **F8** we will exit BASIC and return to Menu ... but we're not ready for that yet.

Since we want Line 10 to read `THIS COMPUTER IS GREAT!`, let's first change the word `ARE` to `IS`. Tap the ▶ key slowly until the cursor is over the first letter of the word `ARE`. Press the **SHIFT** and **DEL** keys same time, 3 times, and delete the word `ARE`. Type `IS` to complete the change.

Nothing new so far ... just like TEXT EDITing. In fact, press the **LABEL** key and see that in EDITor mode, the soft keys are the same as in TEXT.

Advanced EDITing

Now press the **CTRL** key at the same time as the ◀ key to reposition the cursor at the beginning of Line 10. Press **F1** and **G** **ENTER** to search for `GRATE` and we'll change it to `GREAT`. Press ▶ twice to position the cursor over the `A` and type in `E`. The Line now reads:

    `10 PRINT "THIS CONFUSER IS GREATE!"`

Press ▶ twice more to move the cursor over the `E` that we want to remove, and **SHIFT** **DEL** to delete it.

Now we need to change `CONFUSER` to `COMPUTER`. Press **CTRL** ◀ to return the cursor to the beginning of the Line. Type **SHIFT** ▶ three times to put the cursor on the first letter of `CONFUSER`. Press ▶ twice and type `M` followed by **SHIFT** **DEL**. This inserts the `M` (which we want) and deletes the `N` (which we don't want). Follow the same procedure to change the `F` to a `P` and the `S` to a `T`.

Line 10 finally looks like this:

```
10 PRINT "THIS COMPUTER IS GREAT!"
```

Press **F8** (EXIT) to leave the EDIT mode.

> Pressing **ESC** twice does the same thing.

We went into a lot of detail to show that this BASIC EDITor is really just a TEXT editor. That means we can call up *part* or *all* of a BASIC program at one time.

Add:

```
20 REM * EDIT PRACTICE *
30 REM * EDIT PRACTICE *
```

Then:

```
EDIT 20-30
```

and EDIT Lines 20 and 30, just for practice.

Press **F8** to return to BASIC and type:

```
EDIT 10-
```

telling the Computer to EDIT Line 10 and all following Lines.

EDIT Shortcuts

We have just seen how to edit 1 Line, or select a group of Lines for editing.

To load the entire program into the EDITor, simply type `EDIT` **ENTER**.

By pressing the up/down/right/left arrows, we can move the cursor to any part of the program for editing.

Press **F8** to exit the EDIT mode. Notice the shaded `Wait` flashing on the bottom left of the display. The Computer is taking some time to rearrange our program in memory. As we edit longer programs, this wait time will increase. We can hold the wait time to a minimum by selecting only those Lines that need editing, rather than load in the entire program.

Now press **F5** to LIST the program. After the LISTing is complete, type:

> `EDIT.`   **ENTER**   (Note the period)

The Computer placed Line 30 in the EDITor. EDIT. tells the Model 100 to EDIT the last Line in the program or the Line last EDITed or LISTed.

Changing Line Numbers

To put on the final polish, we'll move the REM statement from the last Line to the first. One obvious way is to simply retype the REM statement in Line 5 and delete Line 30. That doesn't teach us anything, however.

We'll do it an easier way, by simply changing the Line number from 30 to 5. This EDITing method has real advantages when reorganizing large programs containing complex equations or long statements. Press **F8**, then:

Type:

> `EDIT 30`   **ENTER**

The display will read:

> `30 REM * EDIT PRACTICE *`

Press **SHIFT** **DEL** twice to remove the number 30. Type:

> `5`

and **F8**

LIST **F5** the program. We now have a new Line 5 along with Lines 10 and 20. 30 is gone.

Learned in Chapter 3

Commands

EDIT

Miscellaneous

`CTRL` ◀ moves cursor to beginning of line
`SHIFT` ◀ moves cursor to beginning of word
◀ moves cursor one letter left
▶ moves cursor one letter right

Chapter 4

The Soft Keys

Each of the built-in programs (BASIC, TEXT, TELCOM, ADDRSS and SCHEDL) have their own specific uses for the function keys. **F8** (Menu) is the only key that remains unchanged from one program to the next.

> One exception: When we are in EDITor, **F8** exits us back to BASIC. The *second* push gives us the MENU.

BASIC Keys

In BASIC, KEYS **F1** through **F5**, and **F8** are predefined. Go to BASIC and press the **LABEL** key to see their names. Each of the "functions" assigned to the F keys in BASIC can also be typed in from the keyboard, so the F keys are not absolutely necessary, as they were in TEXT and other programs. They are just very convenient.

To be technically correct, the so-called "functions" are really BASIC COMMANDS, but somewhere, somehow, the "soft" keys were named "F" keys, for FUNCTION. Just a quirk of computer history. **From here on, it's "soft keys" whenever possible.**

Another way to find out the which commands are available on soft keys is by typing:

```
KEY LIST        ENTER
```

You'll now see a KEY LIST on the top of the display, telling the real names of all the soft keys, and (if you have the **LABEL** key on) the "labels" for all the keys displayed along the bottom of the screen. Note that the label for Files is File, and that Save" and Load" have been shortened to Save and Load.

There just isn't room for more than four letters down there.

KEY LIST

```
Files                    Load "
Save "                   Run
List
                         Menu

Ok
▨

File Load Save Run List          Menu
 ⌐1⌐  ⌐2⌐  ⌐3⌐  ⌐4⌐  ⌐5⌐  ⌐6⌐  ⌐7⌐  ⌐8⌐
```

Predefined Function Keys

Each of these keys will be discussed, later as needed. In a nut shell, here are the assignments given to each F key in BASIC:

    F1 `Files` Displays the files that are stored in memory, similar to MENU, but doesn't exit us from BASIC.

    F2 `Load"` LOADs in a program from our files or from cassette tape.

    F3 `Save"` Stores our hard work in memory or on cassette tape.

    F4 `Run` Types RUN **ENTER** to execute the resident BASIC program.

    F5 `List` Types LIST **ENTER** to LIST the resident program.

    F8 `Menu` Exits BASIC and returns to the main Menu.

Freedom To Function

We can change any of these keys to make them do what we want. We will soon find that some statements and commands are used more than others. We may

find that a PRINT statement is used in most programs. Wouldn't it be handy to have this assigned to one of the unused function keys? Let's define **F6** as PRINT for our convenience.

Type:

```
KEY 6,"PRINT"
```

Look at the LABEL LINE and see that **F6** now means PRIN. (The first 4 characters). From now on and forever more, **F6** will mean PRINT, even if the Computer is turned off. Of course we can change it back the way it was, or to any of many other things we will discover.

Let's try our new function key when typing in these 3 NEW Lines:

```
10 PRINT          use F6
20 PRINT "FUNCTION KEYS SAVE TIME WITH"
30 PRINT "THE EASE OF ONE KEYSTROKE"
```

...and RUN.

Very good!

We can change **F6** back to "empty" by simply typing:

```
KEY 6,""          ENTER
```

The same approach works for all 8 F-KEYS, but since advanced techniques are required to do things like incorporating a " or an **ENTER**, we'd better leave all but **F6** and **F7** alone until we know more about BASIC.

Learned in Chapter 4

Miscellaneous

Soft Keys

"The FOR-NEXT loop is of such overwhelming importance in putting our Computer to work, that few of the programming areas we explore from this point on will exclude it."

Part 2

Speak To Me, Oh Great Computer

Chapter 5

Math Operators

"But Can It Do Math?"

Yes, it can. Basic arithmetic is a snap for the Model 100. So are highly complex math calculations -- when we write special programs to perform them. (More on this later.)

The BASIC Computer language uses the four fundamental arithmetic operations, plus a fifth which is just a modification of two of the others.

    1. Addition, using the symbol +

    2. Subtraction, using the symbol −
(See -- nothing to this. Just like grade school. I wonder whatever happened to ol' Miss... Well, ahem -- anyway)

    3. Multiplication, using the special symbol *
(Oh drat, I knew this was too easy to be true!)

    4. Division, using the symbol /
(Well, at least it's simpler than the old ÷ symbol)

    5. Negation (meaning "multiply times minus one"), using the − symbol.

Of course, we also need that old favorite, the equals sign (=). But wait! The BASIC language is particular about how we use this sign! Math expressions (like

1 + 2 * 5) can only go on the *right-hand side* of the equals sign; the left-hand side is reserved for the *result* of he math equation. In other words, with a Computer we don't say 2 + 2 = 4. We say 4 = 2 + 2. (This all may seem a little strange, but it's really quite simple, as you'll discover in the next few pages.)

Now that wasn't too bad, was it? Be careful. We *cannot* use an "X" for multiplication. Unfortunately, a long time ago a mathematician decided to use "X", which is a letter, to mean multiply. We use letters for other things, so it's much less confusing to use a "*" for multiplication. Confusion is one thing a Computer can't tolerate. To Computers, "*" is the only symbol which means multiply. After using it awhile, you, too, may feel we should completely do away with X as a multiplication symbol.

Putting all this together in a program is not difficult, so let's do it. First, we have to erase the "resident program" from the Computer's memory.

"Resident program" is Computer talk for "what's already in there."

Type the command:

    NEW   ENTER

then press:

    LIST   (**F5**, remember?)

to check that there's nothing left in memory. The Computer will respond with a simple:

    Ok

Putting The Beast To Work

We will now use the Computer for some very simple problem solving. That means using equations. (Oh -- panic.) But then, an equation is just a little statement that says "what's on one side of the equals sign amounts to the same as what's on the other side." That can't get too bad (it says here).

We'll use that old standby equation,

"Distance traveled equals Rate of travel times Time spent traveling."

If it's been a few years, you might want to sit on the end of a log and contemplate that for awhile.

To shorten the equation, let's choose letters (called variables) to stand for the three quantities. Then we can rewrite the equation as a BASIC statement acceptable to the Model 100. Type:

```
40   D = R * T
```

Remember, we have to use the * for multiplication.

What's that 40 doing in our equation? That's the program Line Number. Remember, every step in a program has to have one. We chose 40, but another number would do just as well. The extra spaces in the Line are there just to make the equation easier for us to read; BASIC ignores them. Later, when you write very long programs, you'll probably want to eliminate extra spaces because they take up memory space. For learning, they are helpful, so leave them in.

Here's what Line 40 means to the Computer: "Take the values of R and T, multiply them together, and assign the resulting value to the variable D. So until further notice, D is equal to the result of R times T.

We could not reverse the equation and write: R*T=D. This has no meaning to the Computer. Remember, the left-hand side of the equation is reserved for the Line Number and the value we are *looking for*. The right-hand side is the place to put the values we *know*.

We can use any of the 26 letters from A through Z to identify the values we know as well as those we want to figure out. Whenever you can, it's a good idea to choose letters that are abbreviations for the things they stand for -- like the D, R, and T in the Distance, Rate, Time equation.

To further complicate this very simple example, there's an optional way of writing the equation, using the BASIC statement LET:

```
40   LET   D = R * T            ENTER
```

This use of LET reminds us that making D equal R times T was *our* choice, rather than some eternal truth like 2 = 1 + 1. Some Computers are fussy, and always require the use of LET with programmed equations. Our Model 100 says, "Whatever you want."

Okay -- let's complete the program.

Assume:

> Distance (in miles) = Rate (in miles per hour) multiplied by Time (in hours). How far is it from San Diego to London if a jet plane traveling at an average speed of 500 miles per hour makes the trip in 12 hours?

(Yes, I know you can do that one in your head but that's not the point!)

Type in the following:

```
10 REM   DISTANCE, RATE, TIME PROBLEM    ENTER
20 R = 500           ENTER
30 T = 12            ENTER
40 D = R * T         ENTER
```

Check the program carefully, then:

RUN   (use **F4**)

Hum de dum..........ho-hum..........(this sure is a slow Computer).

```
Ok
```

All it says is Ok. *The Computer doesn't work!*

134 Chapter 5

Yes it does. *It worked just fine.* The Computer multiplied 500 times 12 just like we told it, and came up with an answer of 6000 miles. But we forgot to tell it to give *us* the answer. Sorry about that.

> **EXERCISE 5-1:** Can you finish this program without help? It only takes one more Line. Give it a good try before reading on for the answer. That way, the answer will mean more to you. (Hint: We've already used PRINT to print messages in quotes. What would happen if we said 50 PRINT "D"?...No, we want the *value* of D, not the letter "D" itself. Hmmmm, what happens when we get rid of the quotes?)

> DON'T READ BEYOND THIS POINT UNTIL YOU'VE WORKED ON THE ABOVE EXERCISE!

Look in the back of this Manual for an answer for this 1st Exercise. Also some notes and ideas.

Well, the answer of 6000 is correct, but its "presentation" was no more inspiring than the readout on a hand calculator. This inevitably leads us back to where we first started this foray into the unknown -- the PRINT statement.

Note that we said in Line 50 PRINT D. There were no quotes around the letter D like we had used before. The reason is simple but fairly profound. If we want the Computer to print *the exact words* we specify, we enclose them in quotes. If we want it to print the *value* of a variable, in this case D, we leave the quotes off. That simple message is worth serious thought before continuing on.

> Did you think seriously about it?...Then on we go!

Now suppose we want to include both the *value* of something *and* some *exact words* on the same Line. Pay attention, as you will be doing more and more program design yourself, and PRINT statements give beginners more trouble than any other single part of Computer programming. Type in the following:

```
50 PRINT "DISTANCE IS",D      ENTER
```

Then:

RUN

> REMEMBER: Typing in a statement with a Line number that already exists erases the original Line completely -- and that's what we want to do here.)

The display says:

```
DISTANCE IS         6000
```

How about that! The message enclosed in quotes is printed exactly as we specified, and the letter gave us the value of D. The comma told the Computer that we wanted it to print two separate items on the same Line. We can tell it to print up to two items on the same Line, simply by inserting commas between them.

With this in mind, see if you can change expand and change Line 50 so the Computer finishes the program with the following message:

```
DISTANCE IS         6000
MILES.
```

Break up the quoted message into two parts, and put the variable in between them on the PRINT Line. (Use the EDITor).

```
50 PRINT "DISTANCE IS",D,"MILES."
```

Now what about all that extra space on the display Lines? The reason is that the Computer divides up the display width into two zones. There are 14 characters in the first and the remaining 26 in the second. When a PRINT statement contains 2 or more items separated by commas, the Computer automatically PRINTs them in different PRINT ZONES. *Automatic Zoning* is a very convenient method of outputting tabular information, and we'll explore the subject further later on.

It's possible to eliminate all that extra space in the output display from our Distance, Rate, Time program. EDIT the last version of Line 50, substituting semi-colons (;) for the 2 commas.

```
50 PRINT "DISTANCE IS",D,"MILES."         (old)
50 PRINT "DISTANCE IS";D;"MILES."         (new)
```

RUN

The display now appears:

```
DISTANCE IS 6000 MILES.
```

Look very carefully at the new Line 50. There is no blank space between the S in IS, the D, and the M in MILES. But in the display printout, there *is* a space between IS and 6000, and another space between 6000 and MILES. How come?

Reason: When numbers are printed, leading and trailing blank spaces are automatically inserted. As we do more programming, this feature will become very important.

WHEW!

Well, we have already covered more than enough commands, statements and math operators to solve a myriad of problems.

Math operators? -- they're the + − * / = symbols we talked about earlier.

Now let's spend some time actually writing programs to solve problems. There is no better way to learn than by doing, and *everything* covered so far is fundamental to our success in later Chapters. Don't jump over these exercises! They will plunge you right into the thick of programming, where you belong. Sample answers are in Appendix G, along with further comments.

EXERCISE 5-2: Write a program which will find the time required to travel by jet plane from London to San Diego, if the distance is 6000 miles and the plane travels at 500 MPH.

EXERCISE 5-3: If the circumference of a circle is found by multiplying its diameter times PI, (3.14), write a program which will find the circumference of a circle with a diameter of 35 feet.

EXERCISE 5-4: If the area of a circle is found by multiplying 3.14 times the square of its radius, write a program to find the area of a circle with a radius of 5 inches.

EXERCISE 5-5: Your checkbook balance was $225. You've written three checks (for $17, $35 and $225) and made two deposits ($40 and $200). Write a program to adjust your old balance based on checks written and deposits made, and print out your new balance.

A Bit More On Variable Names

Altho the 26 letter-variables are usually enough for most programs, they can be combined with numbers 0-9 to give us an additional 26*10 = 260. For example:

    A1
    M6
    K9
    etc.

These "extra" variables can be very handy, particularly if we want to label a number of "sub" variables (D1,D2,D3, etc) which combine to make a grand total which we can just call D.

Learned in Chapter 5

Statements	Math Operators	Miscellaneous
LET (Optional)	=	,
	+	;
	−	Variable Names
	*	
	/	

Chapter 6

Scientific Notation

Are There More Stars or Grains of Sand?

In this mathematical world we are blessed with very large and very small numbers. Millions of these and billionths of those. To cope with all this, our Computer uses "exponential notation", or "standard scientific notation" when the number sizes start to get out of hand. The number 5 million (5,000,000), for example, can be written "5E+06" (E for Exponential). This means, "the number 5 followed by six zeros."

Or technically, $5*10^6$, which is 5 times ten to the sixth power: 5*10*10*10*10*10*10

If an answer comes out "5E-06", that means we must shift the decimal point, which is after the 5, six places to the *left*, inserting zeros as necessary. Technically, it means 5×10^{-6}, or 5 millionths, (.000,005). It's really pretty simple once you get the hang of it, and a lot easier to keep track of numbers without losing the decimal point. Since the Computer insists on using it with very large and very small numbers, we can just as well get in the good habit, too.

In our BASIC, that's 5/10/10/10/10/10/10

Type NEW before performing the following exercises.

> **EXERCISE 6-1:** If one hundred million cars drove one million miles in a certain year, how many miles did they drive altogether that year?

Write and run a simple program using zeros (not exponential notation).

_____
_____
_____
_____

Didn't forget the **ENTER** did you? Up till now we've been reminding you to **ENTER** after each Line or command -- but from now on, we'll assume you've got that little routine down pat.

EXERCISE 6-2: Change Lines 20 and 30 in the Car Miles Solution program (from Exercise 6-1) to express the numbers written there in exponential notation, or SSN (Standard Scientific Notaiton). Then RUN it.

_____
_____

Learned in Chapter 6

Miscellaneous

E - notation

Chapter 7

Using ( ) And The Order Of Operations

Parentheses play an important role in Computer programming, just as in ordinary math. They are used here in the same general way, but there are important exceptions:

1. In BASIC, parentheses can enclose operations to be performed. Those operations which are within parentheses are performed before those not in parentheses.

2. Operations buried deepest within parentheses (that is, parentheses inside parentheses) are performed first.

If you want to be sure your problems are calculated correctly, use ( ) around operations you want performed first.

---

3. When there is a "tie" as to which operations the Computer should perform first after it has removed all parentheses, it works its way along the program Line from left to right doing the multiplication and division. It then starts at the left again and performs the addition and subtraction.

Recall the old memory aid, "My Dear Aunt Sally"? In math we are supposed to do Multiplication and Division first (from left to right), then come back for Addition and Subtraction (left to right). The Model 100 uses the same sequence.

---

4. A problem listed as (X)(Y) will *not* tell the Computer to multiply. X*Y is the only scheme recognized for multiplication.

EXAMPLE: To convert temperature in Fahrenheit to Celsius (Centigrade), the following relationship is used:

> The Fahrenheit temperature equals 32 degrees plus nine-fifths of the Celsius temperature. Or, maybe you're more used to the simple formula:

$$F = \frac{9}{5}C + 32$$

Assume we have a Celsius temperature of 25. Type in this NEW program and RUN it.

```
10 REM * CELSIUS TO FAHRENHEIT CONV. *
20 C = 25
30 F = (9/5)*C + 32
40 PRINT C;"DEG. CEL. =";F;"DEG. FAHR."
```

...and RUN.

SAMPLE RUN:

```
25 DEG. CEL. = 77 DEG. FAHR.
```

> Remember what the semi-colons are for?

Notice that Line 40 consists of a PRINT statement followed by four separate expressions -- two variables and two groups of words in quotes called "literals" or "strings". Notice also that everything within the quotes (including spaces) is printed.

Next, note how the parentheses are placed in Line 30. With the 9/5 securely inside, we can multiply its quotient times C, then add 32.

Remove the parentheses in Line 30 and RUN again. The answer comes out the same. Why?

　1. On the first pass, the Computer started by solving all problems

within parentheses, in this case just one (9/5). It came up with (but did not print) 1.8. It then multiplied the 1.8 times the value of C and added 32.

2. On our next try, without the parentheses, the Computer simply moved from left to right performing first the division problem (9 divided by 5), then the multiplication problem (1.8 times C), then the addition problem (adding 32). The parentheses really made no difference in our first example.

Next, change +32 to 32+ and move it to the front of the equation in Line 30. RUN it again, without parentheses.

Did it make a difference in the answer? Why not?

Answer: Execution proceeds from left to right, multiplication and division first, then returns and performs addition and subtraction. This is why the 32 was not added to the 9 before being divided by 5. *Very Important!* If they had been added, we would of course had gotten the wrong answer.

> **EXERCISE 7-1:** Write and run a program which converts 65° Fahrenheit to Celsius. The rule tells us that "Celsius temperature is equal to five-ninths times what's left after 32 is subtracted from the Fahrenheit temperature."

$$C = (F - 32) \times \frac{5}{9}$$

> **EXERCISE 7-2:** Remove the first set of parentheses in the #7-1 answer and RUN again.

> **EXERCISE 7-3:** Replace the first set of parentheses in program Line 30 and remove the second pair of parentheses, then RUN. Note how the answer comes out -- correctly!

EXERCISE 7-4: Insert parentheses in the following equation to make it correct. Write a program to check it out on the Model 100.

30 - 9 - 8 - 7 - 6 = 28

Learned in Chapter 7

Miscellaneous

( )
Order of Operations

Chapter 8

Relational Operators

IF you liked the preceding Chapters, THEN you're going to love the rest of this book!

...because we're just starting to get into the good stuff like IF-THEN and GOTO statements that let your Computer make decisions and take...er, executive action. But first, a few more operators...

Relational Operators allow the Computer to compare one value with another. There are only three:

1. Equals, using the symbol =
(How'd you guess?)

2. Is greater than, using the symbol >

3. Is less than, using the symbol <

Combining these three, we come up with three more operators:

4. Is not equal to, using the symbol <>

5. Is less than or equal to, using the symbol <=

6. Is greater than or equal to, using the symbol >=

> Example: A<B means A is less than B. To help you distinguish between < and >, just remember that the smaller part of the < symbol points to the smaller of the two quantities being compared.

By adding these six relational operators to the four *math* operators we already know, plus new STATEMENTS, called IF-THEN & GOTO, we create a powerful system of comparing and calculating that becomes the central core of everything else that follows.

The IF-THEN statement, combined with the six relational operators above, gives us the *action* part of a system of logic. Enter and RUN this NEW program:

```
10 A = 5
20 IF A = 5 THEN 50
30 PRINT "A DOES NOT EQUAL 5."
40 END
50 PRINT "A EQUALS 5."
```

The display says:

```
A EQUALS 5.
```

This program is an example of using an IF-THEN statement with only the most fundamental relational operator, the equals sign.

The Autopsy
Let's examine the program Line by Line.

Line 10 establishes the fact that A has a value of 5.

Line 20 is an IF-THEN statement which directs the Computer to GOTO Line 50 IF THE VALUE OF A IS EXACTLY 5, skipping over whatever might be in between Lines 20 and 50. Since A *does* equal 5, the Computer jumps to Line 50 and does as it says, PRINTing A EQUALS 5. Lines 30 and 40 were not used at all.

Now, change Line 10 to read:

    10 A = 6

...and RUN.

The display says:

    A DOES NOT EQUAL 5.

Taking it a Line at a time:

> Line 10 establishes the value of A to be 6.
>
> Line 20 tests the value of A. If A equals 5, THEN the Computer is directed to go to Line 50. But "the test fails", that is, A does *not* equal 5, so the Computer proceeds as usual to the next Line, Line 30.
>
> Line 30 directs the Computer to print the fact that A *does not equal* 5. It does not tell us what the *value* of A is, only that it does not equal 5. The Computer then proceeds on to the next Line.
>
> Line 40 ENDs the program's execution. Without this statement separating Lines 30 and 50, the Computer would charge right on to Line 50 and print its contents, which obviously are in conflict with the contents of Line 30.

IF-THEN Vs GOTO

IF-THEN is what is known as a *conditional* branching statement. The program will "branch" to another part of the program *on the condition that* it passes the IF-THEN test. If it fails the test, the program simply continues to the next Line.

GOTO is an *unconditional* branching statement. If we replace Line 40 with:

    40 GOTO 99

and add Line 99:

    99 END

...whenever the Computer hits Line 40 it will *unconditionally* follow orders and GOTO 99, ENDing the run.

For practice, change Lines 40 and 99 as discussed above and RUN.

Did the program work OK as changed? Did you try it with several values of A? Be sure you do so! We will find many uses for the GOTO statement in the future.

Optional THEN With GOTO

When the IF-THEN statement is used with a GOTO statement, either one or both can be used. This can be useful in long program Lines. For example, either of these Lines will work in place of Line 20 in our program:

```
20 IF X = 5 THEN GOTO 99
```

or

```
20 IF X = 5 GOTO 99
```

Now let's see if *you* can accomplish the same thing by using the "does-not-equal" sign:

EXERCISE 8-1: Rewrite the resident program using a "does-not-equal" sign in Line 20 instead of the equals sign, changing other Lines as necessary, so the same results are achieved with your program as with the one in the example.

EXERCISE 8-2: Change Line 10 to give A the value of 6. Leave the other four Lines from #8-1 as shown. Add more program Lines as necessary so the program will tell us whether A is larger or smaller than 5 and RUN.

EXERCISE 8-3: Change the value of A in Line 10 at least three more times, RUNning after each change to ensure that your new program works correctly.

No sample answers are given since you are choosing your own values of A. It will be obvious whether or not you are getting the right answer.

Learned in Chapter 8

Statements	Relational Operators	Miscellaneous
IF-THEN	=	Conditional branching
GOTO	>	Unconditional branching
	<	
	<>	
	<=	
	>=	

Chapter 9

It Also Talks And Listens

Begin this Chapter by typing in the sample answer program to Exercise #8-2:

By now you have probably gotten tired of having to retype Line 10 each time to change the value of A. The INPUT statement is a simple, faster and more convenient way to accomplish the same thing. It's a biggie, so don't miss any points.

Add the following Lines to the *resident* program:

Resident -- remember, that's the program that is now residing in the Computer.

```
5 PRINT "TYPE IN A VALUE FOR A."
10 INPUT A
```

...and RUN.

The Computer will print:

```
TYPE IN A VALUE FOR A
?
```

See the question mark and flashing cursor on the display? It means, "it's your turn -- and I'm waiting..."

Type in a number, press **ENTER** and see what happens. The program responds in exactly the same way as when we changed numbers by *changing* Line 10. RUN the program several more times to get the feel of the INPUT statement.

Pretty powerful, isn't it?

Let's add a touch of class to the INPUT process by changing Line 5 as follows:

```
5 PRINT "TYPE IN A VALUE FOR A";
```

Look at that Line very carefully. Do you see how it differs from the earlier Line 5? It is different -- a *semi-colon* has been added at the end of the Line.

Did you use the EDITor to add the semi-colon?

Think back a bit. We used semicolons before in PRINT statements, but only in the middle to hook several together to print close together on the same display line. In this case, we put a semicolon at the *end*, so the *question mark* from the Line 10 will print on the same line rather than down there by itself. After changing Line 5 as above, RUN. It should read:

```
TYPE IN A VALUE FOR A? ▓
```

We cannot use semicolons indiscriminately at the end of PRINT statements. It is only meant to hook two Lines together, *both* of which print something. The INPUT Line PRINTs the question mark. We will later connect two long Lines starting with PRINT by a "trailing semicolon" so as to PRINT everything on the same Line.

The Model 100 INTERPRETER is able to speak "The King's BASIC" as well as a variety of dialects. The first of the many "short-cuts" we learn combining PRINT and INPUT into one statement.

Interpreter -- is the internal program that allows us to "rap" with the Model 100's insides in the English language. We are studying BASIC, which stands for Beginners All-purpose Symbolic Instruction Code.

> Sometimes the word "dialect" is used when talking about the different forms of a computer language. Just as with dialects in "human" languages, there are differences in the way some computers use BASIC words. That's why I wrote *The Basic Handbook, Encyclopedia of the BASIC Language* available at better computer and bookstores everywhere in English, and translated into French, German, Swedish, Norwegian, Dutch and Italian.

Change Line 5 to read:

```
5 INPUT "TYPE IN A VALUE FOR A";A
```

delete Line 10 by typing:

```
10
```

...and RUN.

The results come out exactly the same, don't they? Here is what we have changed:

1. PRINT to INPUT

2. Both statements on the same Line

3. Eliminated the extra Line

In the long programs which you will be writing, running and converting, this shortcut will be valuable.

Up to now, all our programs have been strictly one-shot affairs. You type RUN, the Computer executes the program, PRINTs the results (if any) and comes back with an Ok. To repeat the program, we have to type RUN again. Can you think of another way to make the Computer execute a program two or more times?

> No -- don't enlarge the program by repeating its steps over and over again -- that's not very creative!

We'll answer that question by upgrading our Celsius-to-Fahrenheit conversion program (Chapter 7). If you think GOTO is a powerful statement in everyday life, wait 'til you see what it does for a Computer program!

Type NEW and the following:

```
10 REM *IMPROVED PROGRAM*
20 INPUT "TEMP IN DEGREES (C)";C
30 F = (9/5)*C = 32
40 PRINT C;"DEG. (C) =";F;"DEG. (F)"
50 PRINT
60 GOTO 20
```

...and RUN.

The Computer will keep asking for more until you get tired or the batteries give out. To stop the program, press the SHIFT key and the **BREAK** key (or CTRL C) at the same time. This is the kind of thing a Computer is best at -- doing the same thing over and over. Modify some of the other programs to make them self-repeating. You'll find they're much more useful this way.

These have been five long and "meaty" lessons, so go back and review them all again, repeating those assignments where you feel weak. We are moving into progressively deeper water, and complete mastery of these *fundamentals* is your only life preserver.

Learned in Chapter 9

Statements

INPUT
INPUT with built-in PRINT

Miscellaneous

; Trailing semicolon

Chapter 10

Calculator Or Immediate Mode

Two Easy Features

Before continuing our exploration of the nooks and crannies of the Computer acting as a *computer,* we should be aware that it also works well as a *calculator.* If we *omit* the Line number before certain statements and commands, the Computer will execute them and display the answer. What's more, it will work as a calculator even when another Computer program is loaded, *without disturbing that program.* All we need, to be in the calculator mode, is the prompt ▓.

EXAMPLE: How much is 3 times 4? Type in:

    PRINT 3 * 4   ENTER

...the answer comes back:

    12

EXAMPLE: How much is 345 divided by 123?

Type:

    PRINT 345/123

...the answer is:

    2.8048780487805

Spend a few minutes making up routine arithmetic problems of your own and use the calculator mode to solve them. Any arithmetic expression which can be used in a program can also be evaluated in the calculator mode. This includes parentheses and chain calculations like A * B * C.

Try the following:

    PRINT (2/3)*(3/2)

The answer is:

    1

Here's a new shortcut. Try:

    ?3*4   ENTER

? is shorthand for PRINT. The Model 100 does the conversion automatically.

Calculator Mode For Troubleshooting

Suppose a program isn't giving the answers we expect. How can we troubleshoot it? One way is to ask the Computer to tell what it knows about the variables used in the resident program.

EXAMPLE: If our program uses the variable X, we can ask the Computer to:

    PRINT X

The Computer will PRINT the present value of X.

Keep this handy tip in mind as you get into more complex programs.

Another thought: *Something* is stored in every memory cell (even if *you* have not put anything there). Enter this instruction in the calculator mode:

    PRINT A;B;C;D;E;F;G;H;I;J;K;L;M;N;O;P;Q;
    R;S;T;U;V;W;X;Y;Z   ENTER

The answers depend on the values last given those variables -- even from much earlier programs.

We will probably get all zeros.

If you turn the Computer off, then on again, all variables will be set to 0. Typing RUN also "INITIALIZES" the variables to 0.

The FRE(0) Command

Since programs do occupy space in the Computer's memory, and program size is limited to how much memory we have purchased, it may be important to know how much memory a given program is occupying. That's what the FRE(0) Command is for.

This manual is meant to be for the Computer operator and programmer, so we are studiously avoiding Computer electronics theory -- when possible.

The least amount of memory available for the Model 100 is "8K". This means there are about 8,000 different memory locations or "Bytes" to store and process programs. If you have "24K" of memory, the number of locations is about 24,000.

BYTE -- is the basic unit of storage for most Computers; normally it is considered as a string of eight binary digits (bits). Thus a byte = 8 bits.

Let's clear out any resident program by typing NEW **ENTER** and see just how much memory is available.

One way to determine the total amount of available memory is to read the value in the Main Menu. Press **F8** and note the Free Byte value shown on the bottom of the display, then return to BASIC.

Now type:

```
PRINT FRE(0)
```
           (Remember, ? can be substituted for PRINT)

Notice that this value is somewhat less than the value found in the Main Menu, 256 less to be precise. BASIC automatically reserves this space in memory for "array variables". Later, we will learn about array variables and see how the array memory space can be changed.

Type in this simple program:

```
10 A = 25            ENTER
```

then measure the memory remaining by typing:

```
PRINT FRE(0)         ENTER
```

0 is a "dummy" value used with FRE. Any number or letter can be used.

A little subtraction tells us that the program took 11 bytes of space. Here is how we account for it:

→ WRONG - NO MEMORY IS OCCUPIED.

1. Each Line number and the space following it (regardless of how small or large that Line number is) occupies 4 bytes. The "carriage return" at the end of the Line takes 1 more byte, even though it does not print on the display. Thus, memory "overhead" for each Line, short or long, is 5 bytes.   → 1 BYTE ONLY

2. Each letter, number and space takes 1 byte. In the above program 5 bytes for overhead + 6 bytes for the characters = 11 bytes.

Go into EDIT and change the Line Number to 9999, then check the memory with PRINT FRE(0). How many bytes used now? Right! Still 11.

EDIT again, removing the spaces on both sides of the =. Did it change the storage used? Yes. 1 byte for each space.

Now, type RUN, then check the memory. We just used up 11 more bytes! When RUN, a simple variable like the A takes up 3 bytes and the numerical value takes up another 8, totaling 11.

We will be studying memory requirements in more detail later.

Obviously, the short learning programs we have written so far are not taking a lot of memory space. This changes quickly, however, as we move to more sophisticated programming. Make a habit of typing PRINT FRE(0) when completing a program to develop a sense of its size and memory requirements.

Learned in Chapter 10

Functions

FRE(0)

Miscellaneous

Calculator Mode
Memory
Byte
Using ? for PRINT

Chapter 11

Saving And Loading BASIC Programs

We will soon write and run long and powerful programs. It becomes tedious to type them in accurately each time we want to use them. So far the program we typed in in Chapter 10 (`10 A = 25`) is stored in the Computer's memory. Let's add one more line:

```
20 PRINT "THE VALUE OF A IS"; A
```

The program remains there when we return to the Main Menu or even if we turn the Computer off. But how can we store this resident program while we work on a new one?

The Model 100 permits several methods. We can save programs in its internal memory or on cassette tape, or we can transfer them via the RS-232 port to another Model 100 or a larger Computer. We can externally store an unlimited number of files, far beyond the Computer's ability to hold them all at the same time.

Internal Storage

To file this program into the Computer's memory from BASIC, press **F3**. The display shows:

```
Save "▒
```

Remember, to turn on the soft keys LABEL line press **LABEL**.

Type:

    XXX"   **ENTER**   (" mark is optional)

To verify that it has been SAVEd, press **F1**. Our program is shown as:

    XXX.BA*

The .BA in XXX.BA means it is a BASIC program. The asterisk is a flag indicating that XXX.BA is the program we are currently working on. Files ending in .DO are TEXT files we created in earlier parts of this book.

F8 to the Main Menu and see that the program is listed without the *.

Return to BASIC and press **F5** to LIST the program. Oops…no program. Once the program is named and SAVEd in memory, the Computer does not retain it as the resident BASIC program. A quick check of the files with **F1** shows XXX.BA without the *, confirming that it is no longer resident.

Press **F2**. The display responds with:

    Load "▒

type:

    XXX"   **ENTER**   (as with Save ", the ending " is optional)

Ok indicates the program was found and was LOADed. Press **F5** to check the LISTing.

Shortcut

There is a quicker way to enter BASIC *and* RUN our program. **F8** to the Main Menu, place the cursor over XXX.BA and **ENTER**.

    THE VALUE OF A IS 25
    OK
    ▒

Chapter 11

We are in BASIC, the program is loaded, and it has even RUN!

Press **F5**, and there's our program.

Cassette Storage

The Model 100 has a built-in "Cassette Tape Interface" which allows us to record and store any program on high quality cassette tape. A full "8K" of memory can be *DUMPed* onto tape or *LOADed* from tape, in under 1 minute. Most programs are shorter and take even less time.

> DUMPed and LOADed are everyday terms used with Computers to indicate "pour out" and "load in" Computer programs.

Recording

Only a little practice is required. Follow the yellow brick road:

Hook up a recorder, just as we did for our TEXT files on page 32.

Press **F3**, and after the Computer says:

```
Save "▨
```

"DUMP" the program to tape by typing:

```
CAS:A        ENTER
```

> CAS tells the Computer that we want this program saved on CAScassette tape under the name "A". We can specify any name of up to 6 letters and numbers.

When `Ok` and the flashing cursor return and the motor stops, the program is SAVEd on tape. It is also in the Computer's memory having only been "copied" out.

Do it again, for safety. This time let's use a short cut. Type C (don't hit **ENTER** yet) then press **F3**. The display shows:

```
CSave "▨
```

Enter the name:

    A   **ENTER**

CSave stands for "Save on Cassette". "A" is again assigned as the program name.

LOADing

Reversing the process and LOADing (copying) the program from tape into the Computer is just as easy.

1. Be sure the tape is fully rewound and the plugs are all in place.

2. Push down the PLAY button until it locks. Set the Volume control to about 5.

IMPORTANT: Too little or too much volume will cause a bad "LOAD".

4. Press F3, and after the Computer displays:

    Load "▓

type in:

    CAS:A   **ENTER**

and the data will flow from the tape into the Computer.

When the Computer finds the file, it displays:

    Found:A

The internal speaker lets us listen to the data as the Computer accepts it. *Digital data sounds terrible!*

When Ok and the flashing cursor returns, the motor will stop and the LOAD is complete. The program also remains on the tape.

> If the load is bad and the recorder does not stop, press **SHIFT** **BREAK** or the RESET button. This will take the Computer out of the LOAD or SAVE mode and return control to the keyboard.

5. RUN the program to see that the data transfer was successful. In the event that it was not, repeat the above steps, being sure that all cables are properly connected, *the volume is set to 5* and the tape recorder heads are clean.

Rewind the tape and prepare the recorder again. This time we'll load using another short cut. Type C (don't hit **ENTER** yet) then press **F2**. The display shows:

```
CLoad "▓
```

Type the name:

```
A        ENTER
```

and the program named A is CLOADed.

Cassette storage is very reliable as long as you use premium quality tapes. With some experience, the noise from the Computer's speaker will even seem to make sense.

CLOAD?

We can compare a program on tape against the one in memory. That way we are sure of getting a good recording before erasing the program from memory.

Rewind the tape. Set it up to play, and type:

```
CLOAD?"A"        ENTER
```

...and RUN.

It looks and sounds like we are loading in a program, but are actually just comparing program "A", character for character, against what's already in the Computer. We are not erasing or changing the memory. If they don't match up for any reason, the test will stop and the display will read:

```
Verify failed
Ok
```

Which means we'd better CSave the program again, maybe on a different tape.

If we just type:

```
CLOAD?
```

without specifying the name of the program, it will check the first program on the tape against memory, and that's normally all we want to do.

KILLing Files

With our program safely stored outside the Computer, we can "free up" some memory space by typing:

```
KILL "XXX.BA"
```
ENTER

What's this, the display displays:

```
?FC Error
```

A quick check of the menu with **F1** indicates that we still have a file called XXX.BA*. Why wasn't it KILLed? The Model 100 cannot KILL a file that is still resident, as indicated by the *. We have to **F8** to the Main Menu, enter BASIC and:

```
KILL "XXX.BA"
```
ENTER

Sometimes the memory gets so full, it won't even allow us to go into BASIC and kill files. If this happens, call up a TEXT file (.DO), delete a paragraph or two, then enter BASIC and proceed to kill files that are no longer needed.

Learned in Chapter 11

Commands	Commands	Miscellaneous
LOAD""	SAVE""	"loading"
LOAD:CAS	SAVE:CAS	"dumping"
CLoad	CSave	
CLoad?	KILL""	

Chapter 12

FOR-NEXT Looping

A major difference between the Computer and a calculator is the Computer's ability to do the same thing over and over an outrageous number of times! This one capability plus larger displays more than any other, separates the two.

The FOR-NEXT loop is of such overwhelming importance in putting our Computer to work, that few of the programming areas we will explore from this point on will exclude it. Its simplicity and variations are the heart of its effectiveness; and its power is truly staggering.

Type NEW and then the following program:

```
10 PRINT "HELP! MY COMPUTER'S BERSERK!"
20 GOTO 10
```

...and RUN.

The Computer is continuously writing:

```
HELP! MY COMPUTER'S BERSERK!
```

It will continue indefinitely until we tell it to stop. When you have seen enough, hit **SHIFT** **BREAK** or **CTRL** **C**. This "breaks" the program RUN.

Endless Loop

We created what is called an "endless loop". Remember our earlier programs which kept coming back for more INPUT? They were a very similar "loop".

Line 20 is an unconditional GOTO statement which causes the Computer to cycle back and forth ("loop") between Lines 10 and 20 forever if not halted. This idea has great potential if we can harness it.

Modify the program to read:

```
8 FOR N = 1 TO 5
10 PRINT "HELP! MY COMPUTER'S BERSERK!"
20 NEXT N
30 PRINT "NO - IT'S UNDER CONTROL."
```

...and RUN it.

Behold:

```
HELP! MY COMPUTER'S BERSERK!
HELP! MY COMPUTER'S BERSERK!
HELP! MY COMPUTER'S BERSERK!
HELP! MY COMPUTER'S BERSERK!
HELP! MY COMPUTER'S BERSERK!
NO - IT'S UNDER CONTROL.
```

The FOR-NEXT loop created between Lines 8 and 20 caused the Computer to cycle through Lines 8, 10, and 20 exactly 5 times, then proceed to Line 30. Each time the Computer hit Line 20 it saw "NEXT N." The word NEXT caused the value of N to increase (or STEP) by exactly 1. The Computer "conditionally" went back to the FOR N = statement that began the loop.

Execution of the NEXT statement is "conditional" on N being less than 5 because Line 8 says FOR N = 1 TO 5. After the 5th pass through the loop, the built-in test fails, the loop is broken and the program execution moves on.

> The FOR-NEXT statement harnessed the endless loop!

In the example we used the variable N. Any single or double letter (or letter/number) variable can be used.

The Step Function

There are times when it is desirable to increment the FOR-NEXT loop by some value other than 1. The STEP function allows that. EDIT Line 8 to read:

```
8 FOR N = 1 TO 5 STEP 2
```

...and RUN.

Line 10 was printed only 3 times (when N=1, N=3, and N=5). On the first pass through the program, when NEXT N was hit, it incremented (or STEPped) the value of N by 2 instead of 1. On the second pass through the loop N equalled 3. On the third pass N equalled 5.

FOR-NEXT loops can be stepped by any decimal number, even negative numbers. Why we would want to step with negative numbers might seem rather vague at this time, but that too will be understood with time. Meanwhile, change Line 8 again:

```
8 FOR N = 5 TO 1 STEP -1
```

...and RUN.

Five passes through the loop stepping *down* from 5 to 1 is exactly the same as stepping *up* from 1 to 5. Line 10 still was printed 5 times. Change the STEP from -1 to -2.5 and RUN again. Amazing! It printed exactly twice. Smart Computer. Change the STEP back to -1.

Modifying the FOR-NEXT Loop

Suppose we want to print both Lines 10 and 30 five times, alternating between them. How will you change the program to accomplish it? Go ahead and make the change.

HINT: If you can't figure it out, try moving the NEXT N Line to another position.

Right -- you moved Line 20 to Line 40 and the display reads:

```
HELP! MY COMPUTER'S BERSERK!
NO - IT'S UNDER CONTROL.
HELP! MY COMPUTER'S BERSERK!
NO - IT'S UNDER CONTROL.
```

... etc. -- 3 more times.

The Pause That Refreshes
Now that the Computer is printing more than 8 lines, the top lines are running off the top of the display.

RUN the program again and press the **PAUSE** key before the first line reaches the top. Press it again and execution continues. With only 8 lines of display space, this key comes in very handy.

DO Looping
How would you modify the program so Line 10 is printed 5 times, then Line 30 is printed 3 times? Make the changes and RUN.

The new program might read:

```
8 FOR N = 1 TO 5
10 PRINT "HELP! MY COMPUTER'S BERSERK!"
20 NEXT N
25 FOR M = 1 TO 3
30 PRINT "NO - IT'S UNDER CONTROL."
40 NEXT M
```

We now have a program with *two* controlled loops, sometimes called *DO-loops*. The first DO-loop *DOes* something five times; the second one *DOes* something three times. We used the letter N for the first loop and M for the second, but any letters can be used. In fact, since the two loops are totally separate we could have used the letter N for both of them -- not an uncommon practice in large programs where most of the letters are needed as variables.

RUN the program, being sure you understand the fundamental principles and the variations we have introduced.

Incremental Looping

There is nothing magic about the FOR-NEXT loop, in fact, you may have already thought of another (longer) way to accomplish the same thing by using features we learned earlier. Stop now, and see if you can figure out a way to construct a workable do-loop substituting something else in place of the FOR-NEXT statement.

Answer:

```
8 N = 1
10 PRINT "HELP! MY COMPUTER'S BERSERK!"
15 N = N + 1
20 IF N < 6 THEN 10
30 PRINT "NO - IT'S UNDER CONTROL."
```

Line 8 *initializes* the value of N, giving it an initial or beginning value of 1. Before initializing to the value we want, N could have been any number from previous program Lines. Note again that a RUN automatically resets all the variables back to 0 before the program executes.

176   Chapter 12

> *Initializes* -- initially, or at the beginning, sets the value of one of our variables (or starts a program back at the beginning).

Line 15 then *increments* it by 1, making N one more than whatever it was before. Line 10 uses one of our relational operators (<) to see that the new value of N is within the bounds we have established. If not, the test fails and the program continues.

> *Increments* -- steps (increases or decreases) values by specific amounts -- by 1's, 3's, 5's, or whatever.

Note that in this system of *incrementing* and testing we do not send the program back to Line 8 as was the case with FOR-NEXT.   What would happen if we did?

___

Answer: We would keep re-initializing the value of N to equal 1, and would again form an endless loop.

The opposite of *incrementing* is *decrementing*.   Change the program so Line 15 reads:

```
15 N = N - 1
```

> To Decrement is to make smaller.

... then make other changes as needed to make the program work.

Answer: The changed Lines read:

```
8 N = 6
15 N = N - 1
20 IF N > 1 THEN 10
```

Putting FOR-NEXT to Work

It isn't very exciting just seeing or doing the same thing over and over, so there have to be a more noble purposes for the FOR-NEXT loop. There are -- many of them; and we will be learning new uses for a long, long time.

Let's suppose we want to print out a chart showing how the time it takes to fly from London to San Diego varies with the speed at which we fly. Remember, the formula is D = R*T. Let's print out the flight time required for each speed between 200 mph and 1000 mph, in increments of 100 mph. The program might look like this:

```
10 REM * TIME VS RATE FLIGHT CHART *
20 CLS
30 D = 6000
40 PRINT"   LONDON TO SAN DIEGO"
50 PRINT"   DISTANCE =";D;"(MILES)"
60 PRINT"RATE (MPH)","TIME (HOURS)"
70 FOR R=200 TO 1000 STEP 100
80    T = D/R
90    PRINT R,T
100 NEXT R
```

Type in the program and RUN. Use the **PAUSE** key as necessary to "freeze" the display. Press **PAUSE** to continue the run.

How about that...? Try doing it on the old slide rule or hand calculator!

It is really solving the D = R*T problem nine times in a row for different values and printing out the result. Your display should look like this:

```
     LONDON TO SAN DIEGO
      DISTANCE = 6000 (MILES)
   RATE (MPH)        TIME (HOURS)
      200               30
      300               20
      400               15
      500               12
      600               10
      700               8.571428571428G
      800               7.5
      900               6.6666666666667
     1000               6
```

Analyzing The Program

Look through the program and observe these many features before we do some exercises to change it:

1. The REM statement identifies the program for future use.

2. Line 20 introduces the CLS (Clear Screen) statement to erase the display so we have a nice place to write. It allows us to write in a *top-down* manner. (RUN the program later leaving out this Line to contrast *top-down* with *scroll* mode.) CLS is a very unfussy statement which you will want to use often just to make your printouts neat and impressive.

3. Line 30 *initializes* the value of D. D will remain at its initialized value.

4. Lines 40 and 50 print a chart heading which is indented for appearance.

5. Line 60 prints the chart column headings, and uses *automatic zone spacing* (the comma) to place those headings.

> Remember zone spacing? The comma (,) in a PRINT statement automatically starts the printing in the next PRINT zone, and the second PRINT zone starts at space 15.

6. Line 70 established the FOR-NEXT loop complete with a STEP. It says, "Initialize the rate (R) at 200 mph, and make passes through the "do-loop" with values of R incremented by values of 100 mph until a final value of 1000 mph is reached." Line 100 is the other half of the loop.

7. Line 80 contains the actual formula which calculates the answer.

8. Line 90 PRINTs the two values. They are positioned under their headings by automatic zone spacing (the comma).

9. Lines 80 and 90 are indented from the rest of the program text. This is a simple programming technique highlighting a do-loop which makes reading and troubleshooting easier. You will see it used increasingly as we move on. *Try to adopt good programming practices like this* as you do the exercises. Indenting does take up a little memory space, and on long programs in their final form it is sometimes omitted.

Take a deep breath and go back over any points you might have missed in this lesson. SAVE this program by pressing **F3** and typing:

FLIGHT"

Our study of FOR-NEXT loops continues in the next Chapter.

Learned in Chapter 12

Commands	Statements	Miscellaneous
CLS	FOR-NEXT	Increment
STEP		Decrement
		Initialize
		BREAK key
		PAUSE key
		Top down Display
		Scroll Display
		Do-Loop

Chapter 13

Son of FOR-NEXT

This is heady stuff. If you turned the Computer off between Chapters, load in the "FLIGHT" program which we SAVEd at the end of the last Chapter.

Modify the program so the rate and time are calculated and PRINTed for every 50 mph increment instead of the 100 mph increment presently in the program and RUN.

Answer: `70 FOR R = 200 TO 1000 STEP 50`

When LISTing a program that has more than 8 Lines and the Lines we want to see scroll off the top of the display, we can use the **PAUSE** key to stop and start it, just as with RUN.

Trouble In The Old Corral

What a revolting development! The printout goes so fast and is so long that we have to continually press the **PAUSE** key to read it. *Aught'a known you can't trust these computers!*

For a really classy display we can build a "pause" routine *into the program*. The display will fill, halt a moment, and automatically go on. Since there is no PAUSE, we have to accomplish it by other means.

The Timing Loop
Start by adding Line:

    9 END

We are going to write and experiment with a second little program using Lines 1-9 without erasing the one already resident. The new one must END without plowing ahead into the "Flight" program, thus, Line 9.

The Egg Timer
It takes time to do everything. Even this foxy box takes time to do its thing, though you may be awed by its speed. Add:

    1 PRINT "DON'T GO AWAY"
    2 FOR X = 1 TO 3300
    3 NEXT X
    4 PRINT "TIMER PROGRAM ENDED."

...and RUN.

> Remember back when we learned not to do this (number Lines in tight sequence)? *Well*...if we hadn't followed that rule with our "FLIGHT" program we wouldn't have this nice space to demonstrate the point.

How long did it take? Well, it did take time, didn't it? About 10 seconds? The Computer can do approximately 330 FOR-NEXT loops per second. That means, by specifying the number of loops, you can build in as long a time-delay as you wish.

Change the program to create a 30-second delay. Time it against your watch or clock to see how accurate it is.

Answer: 2 FOR X = 1 TO 9900

EXERCISE 13-1: Using the space in Lines 1 through 8, design a program which asks how many seconds delay we wish, allows us to enter a number, then executes the delay and reports back at the end that the delay is over, and how many seconds it took. A sample answer is in Appendix G.

How To Handle Long Program LISTings

We now have two programs in the Computer. Let's pull a LIST to look at them. My, my--they are so long it's difficult to PAUSE the LISTing to see our new Lines. Now what do we do?

Rather than wring our hands about the problem, type each of the following variations of LIST, and watch the display very carefully as each does its thing:

```
LIST 40          (Lists only Line 40)
LIST -40         (Lists all Lines up through 40)
LIST 40-         (lists all Lines from 40 to end)
LIST 30-70       (Lists all Lines from 80 thru 84)
LIST 8-88        (Note that these numbers are not even in the program)
LIST .           (Lists the current or last Line number)
LIST .-          (Lists the current or last Line number to end)
```

How's that for something to write home about?

Question: How would you look at the resident program up through Line 9?
Answer: type LIST -9 (Talk about a give away!)

Is There No End To This Magic?

To run the first program resident in the Computer -- we just typed RUN. To run the second one we have a foxy variation on RUN called:

```
RUN ###
```

The ###'s represent the number of the Line we want the RUN to start with.

...and, as you might suspect, it is similar to LIST###. To RUN the program starting with Line 10, type:

```
RUN 10
```

...and that's just what happens.

Will wonders never cease? If there are 20 or 30 programs in the Computer at the same time, we can RUN just the one we want, provided we know its starting Line number. What's more, we can start any program in the middle (or elsewhere) for purposes of troubleshooting -- a matter we will become more involved in as our programs get longer and more complicated.

Meanwhile, Back At The Ranch

We got into this whole messy business trying to find a way to slow down our run on the flight times from London to San Diego. In the process we found out a lot more about the Computer and learned to build a timer loop.

More Than One Way

Another way to STOP the fast parade of information through our display is to put in a STOP. Type in:

```
75 IF R = 400 THEN STOP
```

...and `RUN10`.

We know R is going to increment to 400, and that's about one display full, so 400 is a good choice. See how the chart ran out to 350 mph then hit the STOP as 400 came racing down to Line 75. Your display should display the first part of the chart and:

```
Break in 75
```

This means the program is stopped, or broken in Line 75. We can now study the top part of the chart leisurely. To restart the program merely type:

```
CONT         ENTER
```

...and it will pick up and print the rest, or execute until it hits another STOP.

CONT stands for CONTINUE.

At Last

Our ultimate plan is to build a timer into the program so as not to completely STOP execution, but merely delay it so we can study the display. First, let's erase the Lines in the test program that will not be needed in the timer. Type:

```
1    ENTER
4    ENTER
9    ENTER
```

and type `EDIT`

The cursor is now flashing on Line 2 indicating we are in the EDIT mode. Using what you have already learned about the EDITor, change Lines 2, 3 and 75 to:

```
71 IF R<> 400 THEN 80
72 FOR X = 1 TO 2000
73 NEXT X
```

Press **F8** to exit the EDITor.

...and RUN.

Hey! It really works! As long as R does *not* equal 400 the program skips over the delay loop in Lines 72 and 73. When R *does* equal 400, the test "falls through" and Lines 72 and 73 "play catch" 2000 times, delaying the program's execution for about 7 seconds.

SAVE this program on cassette tape as "LONDON" for a future Chapter.

It's been a long and tortuous route with numerous scenic side trips, but we finally made it. Now that you have picked up so many smarts in these two lessons on FOR-NEXT, it's your turn to put them to work.

EXERCISE 13-2: Design, write and RUN a program which will calculate and PRINT income at yearly and monthly rates, based on a 1/12th-year month. Do this for yearly incomes between $5,000 and $20,000 in $1,000 increments. Document your program with REM statements as necessary to explain the equations you create.

Some of our programs are becoming a little too long for us to leave space in the manual for you to write in your ideas. From now on, use a pad of paper for working up your answers.

EXERCISE 13-3: Here's an old chestnut that the Computer really eats up: Design, write and RUN a program which tells how many days we have to work, starting at a penny a day, so if our salary doubles each day we know which day we earn at least a million dollars. Include columns which show each day number, its daily rate, and the total income to-date. Make the program stop after PRINTing the first day your daily rate is a million dollars or more. (After that ... who cares!)

Answers to these Exercises can be found in Appendix G.

The "Brute Force" Method
(Subtitled: Get A Bigger Hammer)

Much to the consternation of some teachers, a great value of the Computer is its ability to do the tedious work involved in the "cut and try", "hunt and peck" or other less respectable methods of finding an answer (or attempting to prove the correctness of a theory, theorem or principle). This method involves trying a mess of possible solutions to see if one fits, or find the closest one, or establish a trend. Beyond that, it can be a powerful learning tool by providing gobs of data in chart or graph form which would simply take too long to generate by hand. For example:

EXERCISE 13-4: You have a 1000 foot roll of fencing wire and want to create a *rectangular* pasture.

Using all of the wire, determine what length and width dimensions will allow you to enclose the maximum number of square feet? Use the brute force method; let the Computer try different values for L and W and print out the Area fenced by each pair of L and W.

The formula for area is Area = Length times Width, or A = L*W

Learned in Chapter 13

Commands	**Statements**	**Miscellaneous**
LIST###	STOP	Timer Loop
RUN###		"Brute force" or
CONT		optimizing method

Chapter 14

Formatting With TAB

From ▩ To TAB To LPRINT

After those last few chapters, time out for an easy one.

We already know 3 ways to set up our output PRINT format.

We can:
    1. Enclose what we want to say in quotes, inserting blank spaces as necessary.

    2. Separate the objects of the PRINT statement with semicolons so as to print them tightly together on the same Line.

    3. Separate the objects of the PRINT statement with commas to print them on the same Line in the two different print "zones".

A fourth way is using the TAB function, which is similar to the TAB on a regular typewriter. TAB is especially useful when the output is columns of numbers with headings. Type in the following program and RUN:

```
10 PRINT TAB(5);"THE";TAB(15);"TOTAL";
TAB(25);"SPENT"
20 PRINT TAB(5);"BUDGET";TAB(15);"YEAR'S";
TAB(25);"THIS"
```

```
30 PRINT TAB(5);"CATEGORY";TAB(15);"BUDGET";
TAB(25);"MONTH"
```

A semicolon is traditionally used following TAB, as shown, but is optional. Think twice before not using them as they greatly improve readability. Like parentheses, their misuse can sometimes affect answers.

The RUN should appear:

```
THE         TOTAL       SPENT
BUDGET      YEAR'S      THIS
CATEGORY    BUDGET      MONTH
```

EXERCISE 14-1: Rewrite and EDIT the program above using the 3 ways we have so far to format PRINTing. Here is a start:

```
10 PRINT"                                    "
20 PRINT"          ","                    "
30 PRINT"          ";TAB(  );"        ";
TAB(  );"        "
```

Use ordinary spacing for the first Line of the heading, zone spacing for the second Line and TABbing for the third Line.

HINT: This isn't as easy as it looks so may require extensive editing. Since automatic zone formatting is not adjustable, the other formats may have to be keyed to it.

Type (also EDIT) and RUN:

```
10 A = 3
20 B = 5
30 C = A + B
40 PRINT TAB(10);"A";TAB(20);"B";TAB(30);"C"
50 PRINT TAB(10);A;TAB(20);B;TAB(30);C
```

It should appear:

```
         A           B           C
         3           5           8
```

Note that the numbers are indented one space beyond the TAB(#). Keep this in mind when lining up (or indenting) headings and answers.

Change Line 20 to read:

```
20 B = -5
```

...and RUN. See why the indenting is necessary?

When numeric variables are printed, the Computer inserts one space to the left of the number to allow for the − or + sign, plus a following space.

The Long Lines Division

Have you ever wondered what would happen if we had to PRINT a great number of headings or answers on the same Line -- but didn't have enough room on the PROGRAM Line to neatly hold all the TAB statements? You have? Really? You're in luck because it's easy. Type and RUN the following program:

```
10 A = 1
20 B = 2
30 C = 3
40 D = 4
50 E = 5
60 F = 6
70 PRINT "A";TAB(5);"B";TAB(10);"C";
80 PRINT TAB(15);"D";TAB(20);"E";
90 PRINT TAB(25);"F"
100 PRINT A;TAB(5);B;TAB(10);C;TAB(15);
110 PRINT D;TAB(20);E;TAB(25);F
```

It's the trailing semicolon (;) that does the trick. It makes the end of one PRINT Line continue right on to the next PRINT Line without activating a carriage return. The combination of TAB and trailing semicolon allows almost infinite flexibility in formatting the output.

EXERCISE 14-2: Rework the answer to Exercise 13-2 to include the WEEKLY rate of pay in the printout. Use the TAB function to have the chart display all 5 columns side by side.

Learned in Chapter 14

Print Modifiers   **Miscellaneous**

TAB   Trailing Semicolon

Chapter 15

Grandson Of FOR-NEXT

The FOR-NEXT loop didn't go away for long. It returns more powerful than ever. Type this program:

```
10 FOR A = 1 TO 3
20  PRINT "A LOOP"
30   FOR B = 1 TO 2
40    PRINT,"B LOOP"
50   NEXT B
60 NEXT A
```

...and RUN.

For good program readability, add 1 blank space in Line 20 before PRINT; 2 in Line 30 before FOR; 3 in 40 before PRINT; and 2 in 50 before NEXT.

The result is:

```
    A LOOP
            B LOOP
            B LOOP
```

```
         A LOOP
                    B LOOP
                    B LOOP
         A LOOP
                    B LOOP
                    B LOOP
```

This display vividly demonstrates operation of the nested FOR-NEXT loop. "Nesting" is used in the same sense that drinking glasses are "nested" when stored to save space. Certain types of portable chairs, empty cardboard boxes, etc. can be nested. They fit one inside the other for easy stacking.

> When writing programs, be sure to indent Lines to highlight nesting or program flow. It helps when reading them -- and is a great aid when debugging (troubleshooting) program problems.

Let's analyze the program a Line at a time:

Line 10 establishes the first FOR-NEXT loop, called A, and directs that it be executed 3 times.

Line 20 prints A LOOP so we will know where it came from in the program. See how this program Line is indented 1 space to make it stand out as being nested in the "A loop"?

Line 30 establishes the second loop, called B, and directs that it be executed twice. It is indented even more so you can instantly see that it is buried even deeper in the "A" loop.

Line 40 has a comma following PRINT to kick us into the next print zone where B LOOP is printed. Makes for clear distinction on the display between A loop and B loop, eh?

Line 50 completes the "B" loop and returns control to Line 30 for as many executions of the "B" loop as Line 30 directs. So far we have printed one "A" and one "B".

Line 60 ends the first pass through the "A" loop and sends control back to Line 10, the beginning of the A loop. The A loop has to be

executed 3 times before the program run is complete, printing "A" 3 times and "B" 6 times (3 times 2).

Study the program and the explanation until you completely comprehend. It's simple but powerful magic.

OK, to get a better "feel" for this nested loop (or loop within a loop) business, let's play with the program. Change Line 10 to read:

```
10 FOR A = 1 TO 5
```

...and RUN.

Right! A was printed 5 times, meaning the "A" loop was executed 5 times, and B was printed 10 times -- twice for each pass of the "A" loop. Now change Line 30 to read

```
30    FOR B = 1 TO 4
```

...and RUN.

Nothing to it! A was printed 5 times and B printed 20 times. If you are having trouble counting A's and B's as they whiz by, remember what to do? Just press **PAUSE** to stop execution and temporarily freeze the display.

How To Goof-Up Nested FOR-NEXT Loops

The most common error beginning programmers make with nested loops is improper nesting. Change these Lines:

```
50    NEXT A
60 NEXT B
```

...and RUN.

The Computer says:

```
?NF Error in 60
```
            (Next without For in Line 60)

Looking at the program we quickly see that the B loop is *not* nested within the A loop. We have the FOR part of the B loop inside the A loop, but the NEXT part is outside it. This doesn't work!

A later chapter deals with something called "flow charting", a means of helping us plan programs and avoid this type of problem. Meanwhile we just have to be careful.

Breaking Out Of Loops

Improper nesting is illegal, but breaking out of a loop when a desired condition has been met is OK. Add and change these Lines:

```
50    NEXT B
55 IF A = 2 GOTO 100
60 NEXT A
99 END
100 PRINT "A EQUALS 2, RUN ENDED."
```

...and RUN.

As the display shows, we "bailed out" of the A loop when A equalled 2 and hit the test Line at 55. The END in Line 99 is just a precautionary roadblock set up to stop the Computer from running into Line 100 unless specifically directed to go there. That would never happen in this simple program, but we will use *protective ENDs* from time to time to remind us that Lines which should be reached only by specific GOTO or IF-THEN statements must be protected against accidental "hits".

We'll be seeing a lot of the nested FOR-NEXT loop now that we know what it is and can put it to use.

EXERCISE 15-1: Enter the original program found at the beginning of this Chapter. It contains 2 B loops nested within 3 A loops. Make the necessary additions so a new loop called "C" will be nested within the B loop, and will print "C LOOP" 4 times for each pass of the B loop.

Learned in Chapter 15

Miscellaneous

Nested FOR-NEXT loops
Protective END blocks

Chapter 16

The INTeger Function

Integer??? "I can't even pronounce it, let along understand it." Oh, come, come. Don't let old nightmares of being trapped in Algebra class stop you now. It's pronounced (IN-teh-jur) and simply means a whole number like 12, −5, 0, or 3, etc. How difficult can that be? Come to think of it, some folks make a whole career of complicating simple ideas. We're here to do just the opposite.

The INTEGER function, INT(X), allows us to "round off" any number, large or small, positive or negative, into an integer, or whole number.

> Careful -- we're not talking about ordinary rounding. Ordinary rounding gives us the closest whole number, whether it's larger or smaller than X. INT(X), on the other hand, gives us the LARGEST WHOLE NUMBER WHICH IS LESS THAN OR EQUAL TO X. As you'll see in this chapter, this is a very versatile form of rounding -- in fact, we can use it to produce the other, "ordinary" kind of rounding.

Type NEW to clear out any old programs, then type:

```
30 X = 3.14159
40 Y = INT(X)
70 PRINT "Y = ";Y
```

...and RUN.

The display reads:

```
Y = 3
```

Oh -- success is so sweet! It rounded 3.14159 off to 3. Change Line 30 to read:

```
30 X = -3.14159
```

...and RUN.

Good Grief! It rounded the answer DOWN to read:

```
Y = -4
```

What kind of rounding is this? Easy. The INT function ALWAYS rounds DOWN to the next LOWEST WHOLE number. Pretty hard to get that confused! It makes a positive number less positive, and makes a negative number more negative (same thing as less positive). At least it's consistent.

Taking it a Line at a time:

> Line 30 set the value of X (or any of our other alphabet-soup variables) equal to the value we selected, in this case π.

> Line 40 finds the INTeger value of the above number and assigns it a variable name. We chose Y.

> Line 70 prints a little identification (Y =) followed by the value of Y.

Not Content To Leave Well Enough Alone

We can do some foxy things by combining a FOR-NEXT loop with the INTeger function.

Change the program to read:

```
30 X = 3.14159
40 Y = INT(X)
```

```
50 Z = X - Y
60 PRINT "X = ";X
70 PRINT "Y = ";Y
80 PRINT "Z = ";Z
```

...and RUN.

AHA! I don't know what we've discovered but it must be good for something. It reads:

```
X =  3.14159
Y =  3
Z =  .14159
```

We've split the value of X into its INTeger (whole number) value and called it Y, and its decimal value and called it Z.

Line 60, 70, and 80 merely printed the results.

Suppose we only need the value of π accurate to three places, (Of course, we can make X = 3.142, but that's not the point.) Type NEW, then enter this program:

```
10 X = 3.14159
20 X = X + .0005
30 X = INT(X * 1000)/1000
40 PRINT X
```

...and RUN.

Adding .0005 gives our fraction a "push in the right direction." If this fraction has a digit greater than 4 in its 10-thousandths-place, then adding .0005 will effectively increase the thousandth's-place digit by 1. Otherwise, the added .0005 will have no effect on the final result. This results in what's called 4/5 rounding.

Try using other values than π for X (just make sure X*1000 isn't too large for the INT function to handle).

202   Chapter 16

It's easy to change the program to accomplish rounding at a different point. For example, to round X off at the hundredths-place (2 digits to the right of the decimal point), change Lines 20 and 30 to read:

```
10 X = 3.14159
20 X = X + .005
30 X = INT(X * 100)/100
40 PRINT X
```

...and RUN, using several values for X.

> This trick is very useful when you're printing out dollars-and-cents. It prevents $39.995-type prices.

HMMMM!!!

Do you suppose there is any way to separate each of the digits in 3.14159, or in any other number? Do you suppose we would have mentioned it if there wasn't? After all...(mumble, mumble...).

It's really your turn to do some creative thinking, but we'll get it started and see if you can finish this idea. First, wipe out the resident program and retype this program that splits X into an integer and fractional part:

```
30 X = 3.14159
40 Y = INT(X)
50 Z = X - Y
60 PRINT "X = ";X
70 PRINT "Y = ";Y
80 PRINT "Z = ";Z
```

Got any ideas? No? Well, think some more.

Time Out For Creative Thinking!

   (...brief interlude of recorded music...)

Right! If we multiply the value of Z by 10 then Z will become a whole number plus a decimal part: 1.4159. We can then take its integer value and strip off the decimal part, leaving the left hand digit standing alone. Let's label the left-hand digit L and see what happens. Enter:

```
90 M = Z * 10
100 L = INT(M)
110 PRINT "L = ";L
```

...and RUN.

Aha! It reads:

```
X =   3.14159
Y =   3
Z =   .14159
L =   1
```

We peeled off the leftmost digit in the decimal. Can you think of any way we might use a FOR-NEXT loop in order to strip off some more?

After all, these digits might not be just a more accurate value of pi, but a coded message from a cereal box. If you don't have the decoder ring it's tough luck, Charlie -- unless you have a Computer!

     (...More recorded music...)

Enough thinking there on company time! Enter these Lines:

```
95 FOR A = 1 TO 5
120 M = M - L
130 M = M * 10
140 NEXT A
```

...and RUN.

VOILA! The "printout" reads:

```
X =   3.14159
Y =   3
Z =   .14159
L =   1
L =   4
L =   1
L =   5
L =   9
```

Line 95 began a FOR-NEXT loop with 5 passes, one for each of the 5 digits right of the decimal.

Line 120 creates a new decimal value of M (just a temporary storage location) by stripping off the integer part. (Plugging in the values, M = 1.4159 − 1 = .4159)

Line 130 does the same as Line 90 did, multiplying the new decimal value times 10 so as to make the left-hand digit an integer and vulnerable to being snatched away by the INT function. (M = .4159 * 10 = 4.159)

Line 140 moves the control back to Line 95 for another pass through the clipping program...and the rest is history.

Troubleshooting Tools

We can insert temporary PRINT Lines anywhere in any program to follow every step in its execution. The Computer can actually overwhelm us with data. By carefully indicating what we want to know, we can observe the inner details of any process. Start by adding this Line:

```
92 PRINT " #92 M = ";M
```

...and RUN.

The essentials of this "test" or "debugging" or "flag" Line are:

1. It PRINTs something.

2. The PRINT tells the Line number, for analysis and easy location for later erasure.

3. It tells the name of the variable you are watching at that point in the program.

4. It gives the *value* of that variable at *that point*.

This "flagging" is such a wonderful troubleshooting tool in stubborn programs that you will want to make a habit of never forgetting to use it when the going gets tough.

It is most helpful of all when inserted in FOR-NEXT loops -- so:

```
97 PRINT " #97 A = ";A
```

...and RUN.

Wow! The data really comes thick and fast! It tells what is happening during each pass of the loop. Hard to keep track of so much information, and we've barely begun. Is there some way to make it more readable?

Yes, there are lots of ways. Indenting is one simple way to separate the answers from the troubleshooting data. Change Lines 92 and 97 as follows:

```
92 PRINT ,"#92 M = ";M
97 PRINT ,"#97 A = ";A
```

...and RUN.

Ahh. How sweet it is. That is so easy to read, let's monitor some more points in the program. Type:

```
125 PRINT TAB(22);"#125 M = ";M
135 PRINT TAB(22);"#135 M = ";M
```

...and RUN.

Egad, Igor! We've created a monster!

There it is. All the data we can handle (and then some). By using the **PAUSE** key to temporarily halt execution, we can study the data at every step to understand how the program works (or doesn't). Do it. Understand this program and all its little lessons completely. When you are satisfied, go back and erase out the "flags". We have learned quite enough for this Chapter.

EXERCISE 16-1: Enter this straightforward NEW program for finding the area of a circle.

```
10 P=3.14159
20 PRINT "RADIUS", "AREA"
30 PRINT
40 FOR R=1 TO 10
50   A = P * R * R
60   PRINT R,A
70 NEXT R
```

...and RUN.

Area equals π times the radius squared (that is, the radius times itself).

Pretty routine stuff -- huh? Problem is, who needs all those little numbers to the far right of the decimal point. *Oh, you do?* Well, there's one in every crowd. The rest of us can do without them. Without giving any hints, modify the resident program to suppress all the numbers to the right of the decimal point.

EXERCISE 16-2: Now, knowing just enough to be dangerous, and in need of a lot of humility, change Line 55 so that each value of *area* is rounded (down) to be accurate to 1 decimal place. For example:

```
RADIUS                    AREA
   1                       3.1
```

etc.

Ummm -- yaas. Hang in there. It's very simple.

EXERCISE 16-3: Carrying the above Exercise one step further, modify the program Line 55 to round (down) the value of area to be accurate to 2 decimal places.

EXERCISE 16-4: Change the London to San Diego program in Chapter 12 to print out to the nearest 1/10th hour.

Learned in Chapter 16

Functions

INT(X)

Miscellaneous

Flags

Chapter 17

More Branching Statements

It Went That-A-Way

Enter this NEW program:

```
10 INPUT "TYPE A # BETWEEN 1 & 5";N
20 IF N = 1 GOTO 110
30 IF N = 2 GOTO 130
40 IF N = 3 GOTO 150
50 IF N = 4 GOTO 170
60 IF N = 5 GOTO 190
70 PRINT " THE # WAS NOT BETWEEN 1 AND 5
    --- DUMMY!"
```

Notice anything funny about Line 70? It takes up two Lines on the display! That's because it contains more than 40 characters (including Line number and blank spaces). This is perfectly all right, as you may already have discovered in your own programming efforts. In fact, a program Line can contain up to 254 characters (including Line numbers and spaces). To enter or LIST such a long Line takes over four Display Lines; but it's still just ONE NUMBERED PROGRAM LINE!

```
99 END
110 PRINT "N = 1"
```

```
120 END
130 PRINT "N = 2"
140 END
150 PRINT "N = 3"
160 END
170 PRINT "N = 4"
180 END
190 PRINT "N = 5"
```

RUN it a few times to feel comfortable with it, and be sure it is "debugged".

Debugged is an old Latin word which, freely translated, means "getting all the errors out of your Computer program."

This program works fine for examining the value of a variable, N, and sending the Computer off to a certain Line number to do what it says there. If there are lots of possible directions in which to branch, however, we will want to use a greatly improved test function called ON-GOTO which cuts out lots of Lines of programming. Let's examine an ON-GOTO after you do the following:

Erase Lines 20, 30, 40, 50 and 60.

Enter this new Line:

```
20 ON N GOTO 110,130,150,170,190
```

...and RUN a few times, as before.

Works just the same, doesn't it?

The ON-GOTO statement is really pretty simple, though it looks hard. Line 20 says,

if the INTEGER value of N is 1 then GOTO Line 110.

if the INTEGER value of N is 2 then GOTO Line 130.

if the INTEGER value of N is 3 then GOTO Line 150.

if the INTEGER value of N is 4 then GOTO Line 170.

if the INTEGER value of N is 5 then GOTO Line 190.

if the INTEGER value of N is not one of the numbers listed above, then move on to the next Line.

Remember, an INTEGER is just a whole number.

The ON-GOTO statement has its own built-in INT statement. It really acts like this:

```
20 ON INT(N)GOTO...ETC.
```

RUN again and type in the following values of N to prove the point:

1.5
3.99999
0.999
5.999
6.0001

Get the picture?

Variations On A Theme

There are lots of tricks that can be played to milk the most from ON-GOTO. For example, if we want to branch out to 15 different locations but don't want to type that many different numbers on a ON-GOTO Line, we can use several Lines, like this:

```
20 ON N GOTO 110,130,150,170,190
25 ON N-5 GOTO 210,230,250,270,290
30 ON N-10 GOTO 310,330,350,370,390
```

and fill in the proper responses at those Line numbers.

In Line 25, it was necessary to subtract 5 from the number being input as N, since each new ON-GOTO Line starts counting again from the number 1. In Line 30, since we had already provided for inputs between 1 and 10, we subtract 10 from the input N to cover the range from 11 through 15. By using the ON-GOTO statement, we have programmed into 3 Lines what would otherwise have taken 15 Lines. By packing more branching options into each ON-GOTO Line, we could have done it in 2 Lines or less, depending on the number of digits in the Line numbers of the branch locations.

As in most of our examples, we could have used any letter after "ON", not just N. As we just saw, N can be the value of a letter variable, or a complete expression, either calculated in place (as here) or in a previous Line.

Trade Secret

Due to the vagaries of rounding error and the chance the error might just round a number like "N" a tad below the INTeger value expected, it is common to see something like this:

```
50 ON N+.2 GOTO 100,200,300 ETC.
```

The effect of this shifty move is to add just a "pinch" to the incoming value of N, knowing full well that the ON-GOTO statement contains its own INT function. If N happens to have been rounded down to say 1.98 (instead of the 2.000 expected), 0.2 will be added to it making N 1.98 + .2 = 2.18 which the built-in INT will round down to the desired 2. Pretty sneaky. Values between .1 and .5 are often added to the N for this purpose in well-written programs.

Give Me A SGN(X)

Using the ON-GOTO along with a new function called SGN (it's pronounced "sign"), plus a modest amount of imagination, produces a most useful little routine. But first, let's learn about SGN.

The SGN function examines any number to see whether it is negative, zero, or positive. It tells us the number is negative by giving us a (−1). (In computer language, "it returns a −1".) If the number is zero it gives us a (0). If positive, we get a (+1). It's a very simple function.

In order to sneak into the next concept, we will simulate the built-in SGN function with a SUBROUTINE.

So What Is A Subroutine?

Funny you should ask. A subroutine is a short but very specialized program (or routine) which is built into a large program to meet a specialized need. BASIC stores many of them in a special place in memory ready for us to call up as needed.

As an example of how to create functions that are *not* included in our BASIC, we are going to use a five-Line subroutine instead of the "SGN" function to accomplish the same thing. Even though Model 100 BASIC supports the "SGN" function, you should complete this Chapter to be sure you learn about subroutines. We don't want to turn out dummies, you know.

"Scratch" the program now in the Computer by typing NEW, then -- very carefully, so as not to make any mistakes, type in the SGN subroutine:

```
30000 END
30800 REM INPUT X, OUTPUT T= -1,0, OR +1
30810 IF X < 0 THEN T = -1
30820 IF X = 0 THEN T = 0
30830 IF X > 0 THEN T = +1
30840 RETURN
```

"CALLING" A Subroutine -- (Sort of like calling hogs.)

To use a subroutine, use the GOSUB ##### statement.

"#####" represents the Line number.

This statement directs the Computer to GO TO that Line Number, execute what it says there and in the Lines following, and when done RETURN back to the Line containing the GOSUB statement. We will use Line 20 here.

```
20 GOSUB 30800
```

A RETURN is always part of a subroutine, and ours is at Line 30840. We have reserved Line number 30000 to hold a protective END block for all of our subroutines, so the Computer doesn't come crashing into them when it is done with the main program. Try taking it out when we're done and see what happens.

Getting Down To Business

OK, now let's combine GOSUB and SGN (using a subroutine) to see what all this fuss is about. Add:

```
10 INPUT "TYPE ANY NUMBER";X
20 GOSUB 30800
30 ON T+2 GOTO 50,60,70
45 END
50 PRINT "THE NUMBER IS NEGATIVE."
55 END
60 PRINT "THE NUMBER IS ZERO."
65 END
70 PRINT "THE NUMBER IS POSITIVE."
```

...etc. (the subroutine is already typed in)...and RUN.

Try this same program using ON-GOSUB in Line 30. Remember, change Lines 55 and 65 to RETURN and add Line 75 RETURN.

Try entering negative, zero and positive numbers to be sure it works. Most of the program workings are obvious, but here is an analysis:

Line 10 INPUTS any number.

Line 20 sends the Computer to Line 30800 by a GOSUB statement. This is different from an ordinary GOTO, since a GOSUB will return control to the originating Line like a boomerang when the Computer hits a RETURN. The call to GOSUB is not complete and will not move on to the next program Line until a RETURN is found.

Lines 30800 through 30840 contain this rather simple SUBroutine.

Line 30840 contains the RETURN which sends control back to Line 20, which silently acknowledges the return and allows movement to the next Line.

Line 30 is an ordinary ON-GOTO statement, but adds 2 to the value of its variable, in this case "T". Line 30 is really saying, "If T is −1 then GOTO Line 50. If it is zero then GOTO Line 60, and if it is +1 GOTO Line 70. By adding 2 to each of those values we have "matched" them up with the 1, 2, and 3 which are built into the ON-GOTO.

Lines 45, 55, and 65 are routine protective blocks.

By the way, most subroutines are not this simple -- as a matter of fact, they get into rather hairy mathematical derivations. We won't bother trying to explain any of them -- if you're heavy into Math, you go right ahead and play with the numbers...

Preview Of Coming Attractions?

Like so much of what we are learning, this is just the tip of the iceberg. The ON-GOTO and SGN functions have many more clever applications, and they will evolve as we need them. As a hint for restless minds, note that the VALUE of X (which we INPUT) was not used, but it didn't go away. All we did was find its SGN. Hmmm...

Routines Vs Subroutines

We studied a special-purpose routine used as a SUBroutine. It is one of the few that we can both use and really understand. All the routines, understandable or not, can be built directly into any program instead of being set aside and "called" as subroutines. Their main value as subroutines is that they can be "called" repeatedly from different parts of a program, which is often desirable. As ordinary routines they are usually only used once, and Lines containing GOSUB and RETURN are not needed.

One value of using special routines as SUBroutines is that some are exceedingly complex to type without error, and if each is typed once and saved on tape or disk, it can be quickly and accurately loaded into the Computer as the first step in creating a new program.

We'll have more to say in a later Chapter. When you see just how powerful subroutines are, you'll feel like your Model 100 is even smarter than it thinks it is.

Now it's your turn.

EXERCISE 17-1: Remove all traces of the subroutine from the resident program. Use the SGN function to accomplish the same thing we have been doing using a subroutine. Hint: T = SGN(X)

Learned in Chapter 17

Functions	**Statements**	**Miscellaneous**
SGN(X)	ON-GOTO	Debugging
	GOSUB	Subroutines
	RETURN	

Chapter 18

RaNDom Numbers

At Random

A true RANDOM number is one with a value that is unpredictable. A "Random Number Generator" is a device which pulls random numbers "out of a hat". Our Computer can act as such a device, and here is the format for doing so:

```
N = RND(X)
```

where N is the value of the random number.

RND is the abbreviation and symbol for the RaNDom function. X is a control parameter. We can give X a value of 0 or 1. "1" will yield a random number between zero and one. A "0" will produce the value of the previous random number generated by RND, for test purposes.

Type:

```
10 PRINT RND(1);
20 GOTO 10
```

...and RUN (use the **PAUSE** key).

Did you observe:

1. Different numbers appeared each time?

in Exponential notation?

at all these statements are true.

be repeated. Hmmm...

! Virtually all Computer games are
on be playing some and designing

he odds on the next toss are *exactly*
toss is totally independent of what

In the *long run*, however, the number of heads and tails should be exactly the same. (Casinos live off people who go broke waiting for their particular scheme to pay off…"in the long run".) This Computer will give you a complete education in "odds" and various games of chance, and allow you to prove or disprove many ideas involving probability. This is known as Computer "modeling" or "simulation."

Type in this coin toss simulation carefully to avoid errors:

```
10 INPUT "NUMBER OF COIN FLIPS";F
20 CLS
30 PRINT "SIT TIGHT WHILE I'M FLIPPING"
40 FOR N=1 TO F
50 X = INT(RND(1)*2+1)
60 ON X GOTO 90,110
```

```
70 PRINT "BOMBED! NEITHER A 1 NOR A 2."
80 END
90 H = H + 1
100 GOTO 120
110 T = T + 1
120 NEXT N
130 PRINT "HEADS";TAB(10);"TAILS";TAB(20);
"TOTAL FLIPS"
140 PRINT H;TAB(10);T;TAB(20);F
150 PRINT H/F*100;"%";TAB(10);T/F*100;"%"
```

...and RUN. "Flip the coin" 100 times. It comes up with 52 heads, 48 tails, right? RUN it a few more times. Hmmm... how come it comes up with the same answer every time? Well, that's because it is generating random numbers, but it generates the same list of random numbers every time. Later we will learn a way around that, but we need to do some other things first. Now try running it for 1000. Yes, I know it seems to be taking a long time, but that's a lot of numbers -- be patient...Wow! 500/500, that's pretty good!!! Now let's see exactly what's happening in this program.

Program Analysis:

Line 10 inputs the number of flips desired.

Line 20 does a CLear Screen.

Line 30 Prints a "Standby" statement.

Line 40 begins a FOR-NEXT loop that runs "F" times.

Line 50 is the RND generator of our 1's and 2's (heads and tails). Here's what happens. Since the RND(1) gives us random numbers between 0 and 1 (non-inclusive) we multiply RND(1) by 2. Now we have random numbers between 0 and 2. There are two more steps, so don't get bored yet! Next we add 1 to the value of RND(1)*2 and this puts our random numbers between 1 and 3 (remember, the actual range is 1.000...1 to 2.999...). Finally, we take the integer value of

RND(1)*2+1. This gives us a 1 if the random number is in the interval of 1-2 and a 2 if the random number is in the interval of 2-3. And that gives us our heads or tails.

Line 60 has an ON-GOTO test, if X=1 we go to Line 90 where the "Heads" are counted, if X=2 we go to Line 110 where the "Tails" are counted.

Lines 70 and 80 are used as default Lines. If X = other than 1 or 2, the error message will be printed and execution will END. It will never happen, but we want to prove this.

Line 90 sets up H as a "Heads" counter. Each time the ON-GOTO test sends control to this Line (because X=1), H is incremented by one.

Line 100 sends control to Line 120 where NEXT N is executed. When the N Loop has gone through all "F" number of passes, control moves on to Line 130. Until then, the NEXT N sends it back to Line 40.

Line 110 keeps track of the "Tails".

Line 120 passes control to Line 130 when the last "N" is "used up".

Line 130 prints the Headings.

Line 140 prints the values of H, T and F.

Line 150 calculates and prints the percentage of heads and tails.

More Than One Generator At A Time

It is possible to generate more than one random number by using more than one generator in a program. This has special value when the ranges of the generators are different, but is helpful even if their ranges are the same.

> It could also be done with a single generator, but that wouldn't make our point...would it?

To make the point, we will create a Computer game of "Craps" -- where 2 dice are "rolled". Each "die" has six sides, each side having 1,2,3,4,5 or 6 dots. When the 2 dice are rolled, the number of dots showing on their top sides are added. That sum is important to the game. Obviously, the lowest number that can be rolled is 2, and the highest number is 12. We will set up a separate Random Number Generator for each die, give each a range from 1 to 6, and call them die "A" and die "B".

Type NEW, then the following:

```
50 A=INT(RND(1)*6+1)
60 B=INT(RND(1)*6+1)
70 N=A+B
80 PRINT N
90 GOTO 50
```

...RUN.

As you can see, each number PRINTed falls between 2 and 12. We only need to PRINT N since the dice are always both thrown at the same time, and only the *sum* of the two is of interest here.

Remember to press **SHIFT BREAK** to stop the Computer.

Why would the following by wrong?

```
50 PRINT INT(RND(1)*12+1)
```

Answer: Adding random numbers created by two generators, each picking numbers between 1 and 6 will create many more sums which equal 3,4,5,6,7,8,9,10 and 11 than a single generator which picks an equal amount of numbers 1 through 11 (to which we add 1, to make the range 2 through 12).

Rules Of The Game
In its simplest form, the game goes like this:

1. The player rolls the two dice. If he rolls a sum of 2 (called "snake eyes"), a 3 ("cock-eyes"), or a 12 ("boxcars"), on the first roll, he loses and the game is over. That's "craps".

2. If the player rolls 7 or 11 on the first throw, (called a "natural"), he wins and the game is over.

3. If any other number is rolled, it becomes the player's "point". He must keep rolling until he either "makes his point" by getting the same number again to win, or rolls a 7, and loses.

EXERCISE 18-1: You already know far more than enough to complete this program. Do it. Put in all the tests, print Lines, etc. to meet the rules of the game and tell the player what is going on. It will take you a while to finish, but give it your best before you turn over to Appendix H (User Programs) under CRAPS for a sample solution. Good luck!

Making RaNDom Random

Random numbers are unpredictable; properly functioning Computers are not. So how can we get random numbers out of the Computer? We don't: we get PSEUDO-RANDOM numbers.

Each time we use the RND function, the Computer uses an internal "seed number" to produce a random number. The problem is that the Computer starts with the same seed every time a program is RUN, thus the same sequence of numbers is repeated. Here's how to get around the problem.

All we need to do is figure out a way to get an unpredictable number somewhere from in our Computer.

Type the following:

```
PRINT TIME$
```

Hmmm, that's interesting...If we could somehow separate the seconds from the time, we would have essentially unpredictable numbers between 0 and 59. That would give us 60 different seed numbers. Here's how we do it:

```
PRINT VAL(RIGHT$(TIME$,2))
```

The mechanics of that statement will be covered in detail in later Chapters, but for those too curious to wait here is a short analysis: RIGHT$(TIME$,2) means "Peel off the 2 right-most characters in TIME$". VAL means "Make sure those 2 characters are numbers so we can use them in a numeric operation.

We now have the means to write a subroutine for "randomizing" the list. Type NEW and the following:

```
10000 S = VAL(RIGHT$(TIME$,2))
10010 FOR N = 1 TO S
10020    D = RND(1)
10030 NEXT N
10040 RETURN
```

and there's our subroutine. Now let's use it by typing in the rest of the program:

```
10 GOSUB 10000          (Randomize)
20 FOR N = 1 TO 4
30 PRINT RND(1);
40 NEXT N
50 END
```

and RUN several times. Ahhhh! Now we've got it. Instead of only one version of the game, we now have 60 versions. The most important thing to understand right now is that we have developed a RANDOMIZER subroutine, not how it works. The mechanics will be learned later.

EXERCISE 18-2: Add our RANDOMIZE subroutine to the CRAPS game. Check that the game is different each time you RUN it. Can you think of any way to create more than 60 different seed numbers?

Learned in Chapter 18

Functions

RND(X)

Miscellaneous

Random vs. Pseudo-random
Seed numbers

Chapter 19

READing DATA

So far, we have learned how to insert numbers into our programs by two different methods. The first is by building the value into the program:

```
10 A = 5
```

The second is by using an INPUT statement to enter it through the keyboard:

```
10 INPUT A
```

The third principal way uses the DATA statement.

Type in this NEW program:

```
10 DATA 1,2,3,4,5
20 READ A,B,C,D,E
30 PRINT A;B;C;D;E
```

...and RUN.

The DATA statement is in some ways similar to the first method in that a DATA Line is part of the program. It's different, however, since each DATA Line can contain many numbers, or pieces of data, each separated by a comma. Each piece of DATA must be read by a READ statement. Each READ Line can hold a number of READ statements, each separated by a comma.

The display shows that all 5 pieces of DATA in Line 10, the numbers 1,2,3,4 and 5, were READ by Line 20, assigned the letters A through E, and printed by Line 30.

> Keep in mind these important distinctions: DATA Lines can be read *only* by READ statements. If more than one piece of data is placed on a DATA Line, they must be separated by commas. INPUT statements enter data via the keyboard.

DATA Lines are always read from left to right by READ statements; the first DATA Line first (when there is more than one), and *it does not matter where they are in the program*. This may seem startling, but do the following and you will see:

1. Move the DATA Line from Line 10 to Line 25 and run. No change in the printout, right?

2. Move the DATA Line from Line 25 to Line 10000. Same thing -- no change in the printout.
DATA Line(s) can be placed anywhere in the program.

This fact leads different programmers to use different styles. Some place all DATA Lines at the beginning of a program so they can be read first in a LISTing and found quickly so data may be changed.

Others place all DATA Lines at a program's end where they are out of the way and there are additional Line numbers available to keep adding DATA Lines as the need arises. Still others scatter the DATA Lines throughout the program next to the READ Lines. The style you select is of little consequence -- *but consistency is comfortable*.

The Plot Thickens
Since we now know all about FOR-NEXT loops, let us see what happens when a DATA Line is placed in the middle of a loop. Erase the old program with NEW and type in this program:

```
10 DATA 1,2,3,4,5
```

```
20 FOR N = 1 TO 5
30    READ A
40    PRINT A;
50 NEXT N
```

...and RUN.

That DATA Line is outside the loop. Now move it to Line 25 and RUN. What happened?

Nothing different! It is important to observe this fact or we wouldn't have gone to the trouble to do it. Note that as we went through the N loop 5 times, we read the letter A 5 times, and the PRINT statement printed A 5 times, but A's value was different each time. Its value was the same as the value it READ last from the DATA Line. The reason -- each piece of data in a DATA Line can only be read *once* each time the program is run. The next time a READ statement requests a piece of data, it will read the NEXT piece of data in that DATA Line, or, if that Line is all used up, go on to the next DATA Line and begin reading it.

Change Line 20 in the program to read:

```
20 FOR N = 1 TO 6
```

...and RUN.

We, of course, told the READ statement to read a total of 6 pieces of DATA but there were only 5.

```
1 2 3 4 5


?OD Error in 30        (OD = Out of Data)
```

Now change Line 20 so the number of READs is LESS than the DATA available.

```
20 FOR N = 1 TO 4
```

...and RUN.

Chapter 19

The program ran just fine as long as we didn't use all the available data. The point is, each piece of data in a DATA statement can only be read once during each RUN.

Exceptions, Exceptions!

Because it is sometimes necessary to read the same DATA more than once without having to RUN the complete program over, a statement called RESTORE is available. Whenever the program comes across a RESTORE, all DATA Lines are restored to their original "unread" condition, both those that have been read and those that have not, and all are available for reading again, starting with the first piece in the first DATA Line. Change Line 20 of the program back to:

```
20 FOR N = 1 TO 5
```

and insert:

```
35 RESTORE
```

...and RUN.

Oh-oh! The display prints five 1's instead of 1 2 3 4 5. Can you figure out why?

> Line 30 READ A as 1, but Line 35 immediately RESTOREd the DATA Line *to its original unREAD condition*. When the FOR-NEXT loop brought the READ Line around for the next pass it again read the first piece of data, which was that same 1. Same thing with all successive passes.

READ and DATA statements are extremely common. RESTORE is used less often.

Do you begin to see some distant glimmering involving storing business DATA in DATA Lines where it's easily changed or updated without affecting the rest of the program or its formulas?

Learned in Chapter 19

Statements

READ
DATA
RESTORE

"One of the most powerful string handling capabilities is the ability to *compare* them."

Part 3

Strings

Chapter 20

Intermediate BASIC

Intermediate Features Of Model 100 BASIC

Now that we've learned "Elementary" BASIC we can get serious about "Intermediate" BASIC. The next Chapter is sort of a "catch up" and "catch all", showing a lot of little features that didn't find a convenient home previously. Study each of them, do the sample programs and think about them. Each one is brief but important.

Multiple Statement Lines: (Now he tells us!)
Model 100 BASIC allows us to put more than one statement on each numbered Line, separating them by a colon (:). For example, a timer loop such as:

```
100 FOR N = 1 TO 500
110 NEXT N
```

becomes . . .

```
100 FOR N = 1 TO 500 : NEXT N
```

Caveat Emptor *(Don't buy a used computer from a stranger.)*

Control yourself! It's easy to get carried away with this new concept. While we will be using multiple statement Lines often from here on, you will quickly see that it's possible to pack the information so tightly it becomes hard to read, and also very hard to modify.

More Caveat *(or is it more Emptor?)*

Multiple statement Lines require careful understanding. Especially critical are statements of the IF-THEN variety.

Enter the following incorrect program:

```
10 INPUT "TYPE IN A NUMBER";X
20 IF X = 3 THEN 50 : GOTO 70
30 PRINT "HOW DID YOU GET HERE?"
40 END
50 PRINT "X=3"
60 END
70 PRINT "CAN'T GET FROM THERE TO HERE."
```

...and RUN it a number of times with different input values.

Line 20 has an error in logic! If the test in the first statement in the Line passes, control branches off to Line 50. That's OK.

If the test fails, however, control drops to the next Line in the program -- Line 30, not to Line 70. There is no way the second statement in Line 20 (GOTO 70) can ever be executed.

The Message -- if you put an IF-THEN (or ON-GOTO) type-test in a multiple statement Line, it must be the LAST statement in that Line.

Next Message -- we cannot send control TO any point in a multiple statement Line except to its FIRST statement. Look at Line 20. There is no way to address the GOTO 70 portion. It shares the same Line number as the first statement in the same Line. Only the first statement is addressable by a GOTO or IF-THEN. Other statements in a Line are accessed in sequence, IF each prior test is passed.

Variable Names

We know we can use the 26 letters of the alphabet as names for variables. We can also use the numbers 0 through 9 in conjunction with these letters:

```
A3 = 65
F9 = 37
```

etc.

Although the 26 letter variables are usually enough, adding the numbers gives us an additional 26 * 10 = 260. They can be very handy, particularly if we want to label a number of "sub" variables (D1, D2, D3, etc.) which may combine to make a grand total which we can just call D.

In addition, we can use ALMOST any two-LETTER combination for a name. For example:

```
PI = 3.14159
C = PI*D          Circumference = 3.14159 * Diameter
```

(Now that really looks valuable.)

This 2-letter feature gives us another 26 * 26 variables, and if that isn't enough to solve all your problems, nothing will. Nearly a thousand possible variable names so far, and we'll discover several times that many before we're through.

Enter this program and RUN, watching for an error message:

```
10 RATE = 55
20 TIME = 3
30 DISTANCE = RATE * TIME
40 PRINT RATE, TIME, DISTANCE
```

Oops! ?SN got us in Line 30. Is the word DISTANCE too long? Let's EDIT it back to DISTA and RUN again.

OK, that got us past Line 30, but the same problem exists in 40. Cut DISTANCE back to DISTA and try again.

That's more like it. Looks pretty good doesn't it? We can actually use WORDS to name our variables. Add this Line and RUN:

```
35 DIME = 10
```

Another SN error? What's wrong with DIME??

It just so happens that the word DIM (dimension) is only one of a number of "reserved" words, and we can't use them as, or in variable names. DIM is the first 3 letters of DIME. The problem with DISTANCE in Line 30 wasn't length, as we suspected, words can be HUNDREDS of characters long. It contained TAN, another reserved word. Ah, so!

Better take a look now at the list of reserved words in Appendix C.

Okay, how about just cutting back to 2 letters. We know we can use ALMOST any 2 letter combination for a name. (Again -- see Appendix C.)

Now try:

```
35 DI = 10
```

...and RUN.

It ran, but look at the answer! Our variable DISTA was printed with a value of 10 instead of 165. What happened? DISTA surely can't be the same as DI. Well, it might look different, but *the Computer only sees the first 2 letters of any variable,* and they ARE the same. The DI in Line 35 gave the DI in DISTA a new value.

The Lesson here should be pretty clear. It's very easy to get carried away with fancy variable names, and in the process bungle into lots of trouble. Remember KISS? (Keep It Simple, Stupid!)

String Variables

Up to this point we have been using the letters A through Z to hold number variables. They are called *numeric variables*. We can use the same 26 letters to indicate *string variables* by just adding a "$". A$, for example is called "A STRING". String variables can be assigned to indicate *letters, words* and/or *combinations* of letters, numbers and spaces. Type NEW then type:

```
10 INPUT "WHAT IS YOUR NAME";A$
20 PRINT "HELLO THERE ";A$
```

...and RUN.

Hey-hey! How's that for a grabber? If that, along with what you've learned in earlier chapters doesn't instantly make the creative juices flow, nothing will.

That's Two....

Two ways to PRINT words. The first, learned long ago, is to imbed words in PRINT statements (and is called "PRINTing a string"). The second, just seen, is to bring word(s) through an INPUT statement (called "INPUTting a string"). A third way is combining string variables with DATA statements.

Change the program to read:

```
10 READ A$
20 DATA RADIO SHACK MODEL 100
30 PRINT "SEE MY FOXY ";A$
```

...and RUN.

```
SEE MY FOXY RADIO SHACK MODEL 100
```

Let's use 2 string variables to accomplish the same thing, and see how they work with each other. Rework the program to:

```
10 READ A$
15 READ B$
20 DATA RADIO SHACK, MODEL 100
30 PRINT "SEE MY FOXY ";A$;" ";B$
```

Analyzing the program.

> Line 20 contains two pieces of DATA, separated by a comma.
>
> Line 10 READs the first one.
>
> Line 15 READs the second one.
>
> Line 30 contains 4 PRINT expressions. The first one PRINTs `SEE MY FOXY`, leaving a space behind the "`Y`". String variables, unlike numeric variables run everything together, allowing us to insert spaces only where we want them. The second PRINT is A$, `RADIO SHACK`. The third PRINT is the space enclosed in quotes. The last PRINT is `MODEL 100`.

In other words, a semi-colon between STRING variables does NOT cause a space to be PRINTed between them. We have to insert a space using "" marks.

New String Variables
So far we've used A$ and B$ as string variables. We actually have ALL the letters of the alphabet available for strings. And the numbers 0 through 9 too, plus any 2 letter combination. Valid string names include:

```
X$
D8$
PI$        ...etc.
```

Almost a thousand more variable names.

Shorthand
There are several little "shorthand" tricks we can use.

The ′ is shorthand for REM, and is especially nice when documenting the purpose of a Line. It makes program Lines into multiple statement Lines. ′ =:REM.

```
50 X = Z*C/4 + 33   ′ SECRET EQUATION
```

Intermediate BASIC

The only place ' can't be used unaided is in a DATA Line, and that problem can be overcome by actually adding a : to the DATA Line. See Lines 1000 and 1010 in this program.

```
10 CLS            ' CLEAR THE SCREEN
20 READ H,V,N     ' READ DATA
30 V1 = V         ' STORE V FOR RECALL
40 IF N = 0 GOTO 40 ' LOCKING LOOP
50  FOR H = H TO H+2  ' 3 PASSES
60   FOR V=V TO V+N-1 ' COUNTS PRINTING
70    PSET(H,V) ' PSETS LIGHT BLOCK
80   NEXT V      ' CLOSES LOOP
90   V=V1 ' RESETS V TO DATA LINE VALUE
100 NEXT H : GOTO 20 ' CLOSES LOOP
1000 DATA 102,3,9,105,10,1:'DATA IS IN
1010 DATA 108,7,3,111,6,1:'H,V,N ORDER
1020 DATA 114,7,3,117,10,1,120,3,9,0,0,0
```

...but enough graphics. They come later.

The Period . is of minimal value as a BASIC shorthand feature, but if we've just typed a new Line, LISTed one, or EDITed one, we can repeat it without typing its number:

```
110 REM TEST LINE        ENTER
```

then type:

```
LIST.
```

and Line 110 will be LISTed. This works even if the program has been RUN, which can be an aid in troubleshooting a Line without writing down its number. It also works with a Line that keeps popping up due to an error message.

The Enter Key
If you're the very observant type you noticed that program execution begins when you type RUN and the **ENTER** key is PRESSED, not when it's released. Try it on the resident program. This is an important consideration when doing such precision things as setting the Real Time Clock.

Use Of Quotes & Semicolons
Technically, it is not necessary to use quotes to close off PRINT statements, or LOADs and SAVEs.

```
10 PRINT"WHERE IS THE END QUOTE?
```

Note lack of second "

RUNs just fine. Leave it off at your own peril.

A BASIC interpreter that is "too forgiving" is like an airplane that is "too forgiving". It allows us to become sloppy, and when we really need all the skill we can muster, it is absent from lack of practice. You are strongly encouraged not to take these and other "cheap" short-cuts.

INPUT?
When INPUTting several variables in a single INPUT Line, if we fail to INPUT them all at once, separated by commas, the special prompt, ?? alerts us that more DATA must be INPUT. Type this program and enter only one number at a time, followed by **ENTER**. Watch for the ??:

```
10 INPUT A,B,C
```

...and RUN.

RUN again, this time typing all 3 numbers separated by commas. It will "swallow" them all in one gulp.

RUN again and try to INPUT letters instead of numbers. An Error Message instructs:

```
Redo from start
?
```

There is extensive information in Appendix E dealing with Error Messages. REDO reminds us that we can't INPUT a string variable into a request for a numeric one.

Optional Next

FOR-NEXT loops don't always have to specify which FOR we are NEXTing. This can be useful when the loops are nested.

Type this NEW program:

```
10 FOR N = 1 TO 5 : PRINT N
20   FOR Q = 1 TO 3 : PRINT"  ";Q
30     FOR R = 1 TO 4 : PRINT"    ";R
40 NEXT : NEXT : NEXT
```

RUN it several times to get the flavor.

This method of NEXTing should not be used if the program contains tests which might allow a loop to be broken out of. Better then to be specific, as we've already learned, or use this little short-cut.

```
40 NEXT R,Q,N
```

IF-THEN-ELSE

ELSE is an interesting addition to our stable of conditional branching statements. It allows us an option other than dropping to the next Line if a test fails. Try this one:

```
10 INPUT "ENTER A NUMBER";N
20 IF N=0 THEN PRINT"0"ELSE PRINT"<> 0"
```

...and RUN.

POS(N)

POS allows the Computer to tell us the horizontal position of the cursor. This simple program tells all:

```
1 CLS
10 INPUT "A NO. BETWEEN 0 AND 29";A
20 PRINT TAB(10 + A)
30 PRINT POS(N);
40 PRINT"IS THE PRINT POSITION"
```

...and RUN.

Line 30 is the key one, containing POS. The N inside brackets is just a "dummy". Most any other variable or number would work as well -- but something has to be placed there. POS reports back any cursor position up thru 39. Numbers beyond that start over again with zero.

Learned in Chapter 20

Statements	**Functions**	**Miscellaneous**
IF-THEN-ELSE	POS(N)	Multiple Statement Lines
		Variable Names
		Some shorthand
		TABbing
		Quotes and Semicolons
		Multiple INPUTting
		Optional NEXT
		String Variables
		Numeric Variables

Chapter 21

The ASCII Set

The purpose of this Chapter is to learn how to use ASC and CHR$. Before doing so however, we must learn about something called "the ASCII set". (No, they're not like the "horsey set".)

ASCII is pronounced (ASK'-EE) and it stands for American Standard Code for Information Interchange. Since a Computer stores and processes only numbers, not letters or punctuation, it's important that there be some sort of uniform system to specify which numbers represent which letters and symbols. The ASCII Chart in Appendix A shows the relationship between the number system and symbols as used in the Model 100. Take a minute to look at the chart.

Type in this short program:

```
10 FOR N = 33 TO 255
20 PRINT "ASCII NUMBER";N;
30 PRINT "STANDS FOR ";CHR$(N)
40 FOR T = 1 TO 500 : NEXT T
50 NEXT N
```

...and RUN.

As it RUNs, observe that the characters between ASCII code numbers 33 and 191 are displayed. ASCII numbers from 0 to 32 are not printable, but often serve important purposes. ASCII numbers 97 to 122 are just lower-case duplicates of numbers 65 to 90.   Numbers 128 to 255 call forth special Graphics and foreign language characters.

ASCII Applications

If you end up in the Big House serving time for computer fraud, the following little program will make up your license plate combinations, putting CHR$ to good use.

Enter:

```
1 CLS
10 REM *LICENSE PLATE NUMBER GENERATOR*
20 FOR N=1 TO 3 : PRINT INT(RND(1)*10);
30 NEXT N : PRINT " ";
40 FOR N=1 TO 3
50  PRINT CHR$(INT(RND(1)*26+65));" ";
60 NEXT N : PRINT : GOTO 20
```

…and RUN.

The RND generator in Line 20 PRINTs numbers between 0 and 9. Line 50 spits out numbers between 0 and 25. We add 65 to each number to make the sum fall in the range between 65 and 90. What do we see on the ASCII conversion chart between 65 and 90.   Hmmmm???

So What Is CHR$(N)?

We have used CHR$ (pronounced character string) without describing it, but you undoubtedly figured it out anyway. CHR$(N) produces the ASCII character (or control action) specified by the code NUMBER N. It is a one-way converter from the ASCII CODE NUMBER to the ASCII CHARACTER, and allows us to throw characters around with the ease of throwing around numbers. The word "string" refers to any character (letter, punctuation or numeral) . It may also be more than one character.

Enter this simple program:

```
10 INPUT "TYPE ANY NUMBER 33 - 125";N
```

```
20 PRINT CHR$(N)
30 PRINT : RUN
```

...and RUN.

Note Line 30. Instead of the more traditional: `GOTO 10`, we used `RUN`, which RUNS the program again. **Question:** In what sort of program would this use of RUN have a different effect? **Answer:** Those containing DATA statements. They would all be restored each time RUN was executed.

Almost all of our activity with ASCII numbers will be confined to the range between 33-125. However, these "quickie" programs show how to use several ASCII numbers that stand for ACTIONS instead of numbers, letters or characters. Give them a try:

> **EXERCISE 21-1:** Using the ASCII chart (Appendix A) and the CHR$ function, create a program which will print the name: MODEL 100.

What Then Is ASC($)?

ASC is the exact opposite of CHR$(N). ASC is a one-way converter from the ASCII CHARACTER to its corresponding ASCII NUMBER.

Type:

```
10 INPUT "TYPE NEARLY ANY CHARACTER";A$
20 PRINT A$;" ASCII NUMBER IS";ASC(A$)
30 PRINT : GOTO 10
```

...and RUN.

It will print the ASCII number of almost all characters. (Try special code characters which use the **CODE** key, too. It doesn't work with the comma (,), the quotation mark ("), the space bar, and some others, but then strings can be a real mystery at times, as we will see.

Before we can really understand what we are doing, we must learn a lot more about strings. Before we could learn about strings we had to learn something about ASCII. It's like "catch Model 100".

Learned in Chapter 21

Functions

CHR$
ASC

Miscellaneous

ASCII Codes

Chapter 22

Strings In General

It was not our intention to "string you along" in the previous Chapter, but we really can't understand how strings work without first understanding the ASCII concept of numbers standing for letters, numbers and other characters and controls.

Comparing Strings

One of the most powerful string handling capabilities is the ability to *compare* them. We compare the numbers between *numeric* variables all the time. How can we compare strings of letters or words? Well, why do you suppose we put the ASCII Chapter just before this one? RIGHT! The Computer can compare the ASCII *code numbers* of letters and other characters. The effective result is a comparison of what's in the corresponding strings.

Type in this NEW program:

```
10 INPUT "WHAT IS YOUR NAME";A$
20 IF A$ = "ISHKIBIBBLE" THEN 50
30 PRINT "SORRY, WRONG NAME!"
40 END
50 PRINT "FINALLY GOT IT!"
```

...and RUN.

If the Computer can compare THAT name it should be able to compare anything!

During the process of comparing what you enter as A$ in Line 10 to what's already in quotes in Line 20, the ASCII code numbers of each letter found in one string are compared, letter for letter, from left to right with those in the other. Every one must match, or the test fails.

Strings and "quotes" go together like beer and chocolate cake. *(Beer and chocolate cake ...?)* You know this from earilier chapters where every PRINT"XXX" has its string enclosed in quotes. (PRINT"XXX" is called a string *constant*, compared with A$, a string *variable*.) RUN the above program again, this time answering the question with "ISHKIBIBBLE", but enclosed in quotes.

Sure -- it ran OK. Worked either with or without quotes. BASIC has become increasingly lenient about this matter, but every once in a while the rules come up from behind and bite us if we play fast and loose with them.

If we READ a string, and it has no commas, semicolons, leading or trailing spaces in it, we don't need to enclose it in quotes. We will never go wrong by ALWAYS enclosing strings in quotes, but that can be a nuisance.

> **EXERCISE 22-1:** Write a program that will compare two strings entered from the keyboard. PRINT them in alphabetical order.

Erase the resident program and type in this next one, which READs string data from a DATA Line.

```
1 CLS
10 READ A$,B$,C$
20 PRINT A$
30 PRINT B$
40 PRINT C$
100 DATA COMPUSOFT PUBLISHING
110 DATA SAN DIEGO, CA, 92119
```

...and RUN.

Look carefully at the results. The display shows:

```
COMPUSOFT PUBLISHING
SAN DIEGO
CA
```

That's fine, but where is the ZIP CODE? And why weren't SAN DIEGO and CA printed on the same line? The answer, my friend, is blowing in the ...er, in the commas.

Because of the commas in the DATA Lines, the READ statement sees 4 pieces of DATA, but only READs 3 of them. What do we have to do in order to PRINT a comma as part of a string? Right -- enclose it, or the string containing it, in quotes.

```
EDIT110
```

and change Line 110 to read:

```
110 DATA "SAN DIEGO, CA", 92119
```

...and RUN.

```
COMPUSOFT PUBLISHING
SAN DIEGO, CA
92119
```

Aaaah! That's more like it. Notice that we didn't have to enclose all pieces of string DATA in separate quotes, but we could have.

What would happen if we also enclosed *entire* DATA Line in quotes, leaving the existing quotes in there? (Think about it, then try it. Every question raised has a specific purpose.)

Our editor is so easy to use, let's make it read:

```
110 DATA""SAN DIEGO, CA", 92119"
```

...and RUN.

Awwk! Disaster...A syntax error? Yes, there is no straight-forward way to print quotes as part of a string constant, even by enclosing them inside another pair of quotes. The Computer just isn't smart enough to figure out which quote mark is which. The usual way to overcome this BASIC language deficiency is to substitute ' for ", inside other quotes. Let's try it:

```
110 DATA"'SAN DIEGO, CA', 92119"
```
...and RUN.

Ooops, ?OD (OUT OF DATA) error in 10? Of course. With quotes surrounding the whole works in Line 110, there are now just *two* pieces of DATA, and we are trying to read 3 pieces. Let's change Line 10 to read two pieces:

```
10 READ A$,B$
```

...and RUN.

There we go. Might look a little strange, but it proves the point and warns us a little about the "touchiness" of strings.

When it comes to strings, that classic old ballad from the hills is so appropriate:

> *"Ah-cigareets, and whuisky, and wild computers, they'll drive you crazy, they'll drive you insane!"*

But, undaunted by this high class philosophy, we steer our vessel towards the next Chapter.

As the sun sinks slowly in the west, tropical breezes fill the sails and water laps against the bow. Stars appear, and from the beach fires plaintive native chants are heard, calling...

Learned in Chapter 22

Miscellaneous

String comparison

Chapter 23

Measuring Strings

One of the most frequently needed facts about a string is its length. Fortunately, the LEN function makes that easy to find. Type:

```
1 CLS : PRINT
10 PRINT "TYPE A STRING OF CHARACTERS"
20 INPUT A$
30 L = LEN(A$)
40 PRINT A$;" HAS";L;"CHARACTERS"
```

...and RUN.

RUN several times, entering your name and other combinations of letters and numbers. Try entering your name, last name first, with a comma after your last name.

AHA! Can't input a comma. How about if we put it all in quotes? Try again.

Yep. Just like it said in the last Chapter.

LEN has one significant variation, and it's not all that useful -- unless you really need it. LEN can evaluate the length of a string placed between quotes. For example:

```
PRINT LEN("ABC")
```

displays the number 3 telling us there are 3 characters between the quotes. Like we said, this second way to use LEN has its limitations, but does tell us the length of what's there.

DEFSTR -- For Thrill Seekers Only

Those among us who attract trouble will love this next one. As if handling strings isn't complex enough, this very powerful statement looks nice and clean but can be the greatest source of heartburn since the horseradish pizza.

DEFSTR (pronounced "DEFine STRing") allows us to define which variables are to be string variables, so we don't have to use $ any more. (Hmm...Uncle Sam could put some of this DEFSTR business to good use.) Add this Line:

```
5 DEFSTR A
```

and use the Editor to remove the $ in Lines 20, 30, and 40. Then RUN.

Works great, doesn't it. A was declared by Line 5 to be a string variable. So what's all the fuss about?

Well, this is a very simple program, but let's change 5 to read:

```
5 DEFSTR A-Z
```

which makes *all* letters STRing variables.

...and RUN.

Crasho again! Too much of a good thing. The L in Line 30 is now *also* a string. Since LEN gives us the length of a string as a number, it doesn't set at all well with the L (really L string). Imagine the fun this can create in a long program.

Good thing we can learn by our errors!

DEFSTR is best used to define individual variables. For example:

```
DEFSTR A,N,Z
```

defines only A, N and Z as string variables.

It Came Upon A Midnight CLEAR

When the Computer entered BASIC, 256 bytes of memory space were automatically set aside for use by strings --*all* strings combined. Not very much space if we're into a biggie. At the command level, type NEW, then:

```
PRINT FRE(A$)
```

The Computer responds with 256.

FRE asks the Computer "how much space is left for strings?" Not only A$, but *all* strings. The "A$" is just a "dummy" we have to use with FRE. B$, C$, or anything similar would work as well. PRINT FRE(X) (using most any character, but without the $ sign) tells us the same thing as when we first entered BASIC -- how much *total* memory space is available.

The CLEAR command/statement allows us to change the amount of reserved string space to anything we want, up to almost the total available memory. Going the other way, we can eliminate all reserved space, leaving all memory for nonstring use. Let's play around with some combinations and see what happens:

```
CLEAR 0              ENTER
PRINT FRE(A$)        ENTER
0
```

Is that what you got? CLEARed 0 and got 0? Good.

Type NEW and measure again.

```
NEW
PRINT FRE(A$)
0
```

What? Still zero? That's right. The CLEAR command is a high level one and is not affected by NEW. Entering BASIC automatically sets aside 256 bytes, and wherever we reset it, there it stays until it's reset again.

Press **F8** and return to Main Menu. Record the amount of Free Bytes and return to BASIC.

Type:

```
PRINT FRE(A)
```

and notice that we have 256 bytes less memory than in the Main Menu. That space was taken for string storage.

Now type:

```
CLEAR 0
PRINT FRE(A)
```

and the available memory has increased to the Main Menu value.

Controlled CLEARing
Try:

```
PRINT FRE(A)
CLEAR FRE(A)/4
PRINT FRE(A$),FRE(A)
```

We just arbitrarily said, "Let's set aside a fourth of the memory for use by strings." CLEAR FRE(A)/4 did it. If it turns out to be too much (wasteful) or too little (Computer will say ?OS)(Out of string Space) it's easily changed. A very adept programmer could even come up with an error-trapping routine that would CLEAR additional memory as needed if an ?OS message came through, and the operator wouldn't even know that something happened.

> Be careful with CLEAR. It removes anything stored in variables.

PRINT FRE(X$) can also be used as a program statement. Try it in any program using strings to watch what happens.

Type:

```
CLEAR 256
```

and get us back to "normal".

Concatenation

Concatenation? Concatenation??? Now what is that supposed to mean? Isn't even in the dictionary. Did you ever wonder who pays whom to sit around and think up such nondescriptive words? Must have been done on a government grant. Wait till Senator Proxmire hears about it.

Concatenation (pronounced con-cat-uh-na'tion) is a national debt-sized word which means "add". In our case it means "add strings together". It's easier to do than to pronounce.

Type this NEW program:

```
1 CLS : PRINT
10 CLEAR 100
20 FOR N = 1 TO 16
30 READ A$
35 B$ = B$ + A$
40 PRINT B$
50 NEXT N
100 DATA ALPHA,BRAVO,CHARLIE,DELTA,ECHO,FOXTROT,GOLF,HOTEL
110 DATA INDIA,JULIETT,KILO,LIMA,MIKE,NOVEMBER,OSCAR,PAPA
```

Check it carefully but don't RUN it yet. The key Line is 35, which simply says B$ (a new variable) equals the old B$ (which starts out as nothing) plus whatever is in A$. It then cycles around and keeps adding what is in B$ to what is READ from DATA as A$. Now RUN.

Gotcha! We ran out of string space, says the ?OS Error in 35. B$ just keeps growing and growing until the 100 bytes set-aside in Line 10 isn't enough.

How much is enough? Easy question, tough answer. The VARPTR statement can give us the answer, but its use requires a PhD from the funny farm where they only talk in ones and zeros.

The easiest way is to stay within the noblest engineering tradition -- add some more string space and see what happens. It's "cut and try" time.

```
10 CLEAR 125
```

...and RUN.

Getting closer. Let's try again. (This warms the cockles of any true experimenter's heart -- and drives a true theoretical scientist right up the wall.) *(Chuckle.)*

```
10 CLEAR 150
```

...RUN.

Still not enough. Looks close though, doesn't it?

```
10 CLEAR 175
```

...RUN.

Sweet success. All due to our extensive planning, no doubt.

Better do a quick

```
PRINT FRE(A)
```

to see that there's plenty of free space left -- and there is.

The purist will keep experimenting and find out that we need exactly...*message garbled in transmission*...bytes of string space to make the program RUN, yet not waste any. (Hint: If you add the number of characters in the last group printed to those in the next-to-last group, you'll be so close to the answer it may bite you. We *could* even figure that one out in advance.)

Anyhoo, the point of all this is *concatenation*. Line 35 just did it, and that's about all there is to it. We added strings together.

Not done playing you say? OK, you non-believers, have some fun with this simple program:

```
1 CLEAR 35
10 REM * CLEAR DEMO *
20 A$="0" : B$="/"
30 PRINT A$;LEN(A$)
40 A$ = A$ + B$
50 GOTO 30
```

We'll soon learn how to tear strings into little pieces. We've just learned how to put them back together. (Somebody got something backwards here...)

EXERCISE 23-1: Use the LEN function to check the length of a string INPUTted from the keyboard. Print a message telling us if the string exceeded 10 characters.

EXERCISE 23-2: Input a word from the keyboard and compare it to a secret password. If there is a match, print "CORRECT PASSWORD - ENTER". If not, print "WRONG PASSWORD - GET LOST". Store the ASCII number for each letter of the password in a DATA Line. READ each value and use CHR$ to build (concatenate) the password string.

Learned in Chapter 23

Statements	**Functions**	**Miscellaneous**
DEFSTR	LEN	Concatenation (+)
CLEAR	FRE(A$)	

Chapter 24

VAL and STR$(N)

The "hassle factor" is very high when converting back and forth between strings and numerics.

By definition, if we convert a *numeric* variable (can hold only a number) to a *string* variable (can hold almost anything), the *content* of that new string is still the original number. No letters or other characters were converted (except for a leading space) since they weren't in the numeric variable to start with.

Conversely, if we change a *string* variable to a *numeric* variable, we can't change any letters or other characters to numbers. Only the *numbers* in a string can be converted to a numeric variable. (Don't get this confused with ASCII conversions.)

If you'll keep the two previous paragraphs in mind, it'll save an awful lot of grief in dealing with strings.

VAL

Let's give string-to-numeric conversion a shot. The VAL function converts a *string* variable holding a *number* into a *number*, if the number is at the beginning of the string. Try this VAL program:

```
1 CLS : PRINT
10 INPUT"ENTER A STRING ";A$
20 A = VAL(A$)
```

```
30 PRINT "NUMERIC VALUE OF ";A$;" IS";A
90 PRINT : GOTO10
```

...and RUN.

Try lots of different INPUTs, such as:

```
12345
ASDF
123ASD
ASD123
1,2,3
A,B,C
```

and the same ones over again, but enclosed in quotes.

The display tells all.

BREAK out of the program, then take the $ out of Lines 10, 20, and 30 and RUN, INPUTting both numbers and letters.

What you're seeing is typical of the frustrations that bedevil string users who don't follow the rules. VAL only evaluates STRINGs, and we've put A, a numeric value, in where a string belongs.

Trying to mix numbers with strings is called a TYPE MISMATCH.

Let's put that A in quotes and see what happens.

```
20 A = VAL("A")
```

...and RUN.

No help at all! The rule remains unchanged. VAL converts a STRING holding a *number* into that *number*. Looking at the display, we see it's just not in the cards. Remember this frustration when you get in the thick of debugging a nasty string-loaded program.

STR$

Now let's try the opposite, converting a numeric variable to a string variable. Change the program to read:

```
1 CLS : PRINT
10 PRINT "CONVERT THIS NUMERIC ";
20 INPUT "TO A STRING";A
30 A$ = STR$(A)
40 PRINT "STRING VALUE OF";A;"IS";A$
90 PRINT : GOTO 10
```

...and RUN, using the same INPUTs we used when wringing out VAL.

There it is. A short but very important Chapter. You should spend as much time on this one as any other Chapter. If you really learn the pitfalls in using these two powerful functions, the time spent will come back manyfold in future debugging time.

> **EXERCISE 24-1:** Input your street address (e.g. 2423 LA PALMA). Use VAL to extract the street number. Add the number 4 to the street number and report this new number as your neighbor's street number.

> **EXERCISE 24-2:** Write a program using STR$ to print the following 20 store item stock numbers: 101WT, 102WT, 103WT, ... 120WT. Hint: Looks like a natural for a FOR-NEXT loop.

Learned in Chapter 24

Functions

VAL
STR$

Chapter 25

Having A Ball With Strings

LEFT$, RIGHT$, MID$

Three different, yet very similar, functions are used for playing powerful games with strings. They are LEFT$, RIGHT$, and MID$. Let's start with this program:

```
1 CLS : PRINT
30 S$ = "KILROYWASHERE"
60 PRINT LEFT$(S$,6)
70 PRINT MID$(S$,7,3)
80 PRINT RIGHT$(S$,4)
```

...and RUN.

The display shows:

```
KILROY
WAS
HERE
```

(How about that one, nostalgia buffs?)

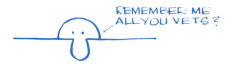

Learning to use these functions is exceedingly simple. Study the program slowly and carefully as we explain what happened.

    LEFT$ PRINTed the left-most 6 characters in the string named S$.

    MID$ PRINTed 3 characters in the string named S$, starting with the 7th character from the left. (Count 'em.)

    RIGHT$ PRINTed the 4 rightmost characters in the string named S$.

Let's move some Lines around to exercise our new-found power. Move Line 70 to Line 50:

```
50 PRINT MID$(S$,7,3)
```

and we get:

```
WAS
KILROY
HERE
```

Now move Line 80 to Line 40:

```
40 PRINT RIGHT$(S$,4)
```

and we get:

```
HERE
WAS
KILROY
```

These three functions can really do wonders with strings. Let's type in a NEW

program and examine each in more detail:

```
1 CLS : PRINT
10 FOR N = 1 TO 15
20 PRINT "N =";N,
30 S$ = "KILROY WAS HERE"
40 PRINT LEFT$(S$,N)
50 FOR T=1 TO 200 : NEXT T
60 NEXT N
```

...and RUN.

The "slow motion" picture tells it faster than we can in words. LEFT$ picks off "N" letters from the *left* side of string, and we PRINT them. See how this could be used to strip off only the first three digits of a phone number, or the first letter of a name, when searching and sorting?

Change Line 10 to read:

```
10 FOR N = 1 TO 20
```

...and RUN.

As we see, even though there are only 15 characters in the string, the overrun is ignored. (Change Line 10 back to N = 1 TO 15.)

RIGHT$ works the same way, but from the RIGHT:

Change Line 40 to read:

```
40 PRINT RIGHT$(S$,N)
```

...and RUN.

It's the mirror image of LEFT$.

Now let's exercise MID$ and see where it goes. Change Line 40 to:

```
40 PRINT MID$(S$,N,1)
```

...and RUN.

It very methodically scanned the string, from left to right, picking out one letter at a time.

With only a slight change we can make MID$ act like LEFT$. Change Line 40 to:

```
40 PRINT MID$(S$,1,N)
```

...and RUN.

It printed N characters, counting from number 1 on the left.

MID$ can also simulate RIGHT$. Change Line 40:

```
40 PRINT MID$(S$,16-N,N)
```

...and RUN.

Would you believe RIGHT$ backwards, one at a time?

```
40 PRINT MID$(S$,16-N,1)
```

...and RUN.

How about a sort of "histogram" type graph:

```
40 PRINT MID$(S$,N,N)
```

...and RUN.

(Make notes below for future reference. If all these examples don't spark some ideas for your future use, I give up.)

Let's select a specific position in the string and print its character. Make the program read:

```
1 CLS : PRINT
10 INPUT "CHARACTER # TO PRINT";N
30 S$ = "KILROY WAS HERE"
40 PRINT MID$(S$,N,1)
```

...and RUN.

Just to make the point, we can assign any of these statements to a variable. That variable could in turn be used in tests against other variables. Change:

```
40 V$ = MID$(S$,N,1)

45 PRINT V$
```

...and RUN.

A short book could be written about these three functions, but I think we've made the point. They are used *very* frequently in complex *sort* and *select* routines. If we remember to dissect them into their simple components, they *can* be understood. The next section is a good example.

EXERCISE 25-1: Write a program that asks the question "ISN'T THIS A SMART COMPUTER". Input a YES or NO answer. If the first character in the answer is a Y, print "AFFIRMATIVE". If the first character is an N, print "NEGATIVE". Otherwise print "THIS IS A YES OR NO QUESTION" and send control back to the INPUT statement.

EXERCISE 25-2: READ in the following part numbers: N106WT, A208FM, and Z154DX. Use MID$ to find the numbers. PRINT the number with the largest numeric value.

Searching With INSTR

INSTR (pronounced, "In-string") is a function that can be of value when searching for a needle in a haystack. It compares one string against another to see if they have anything in common.

Suppose we have a list of names and want to see if another name (or part of that name) is in our list. It's the "part of" which makes this operation very different from a straight comparison of name-against-name, which we already know how to do with ordinary string-against-string comparisons. Here we learn how to locate a name (and similar names) by asking for just a small part of it.

Let's start our NEW program by entering the list of Names:

```
10000 DATA SMITH, JONES, FAHRQUART, BROWN
10010 DATA JOHNSON, SCHWARTZ, FINKELSTEIN
10020 DATA BAILEY, SNOOPY, JOE BFTSPLK, *
```

That was the easy part.

We have to provide a means of READing these names, one at a time and comparing them, or parts of them, with the name or part of a name which we INPUT. Add these Lines:

```
10 CLEAR 100 : CLS
20 INPUT"ENTER THE NAME YOU NEED ";N$
30 PRINT
40 READ D$
50 IF D$ = "*" THEN GOTO 999
60 IF INSTR(1,D$,N$) = 0 THEN GOTO 40
70 PRINT N$;" IS PART OF ";D$
80 GOTO 40
999 PRINT"END OF SEARCH" : END
```

SAVE this program in memory as "INSTR", we'll be needing it later.

Now this takes a bit of explaining:

Line 10 CLEARs 100 bytes for strings, and CLears the Screen (display).

Line 20 INPUTs the name, or part of the name we are trying to locate.

Line 30 PRINTs a blank space for easier reading to give this book some class.

Line 40 READs a single name from our DATA file.

Line 50 checks to see if we're at the end of the DATA file, IF so, it branches to Line 999.

Line 60 uses the INSTRing function which does all the searching. The number following INSTR tells it to look at D$ starting with the 1st character to see if the characters we INPUT in N$ match the characters taken from D$. If its INSTR returns the value of 0 it means no such name (or part) was found, and we should READ the next one. If it was found, INSTR returns a number which is the number of characters it counted in N$ before a match was found. Since this number is not 0, and we drop to

Line 70 which PRINTs both what we're looking for and what we found.

Line 80 sends us back to READ another name from DATA.

RUN it a few times to get the hang of what's going on.

Now that wasn't too bad, was it? ('Twarnt nothin', really.) It doesn't matter how hard a program seems, when broken down to its individual parts it isn't very hard. Like we've pointed out before, "The BASICs Are Everything". A little time beside the pool reflecting on the logic will do wonders.

For those with only a silver fingerbowl, but no pool, these changes will show the inner machinations of INSTR.

```
60 L = INSTR(1,D$,N$)
65 IF L = 0 THEN GOTO 40
70 PRINT N$;" IS CHARACTER#";L;"IN ";D$
```

Run it through a number of times trying different combinations of letters, halting execution as necessary. It really does make sense!

To see the effect the starting number following INSTR has on our program, change Line 60 to:

```
60 L = INSTR(2,D$,N$)
```

INSTR will now look at D$ starting with the 2nd character.

RUN and type in the letter S. Notice how it skipped SMITH, SCHWARTZ and SNOOPY. Play around with the starting number in INSTR until you have a good handle on what it is doing to INSTR.

EXERCISE 25-3: ReLOAD the "INSTR" program and change the DATA in Lines 10000, 10010 and 10020 to:

```
10000 DATA P-RUTH, OF-MANTLE, SB-MORGAN
10010 DATA SS-LEOTHELIP, P-KOUFAX
10020 DATA C-CAMPANELLA, P-FELLER,*
```

What string would we enter to LIST the pitchers only?

    A. P
    B. PITCHER
    C. P-
    D. None of the above

Snarled String

In the last Chapter we learned about STR$, which lets us convert a numeric variable to a string variable. For the purpose of confusion (no doubt), there is another "string-string" that does something completely different. Fortunately, it is written differently.

STRING$(N,A) is a specialized PRINT *modifier* which allows us to PRINT a single ASCII character, represented by A, a total of N times. Quite simple, really.

Type:

```
5 CLEAR 50
10 PRINT STRING$(12,42);
```

```
20 PRINT "STRING$ FUNCTION";
30 PRINT STRING$(12,42);
```

...and RUN.

Wow! That really moves. It printed ASCII character number 42, which is a *, 12 times, then PRINTed the phrase STRING$ FUNCTION, then PRINTed * 12 more times. This just has to have some good applications.

Suppose we need to type a "header" across the top of a report - let's say the first line of it is to be solid dashes. What is the ASCII code for a dash? Forgot? *me too*. Everybody back to Appendix A to find the code number.

45 it is. We want to PRINT, 40 times, the character represented by ASCII code 45. That's the full width of a line on our display. The NEW program should look something like:

```
5 CLEAR 20
10 PRINT STRING$(40,45)
```

Let's RUN it and see what happens:

```
?OS Error in 10        (Out of String space in Line 10)
```

Suckered in again! Tho STRING$ is really a sort of PRINT statement, it's also a STRING function, so is subject to the string space restriction. Now what do we do?

Change:

```
5 CLEAR 40
```

...and RUN.

That's more like it.

An even easier way to use STRING$ is by replacing the ASCII code of the character we wish to PRINT with the actual character itself. (It must be enclosed in quotes.) This works fine with characters that really PRINT, such as letters, numbers and punctuation marks. Change Line 10 so the program reads:

```
5 CLEAR 40
10 PRINT STRING$(40,"-")
```

...and RUN.

Works nice doesn't it, and we didn't have to look up an ASCII code.

As with most string functions, we can bring in the string via a string variable. This simple program shows a variation on the theme, and may trigger some ideas:

```
5 CLEAR 100
10 PRINT "ENTER ANY LETTER, NUMBER OR "
20 INPUT "SYMBOL";A$
30 PRINT STRING$(40,A$)
40 PRINT : GOTO 10
```

Play around with STRING$ a while. It's really very helpful when we need it, particularly for giving our printouts some class. An obvious advantage is its ability to do a lot of PRINTing with very little programming.

EXERCISE 25-4: Print a string of 20 asterisks centered at the top of the display.

On The Lighter Side

The specialized string functions allow us to do all sorts of exotic things. Here is the beginning of a simple but fun program which uses LEN and MID$. You can easily figure it out, especially after you've seen it RUN.

Enter:

```
1 REM * TIMES SQUARE BILLBOARD *
10 CLEAR 400
20 CLS:N=0:READ A$
```

Having a Ball with Strings 279

```
30 L=LEN(A$) : F=1
80 IF L>N THEN L=N+2
90 B$ = MID$(A$,F,L)
100 PRINT TAB(38-N);B$
190 IF N=38 GOTO 220
200 N=N+1 : IF N<38 GOTO 290
220 L=L-1 : F=F+1 : IF L<0 THEN L=0
230 IF L=15 GOTO 20
290 CLS : PRINT : PRINT : PRINT : GOTO 80
500 DATA"LUCKY LINDY HAS LANDED IN PARIS"
510 DATA"MET BY LARGE CROWD AT LEBOURGET AIRPORT"
```

...and RUN.

Your assignment, if you choose to accept it, is to complete the program so it repeats, ends, or otherwise does not crash.
Good luck!.

.
 .
  .
   .
    ....Fsssss!

Learned in Chapter 25

Functions

LEFT$
INSTR
MID$
RIGHT$
STRING$

"As if life isn't complicated enough, the LOGarithm system is centered around what are called *natural* logs. Exactly what that means is the subject of another discussion, but we're stuck with it anyway."

Part 4

Variable Precision and Math

Chapter 26

What Price Precision?

Unless told otherwise, Model 100 BASIC stores and displays variables to an accuracy of 14 digits. This is called "double precision" and is more than adequate for most applications.

> The old slide rule was accurate to only 3 digits.

These high precision numbers are fine for large businesses and special scientific applications. However, we pay a price for this precision both in the additional memory it takes to store and process long numbers, and the extra time required to process them.

When speed and preservation of memory space is more important than "double precision" we can specify the faster and generally more useful "single precision" accuracy. By telling the Computer to go "single precision", it will store and display numbers accurate to 6 digits.

Enter this double precision program:

```
1 CLS : PRINT
20 X = 1234567890987654321           (check 'em)
30 Y = .00000000123456789            (check 'em)
40 Z = X * Y
50 PRINT X;"TIMES";Y,"EQUALS";Z
```

and ... RUN.

```
1.2345678909877E+18 TIMES
1.23456789E-10 EQUALS 152415787.62384
```

Ummm-hmmm. A very large number times a very small number -- both expressed in Exponential notation, and the answer is clipped to 14 places. (The 'E' stands for *Exponential notation*. E+18 means the number ahead of it times 10 to the +18th power. E−10 means the number ahead of it times 10 to the −10th power).

Single Precision

We can easily convert storage, processing and printing of X, Y and Z to single precision. The BASIC Statement is an easy one:

```
10 DEFSNG A-Z
```

DEFSNG stands for "DEFine as SiNGle precision", and A-Z means "every variable from A through Z".

Add the Line and RUN.

```
1.23457E+18 TIMES 1.23457E-10 EQUALS
152416000
```

Quite a difference, eh? We lost several digits out in the hinterland, and reduced our accuracy from 14 places to 6, the 0's in the answer simply holding the decimal place.

Since we are only using 3 variables, X, Y and Z, there is really no point it DEFining more than them to be Single Precision. We can tell the Computer to handle only those 3 as single precision, and leave any other variables (of which there are none, right now) alone. Change Line 10 to:

```
10 DEFSNG X-Z
```

...and RUN.

Same results.

Overruled!

There are times when we will want to *temporarily* override the DEFSNG declaration, converting a number or answer back to double precision. Suppose we want Z to be printed as double precision. We override the Line 10 declaration by changing only those Lines which contain Z. Do it:

```
40 Z# = X * Y
50 PRINT X;"TIMES";Y;"EQUALS";Z#
```

...and RUN.

```
1.23457E+18 TIMES 1.23457E-10 EQUALS
152416308.49
```

Our "raw" data and the calculating was done in single precision, but our final answer is printed out with double-precision accuracy -- just what we asked for. It goes without saying that since the input numbers are less accurate than he output number, the output can only be trusted to the same level of accuracy as the input. A classic case of Garbage In, Garbage Out.

A very *specific* declaration (like the #, which stands for "double precision"), always takes precedence over a *global* declaration like Line 10. (Global means "valid for the entire program", not just one character or one Line.)

SiNGle Precision -- Simplified

There's another way to calculate with single precision but print the answer in double precision. Since double precision is the "default" mode, we can simply NOT include Z in the DEFine Line 10.

Change Lines 10, 40 and 50 and RUN.

```
10 DEFSNG X,Y         (or DEFSNG X-Y)
40 Z = X * Y
50 PRINT X;"TIMES";Y;"EQUALS";Z
```

Same results.

Global Override

It is possible to override the "global" DEFSNG declaration with a global double precision declaration. DEFDBL will change everything back to single precision. Let's try it by changing and adding these Lines:

```
60 DEFDBL X-Y
70 PRINT X;"TIMES";Y;"EQUALS";Z
```

...and RUN.

Good Grief -- our "double-precision" numbers turned to zeros!

Well, it turns out that X *SiNGle precision* is a completely separate variable from X *DouBLe precision*. It's as different from X as is Y, or any other variable. If we want to use X and Y again as double-precision numbers, we have to go back and assign them values *after* declaring them to be *DouBLe precision*. Hmmmm. This is getting complicated.

A cheap and dirty way to show the point is to change Line 70 to:

```
70 GOTO 20
```

...and RUN -- hitting the **SHIFT BREAK** key after both single and double precision versions are printed in Line 50.

Line 60 reDEFines X and Y as double precision, then control returns to Line 20 and the calculations are performed again. (Fortunately, there is rarely reason to *reDEFine* a variable within a program. If necessary, we can do it with conventional string techniques.)

SiNGle Precision, Another Way

Instead of a "global" declaration of accuracy, we can do it one variable at a time. Change the resident program to read:

```
1 CLS : PRINT
20 X! = 1234567890987654321
30 Y! = .0000000000123456789
40 Z! = X! * Y!
50 PRINT X!;"TIMES";Y!,"EQUALS";Z!
```

...and RUN.

"OOOOOOOOOOOO"
?

GARBAGE IN
GARBAGE OUT!

Same results as before. The ! sign declares that the variable letter preceding it is to be handled as SiNGle precision, overriding the normal presumption that it is DouBLe precision.

Remember, X! is not the same as X. It is an entirely different variable. Same with Y! and Z!. To nail this point down, add:

```
10 X = 4.321
60 PRINT "X =";X
```

...and RUN.

The values of X! and X had no effect on each other, did they?

INTeger Precision

In those frequent cases where the numbers used are integers (and in the range between -32768 and +32767), execution can be speeded up by declaring them to be INTegers using the % sign or the DEFINT statement. Type this NEW program:

```
20 FOR N = 1 TO 3500
30 NEXT N
80 PRINT : LIST
```

...and RUN.

Using a stopwatch or clock with a second hand, measure the time it takes for the 3500 passes thru the FOR-NEXT LOOP. Should be around 10 seconds. By default, the Model 100 processed the values of N in double precision.

Now, let's declare N to be an INTeger, (which is all the accuracy we need) and time it again.. Add:

```
10 DEFINT N
```

...and RUN.

Aha! It took only about 4 seconds. Cut the processing time by more than half.

What Price Precision?

We can accomplish the same thing using specific declarations instead of the global DEFINT. Delete Line 10 and change the program to read:

```
20 FOR N% = 1 TO 4000
30 NEXT N%
```

...and RUN.

Same fast results.

One More Way

The conversion functions CSNG(#), CDBL(#) and CINT(#) provide 3 additional ways to declare numbers as SiNGle, DouBLe or INTeger precision. Enter this NEW test program:

```
1 CLS : PRINT
20 X = 12345.67890
30 PRINT X
40 PRINT CDBL(X)
50 PRINT CSNG(X)
60 PRINT CINT(X)
```

...and RUN.

It tells the whole sordid story:

```
12345.6789
12345.6789
12345.7
12345
```

Line 30 printed the value of X, the same as we specified in Line 20, accurate to 14 digits. There just weren't 14 digits to print.

Line 40 printed the DouBLe precision value of X.

Line 50 printed the SiNGle precision value of X.

Line 60 printed the INTeger value of X. No surprises here.

Let's make the value of X negative and see what happens. Change Line 20 to:

```
20 X = -12345.67890
```

...and RUN.

Same answers, except negative.

CINT acted like INT by removing all the numbers to the right of the decimal point. Unlike most other computers' handling of INT in BASIC, it does not round up or down, just chops off the numbers to the right of the decimal point.

To refresh our memory as to how INT usually works, try typing:

```
PRINT INT(-12345.67890)
```

We get 12346. INT rounded down.

> This difference between the way the Model 100 and most other BASIC speaking computers handles CINT is worth noting.

Do SiNGles Have More Fun?

Now let's go back and declare the value of X to be SiNGle precision, change it to a positive number, and do all our PRINTing in SiNGle precision. The new program will read:

```
1 CLS : PRINT
20 X! = 12345.67890
30 PRINT X!
40 PRINT CDBL(X!)
50 PRINT CSNG(X!)
60 PRINT CINT(X!)
```

...then RUN.

and the display reads:

```
12345.7
12345.7
12345.7
12345
```

All makes sense, and all quite predictable, isn't it?

Caveat

Degrees of precision may not be the most inspiring subject, nor always seem to be the most consistent. But, if we're at least aware of the differences in precision, we'll not be caught off guard and be deceived by numbers that never were.

Learned in Chapter 26

Statements	Functions	Miscellaneous
DEFSNG	CSNG	Single precision (!)
DEFDBL	CDBL	Double precision (#)
DEFINT	CINT	Integer precision (%)

Chapter 27

Intrinsic Mathematical Function

The BASIC language includes a number of mathematical Functions. These math Functions are all very straightforward and easy to use, but if your math skills are a bit rusty, you will want to refresh them to fully understand what we're doing. We'll keep everything here at the 9th grade Algebra level so there's no need to panic (unless maybe you're in the 6th grade...but even so, just hang on and you'll be OK).

INT(N)
We studied the INTeger function in some detail in an earlier Chapter so we won't cover that ground again. INT stores and executes whole numbers with no more than single precision accuracy.

FIX(N)
FIX is just like INT, but instead of rounding negative numbers downward, it simply chops off everything to the right of the decimal point.

Try this simple test at the command level:

    `PRINT INT(-12345.67)`   **ENTER**

produces `-12346`

    `PRINT FIX(-12345.67)`   **ENTER**

produces `-12345`

The one we use depends on what we want.

SQR(N)
The SQuare Root function is simple to use.

Type this:

```
10 INPUT"THE SQUARE ROOT OF";N
20 PRINT "IS";SQR(N)
30 PRINT
40 GOTO 10
```

...and RUN some familiar numbers.

Another way to take the square (of any) root of a number is by using the up-arrow, or carat, above the #6 key. It of course means "raised to the power". Finding the square root of a number is the same as raising it to the 1/2 power. Change Line 20 to:

```
20 PRINT "IS";N^(1/2)
```

...and RUN.

The same logic which allows us to find the *square* root with the up-arrow will let us find any *other* root. (Even the thought of doing that is pre-computer days drove men mad.) Out of the sheer arrogance of power, let's find the 21st root of any number. Change the first two Lines:

```
10 INPUT"THE TWENTY-FIRST ROOT OF";N
20 PRINT "IS";N^(1/21)
```

...and RUN.

Now there is real horsepower! Problem is, how are we sure that the answers are right? Well, it's easy enough to add a few Lines that compute the root back to its 21st power to find out. Let's clean up the program a bit and make it read:

```
10 INPUT"THE TWENTY-FIRST ROOT OF";N
15 R=N^(1/21)
```

```
20 PRINT"IS ";R
30 PRINT
33 PRINT R;"TO THE 21ST POWER = ";R^21
36 PRINT
40 GOTO 10
```

...and RUN.

They come out pretty close, don't they? This "proof" process might not stand up under rigorous scrutiny, but the answers are correct.

> **EXERCISE 27-1:** Pythagoras discovered that the sides of a right triangle always obey the rule:
>
> $$C^2 = A^2 + B^2$$
>
> where C is the longest side (hypotenuse). Stated another way: "The length of side C equals the square root of the sum of the squares of sides A and B. $(C = \sqrt{A^2 + B^2})$.
>
> If side A = 5 and side B = 12, write a program to calculate the length of side C.

ABS(N)

ABSolute Value has a lot to do with signs, or without them. The absolute value of any number is the number *without* a sign. If you've forgotten, this NEW program will quickly refresh the memory:

```
10 INPUT"ENTER ANY NUMBER ";N
20 A = ABS(N)
30 PRINT A
40 PRINT
50 GOTO 10
```

...and RUN.

Respond with various large and small, positive and negative, numbers, and 0.

They all come out as they went in didn't they? Except the sign is missing.

LOG(N)

No, a log isn't what you build cabins with. But even the swiftest among us have to refresh their memory from time to time to keep all the details straight.

A LOG (Logarithm) is an *exponent*. Exponent of what? The exponent of a *base*. What's a *base*? A *base* is the number that a given number *system* is built on. Aren't all number systems built on 10? 'Fraid not.

$10^3 = 1000$

10 is the BASE.
3 is the LOG(exponent) and
1000 is the answer.

(Think it has something to do with "new math", but I was too old to take it, too young to teach it, and grateful for having missed learning it from those who didn't understand it.)

As if life isn't complicated enough, the LOGarithm system is centered around what are called *natural* logs. Exactly what that means is the subject of another discussion, but we're stuck with it anyway. Natural logs use the number 2.718282 as their base. (Really makes your day, doesn't it!) Some BASICs provide a second LOG option using 10 as the base, as in our decimal system, but making the conversion isn't too bad -- and we still do have to live with it.

Type this NEW program:

```
10 INPUT"ENTER ANY POSITIVE NUMBER";N
20 L = LOG(N)
30 PRINT "THE LOG OF";N;
40 PRINT "TO THE NATURAL BASE =";L
50 PRINT : GOTO 10
```

The LOG function is not valid for negative numbers or zero.

...and RUN.

Ummm Hmmm. Can't relate to the conclusion? Respond with the number 100 and we should get the answer 4.605170185988. Being in double precision, the answers are a bit messy. After we learn the principles, you can change the PRINT Lines to reduce accuracy to Single Precision or below.

What it means is, 2.718282 to the 4.60517 power = 100. Lay that one on them at the next meeting of the Audubon Society and they'll think you're weird for sure.

Let's jack this thing around to where the vast majority of us who have to work with LOGs can use it...into the decimal system.

Decimal-based Logs are called "common", or "base 10" Logs. Add these Lines:

```
45 PRINT "THE LOG OF";N;
47 PRINT "TO THE BASE 10 =";L*.4342945
```

...and RUN, using 100 as the number.

Ahhh! That's more like it. We can clearly see that 10 to the 2nd power equals 100. It's good to be back on *relatively* solid ground.

The magic conversion rules are:

To convert a natural log to a common log, multiply the natural log times .4342945.

To convert a common log to a natural log, multiply the common log times 2.3026.

And that's the name of that tune.

This final NEW program scoops it all up and spreads it out:

```
1 REM * LOGARITHM DEMO *
10 CLS : PRINT
```

```
20 INPUT "ENTER A POSITIVE NUMBER";N
30 PRINT
40 PRINT "NATURAL LOG";
50 PRINT TAB(20);"COMMON LOG"
60 PRINT LOG(N);TAB(20);LOG(N)*.4342945
70 PRINT : GOTO 20
```

EXP(N)

EXP is sort of the opposite of LOG. EXP computes the value of the answer, given the EXPonent of a *natural* log. (Another winner.)

2.718282 raised to the EXP power = the answer

Type in this NEW program:

```
10 INPUT"ENTER A NUMBER";N
20 A = EXP(N)
30 PRINT "2.718282 RAISED TO THE";N;
40 PRINT "POWER =";A
50 PRINT : GOTO 10
```

…and RUN, responding with a number smaller than about 145.

The number we entered is the EXPonent, so it's easy to respond with a number too big for the Computer and cause it to OVerflow.

As a benchmark against which to test the program, enter this number:

4.6051702

The BASE of the natural log system raised to this power should equal 100 (or be very close).

When you're done playing, respond with 150 to see the OVerflow Error message.

If you are really into math, and logs, do the exercise below, checking the results against a LOG table. If you're not too comfortable with all this…forget it, and *try making a log cabin with the remainders!*

EXERCISE 27-2: (for math fans only) Convince yourself that LOG and EXP functions are inverses of each other. (Hint: LOG(EXP(N)) = N.) Try using the two functions in the opposite order, then using both positive and negative values for N. Why do the negative values create havoc?

Learned in Chapter 27

Functions

INT
FIX
SQR
ABS
LOG
EXP

Miscellaneous

Natural Logs
Common Logs

Chapter 28

The Trigonometric Functions

Since this is about as deep as we'll get into mathematics, I have to assume you know something about elementary trig.

Trigonometry, of course, deals with triangles, their angles, and the ratios between the lengths of their sides. In the triangle below, the Sine (abbreviated SIN) of angle A is defined as the *ratio* (what we get after dividing) of the *length* of side **a** to the *length* of side **c**. COSine and TANgent are defined similarly:

SIN A = a/c
COS A = b/c
TAN A = a/b

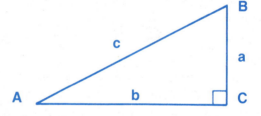

From these relationships, we can find any ratio if we know the corresponding angle. Let's try this simple program:

```
10 PRINT "ENTER AN ANGLE"
20 INPUT "BETWEEN 0 AND 90 DEGREES";A
30 S = SIN(A*.0174533)
40 PRINT "THE SIN OF";A;"DEGREES IS";S
50 PRINT : GOTO 10
```

...and RUN, responding with any number between 0 and 90.

The Trigonometric Functions

It really works! Try the old "standard" angles like 45°, 30°, 60°, 90°, 0°, etc.

Unless you're right up to snuff on trig, Line 30 undoubtedly looks strange. Well, it turns out that most Computers think in radians, not degrees (always has to be some nasty twist doesn't there...!) A radian is a unit of measurement equal to approximately 57 degrees. In order to convert from degrees (which most of us use) to radians, we changed the degrees we INPUT in Line 20 to radians. The SIN function will not work correctly without this conversion.

> To convert angles from degrees to radians, multiply the degrees by 0.0174533.

> To convert angles from radians to degrees, multiply the radians by 57.29578.

Failure to make these conversions correctly is *by far* the greatest source of Computer users' problems with the trig functions.

COSine and TANgent work the same way. Change the resident program to:

```
10 PRINT "ENTER AN ANGLE"
20 INPUT "BETWEEN 0 AND 90 DEGREES";A
30 C = COS(A*.0174533)
40 PRINT "THE COS OF";A;"DEGREES IS";C
50 PRINT : GOTO 10
```

...and RUN.

Most answers are pretty close, very good for such a small Computer. We know that COS(90) should be zero. Unfortunately, the Computer is slightly off because it calculates these functions by approximation. It's doing the best that it can...Honest!

For Tangent, RUN this program:

```
10 PRINT "ENTER AN ANGLE"
20 INPUT "BETWEEN 0 AND 90 DEGREES";A
30 T = TAN(A*.0174533)
40 PRINT "THE TAN OF";A;"DEGREES IS";T
50 PRINT : GOTO 10
```

> The TAN function is not even defined for 90°, tho the Model 100 will TRY to calculate it for us.

This next NEW simple program displays all three major trig functions at the same time. Note in Line 30 we *divide* our incoming angle by 57.29578 instead of multiplying it by 0.0174533. The results are the same.

```
10 CLS
20 PRINT"ENTER AN ANGLE"
30 INPUT "BETWEEN 0 AND 90 DEGREES";A
40 A = A/57.29578
50 PRINT
60 PRINT "ANGLE =";A*57.29578
70 PRINT "SIN =";SIN(A)
80 PRINT "COS =";COS(A)
90 PRINT "TAN =";TAN(A)
```

Inverse Trig Functions

The opposite of finding a *ratio* between two sides of a triangle when an angle is known, is finding an *angle* when the ratio of two sides is known. There are three functions commonly used in trig to do this, but most Computers only make provisions for one, called ATN (Arc of the TaNgent).

The following simple program takes the angle we INPUT, converts it to radians and computes and PRINTs its TANgent. Then, as a "proof check", takes that TANgent value and reverses the process by computing its arc (angle).

The letter "I" in Line 60 stands for "inverse" (sort of the "opposite"). ArcTANgent is commonly referred to as an "inverse function". In Line 40 we convert from degrees to radians, *before* the trig computation. In Line 60 the conversion from radians to degrees, *after* the trig computation.

```
1 CLS
10 REM * ATN DEMO *
20 PRINT "ENTER ANY ANGLE"
30 INPUT "BETWEEN 0 AND 90 DEGREES";A
```

```
40 T = TAN(A/57.29578)
50 PRINT : PRINT "TANGENT =";T
60 I = ATN(T) * 57.29578
70 PRINT "ARC OF THE TANGENT =";I
```

If you're one of those rare types who is very familiar with trig you can probably throw numbers around in such a fashion that the other 2 "inverse" trig functions, ARCSIN and ARCCOS are not needed. But for those of us who still get confused when we run out of fingers, the last two functions are built into a simple NEW program by way of special routines. The accuracy is close enough for "government" work. Give it a try:

```
10 CLS : ' * INV FUNCTION DEMO PROGRAM *
20 PRINT "ENTER A NUMBER - THE RATIO"
30 INPUT "OF 2 SIDES OF A TRIANGLE";R
40 AS = 2 * ATN(R/(1+SQR(ABS(1-R*R))))
 * 57.29578
50 AC = 90-AS : PRINT
60 PRINT "RATIO =";R
70 IF ABS(R)>1 THEN 110
80 PRINT"ARCSIN =";AS:PRINT"ARCCOS =";AC
90 PRINT "ARCTAN =";ATN(R)*57.29578
100 PRINT : GOTO 20
110 PRINT "ARCSIN = U":PRINT"ARCCOS = U"
120 PRINT "ARCTAN =";ATN(R)*57.29578
130 PRINT : GOTO 20
```

...and RUN. Respond with a ratio number between −1 and +1. The rest should now be obvious.

Other trig function routines can be found in *The BASIC Handbook*, available from CompuSoft Publishing and all good book and computer stores.

Remember, when our ratio moves outside the range −1 to 1, arcTAN and arcSIN are both "undefined." Also, arcTAN and arcSIN produce angle measures between −90 and 90 degrees, but arcCOS can range between 0 and 180 degrees.

Learned in Chapter 28

Functions

SIN
COS
TAN
ATN

Miscellaneous

Degrees
Radians

"For graphic use, the display is divided into a large number of blocks or 'pixels'..."

Part 5

Graphics and Display Formatting

Chapter 29

Video Display Graphics

And It Draws Pictures Too!

Our Model 100 can draw an endless variety of pictures on the Video Display. We will learn some of the basic procedures and capabilities in this Chapter. After that, what you create is limited only by your own imagination. Who knows...you may write a graphics program artistically equivalent to the Mona Lisa.

Now, the 2 most basic of the 4 graphic commands:

PSET turns on (darkens) a particular section or block on the display.

PRESET turns off (lightens) a particular block.

For graphic use, the display is divided into a large number of blocks or "pixels" (see the Video Display Worksheet on the next page). To get a good idea of how many dots will cover the display, turn the Display Adjustment Dial until the display becomes fairly dark. If we look close enough, we can see a grid of very thin lines, chopping the display into many little dots. Each of these dots representing a "part" of the display is called a "pixel".

Each block is a square section 1/48 the size of a regular character (1 character uses 48 pixels), and each pixel has its own "address".

For example:

```
PSET(55,32)
```

means -- "turn on the light" at the junction of 55th "H" Street and 32nd "V" Avenue.

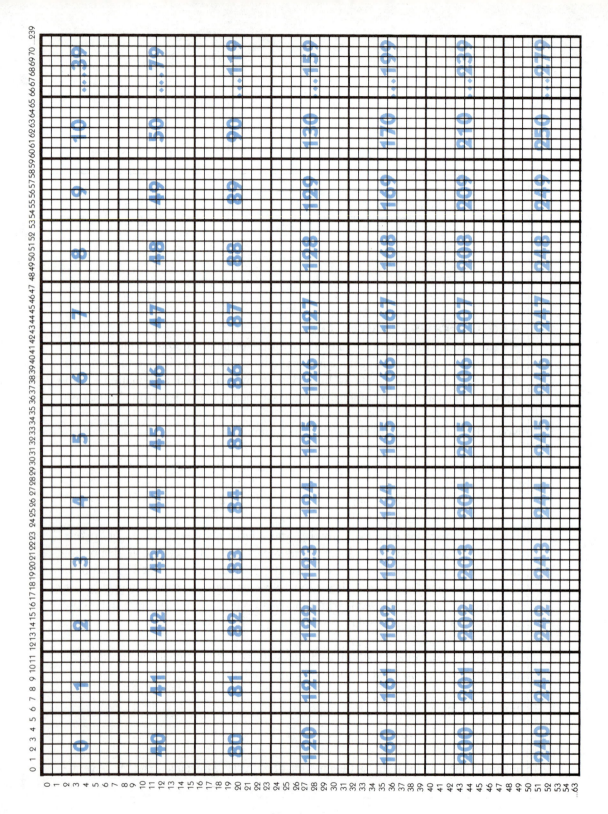

Video Display Worksheet

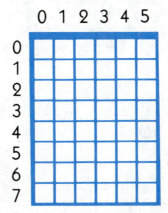

H is the horizontal address counting across from the left-hand side of the display. V is the vertical address, counting down from the top of the display. All "street addresses" start counting from the upper left-hand corner. H and V as used here are the same as X and Y used in the first quadrant of mathematical coordinate grid systems. H and V are more descriptive and easier to work with while learning.

Type in

    50 CLS : PSET(55,32)

...and RUN.

Look carefully for the dot because it is very tiny (there are approximately 32 dots per inch). Check the Video Display Worksheet carefully to find the address of that pixel. Did it show up in about the right place?

Careful now, don't mess up the display. Type:

    50 PRESET(55,32)

...and RUN.

How about that. We found the ON-OFF switch!

Want to really press your luck? Try re-darkening the block. That's right, type:

    50 PSET(55,32)

...and RUN several times.

Oh well, can't win 'em all. Why didn't it work? It *did* work! Then why didn't the fool light stay ON.

Answer: The Line Feed keeps moving it up away from its original address, and only what's at a specific address stays turned ON. When the cursor gets to the bottom of the display, another line feed moves the display up and the dot gets zapped!

The point of all this obviously is that we can control whether each block on the displays is dark or white (on or off) by "talking" to it at its individual address with PSET and PRESET statements.

Flying Saucers or Lightning Bugs?

If one has an ON-OFF switch, what does one do with it? With a little imagination we could create blocks that go ON and OFF, to attract attention...*by blinking*. This simple program shows how to set up a "blinker". RUN it:

```
10 CLS
20 H = 60
30 V = 25
40 PSET(H,V)
50 PRESET(H,V)
60 GOTO 40
```

Simple FOR-NEXT loops at 45 and 55 could control the blinking rate.

Once Again, More Heavily

In the Horizontal direction, there are 240 addresses, numbered 0 to 239. 0 is at the far left, 120 is near the middle and 239 is at the far right.

In the Vertical direction, there are 64 light blocks addresses, 0 is at the top and 63 is at the bottom.

The statement "PSET(H,V)" darkens the block which is the Hth block from the left in the horizontal direction and the Vth one down from the top in the vertical direction. And, you've figured out that PRESET works in the same way except that it lightens the block.

Let's exercise it more aggresively. This NEW program will darken any one block of your choosing. Type:

```
10 INPUT "HORIZONTAL (0 TO 127)";H
```

```
20 INPUT "VERTICAL (0 TO 63)";V
30 CLS
40 PSET(H,V)
```

...and RUN a number of times using various values of H and V.

You may have noticed that if a block is lit in the upper left-hand corner, the Ok will destroy it. If it lands on the flashing cursor, it will alternate between dark and light. Try H = 3 and V = 4. Then H = 3 and V = 12. We can avoid this problem by not returning control to the prompt -- by adding:

```
99 GOTO 99
```

This Line locks the Computer in an endless loop. RUN the program trying value of H = 5 and V = 5. To break the loop, press the **SHIFT** **BREAK**.

CLS is a single statement which PRESETs every block on the display to "OFF" in one operation; we don't have a similar statement to turn them all "ON".

However, we can easily write a program that "darkens" or "paints" the entire display. It uses one CLS (not really a *must,* but always a good habit to use in graphics programs), two FOR-NEXT loops and one endless "locking loop". Type this:

```
10 CLS
20 FOR H = 0 TO 239
30  FOR V = 0 TO 63
40   PSET(H,V)
50  NEXT V
60 NEXT H
99 GOTO 99
```

...and RUN.

The program fills the display from left to right. Redesign it so it starts at the top and fills to the bottom.

Answer:

```
10 CLS
20 FOR H = 0 TO 239
30   FOR V = 0 TO 63
40     PSET(H,V)
50   NEXT V
60 NEXT H
99 GOTO 99
```

Rewrite the program so it starts painting at the bottom and fills to the top.

Answer:

```
10 CLS
20 FOR V = 63 TO 0 STEP-1
30   FOR H = 0 TO 239
40     PSET(H,V)
50   NEXT H
60 NEXT V
99 GOTO 99
```

Did you forget it could STEP backwards?

Rewrite it so it starts painting at the upper right-hand side and fills to the lower left-hand side.

Answer:

```
10 CLS
20 FOR H = 239 TO 0 STEP-1
30   FOR V = 0 TO 63
40     PSET(H,V)
50   NEXT V
60 NEXT H
99 GOTO 99
```

Just for practice, RUN the program using other positive and negative STEP increments...

Fantastic -- now we can paint the old barn at least four ways!

EXERCISE 29-1: Write a program which will allow painting only a small part of the display (you determine which part). Allow keyboard INPUT of the starting and ending block numbers in both the horizontal and vertical directions.

Getting the hang of it? Great. Enough playing with blocks...let's draw some lines. Erase the resident program.

> You haven't forgotten how to do that have you! Type ERASE...no, no! Type NEW.

We'll start our artistry with a straight line. This program PSETs a straight horizontal line across the entire display. Type:

```
10 INPUT "VERTICAL (0 TO 63)";V
20 CLS
30 FOR H = 0 TO 239
40   PSET(H,V)
50 NEXT H
99 GOTO 99
```

...and RUN several times.

We can just as easily create a straight vertical line. Try this.

```
10 INPUT "HORIZONTAL (0 TO 239)";H
20 CLS
30 FOR V = 0 TO 63
40   PSET(H,V)
50 NEXT V
99 GOTO 99
```

...and RUN a number of times.

Now, let's see if we can modify this last program to allow us to INPUT both the starting vertical address and the length (in pixels):

```
12 INPUT "VERT START ADDR# (0 TO 63)";V
14 INPUT "NO. OF VERTICAL PIXELS";N
16 IF V + N < 64 GOTO 20
18 PRINT "TOO MANY VERTICALS"
19 END
30 FOR V = V TO V + N
```

Now that we can draw straight lines, we can form figures -- like squares and rectangles. This program forms a rectangle. After NEW, type:

```
10 INPUT "HORIZ START NO. (0 TO 239)";H
20 INPUT "VERT START NO. (0 TO 63)";V
30 INPUT "LENGTH OF SIDES (0 TO 63)";S
40 CLS
50 FOR L = H TO H + S
60   PSET(L,V)
70   PSET(L,V+S)
80 NEXT L
90 FOR M = V TO V+S
100   PSET(H,M)
110   PSET(H+S,M)
120 NEXT M
999 GOTO 999
```

Remember, we can't draw pictures off the display. If you get an error message like: ?FC Error in 70, that means you tried to do it.

...and RUN.

> You may want to come back later for some heavier study.

Press on...

A Little Diversion

All our graphics work so far has been drawing dark lines on the display. We can do just the reverse by painting the display dark first, then lightening the desired areas with PRESET. This NEW program draws a white horizontal line on a black background. Type:

```
10 INPUT "VERT POSITION (0 TO 63)"; V
20 CLS
30 FOR H = 0 TO 239
40   FOR  J = 0 TO 63
50     PSET(H,J)
60   NEXT J
70 NEXT H
80 FOR H = 0 TO 239
90   PRESET(H,V)
100 NEXT H
999 GOTO 999
```

...and RUN.

If you're interested, go back and try similar easy modifications to other demonstration programs and have some fun with these reverse (or "negative") displays.

> **EXERCISE 29-2:** Rewrite the opening section of the last program to speed up the display "painting". HINT: Use the CHR$ function and the ASCII chart in Appendix A.

Learned in Chapter 29

Statements

PSET
PRESET

Miscellaneous

Pixel

Chapter 30

Intermediate Graphics

We can draw other straight (more or less) lines by just changing H and V addresses of PSET in the FOR-NEXT loop. Try this next program to draw a diagonal line:

```
10 INPUT "HORIZ START NO. (0 TO 239)";H
20 INPUT "VERT START NO. (0 TO 63)";V
30 INPUT "DIAGONAL LENGTH";D
40 CLS
50 FOR L = 0 TO D
60   PSET(H+L,V+L)
70 NEXT L
99 GOTO 99
```

Once we have the diagonal line, we can form a right triangle by adding:

```
70   PSET(H,V+L)
80   PSET(H+L,V+D)
90 NEXT L
```

or

```
70   PSET(H+D,V+L)
```

```
80   PSET(H+L,V)
90 NEXT L
```

Try them both.

Question: What is the difference in the displays?

Answer: They are inverted, mirror images of each other.

Remember, you can't draw pictures off the display.

Broken Lines

In every prior graphics program we could have made the lines "broken" by introducing a STEP other than "1" in the FOR-NEXT loops. For example, try drawing a broken horizontal line with:

```
10 INPUT "VERTICAL ADDRESS (1 TO 63)";V
20 INPUT "STEP SIZE";S
30 CLS
40 FOR H = 0 TO 239 STEP S
50   PSET(H,V)
60 NEXT H
99 GOTO 99
```

RUN this program with various values of S. Note that as you increase S, the line is drawn much faster (since the Computer has less work to do). In fact, for S = 10 or more, we can hardly see the line being drawn. This is how a TV picture is created -- since it too is drawn one unit at a time (but so fast we don't notice the "drawing time").

Make the following program changes:

```
11 REM * V MUST BE LARGER THAN 0 *
55   PRESET(H,V-1)
70 V = V + 1
80 IF V < 64 GOTO 40
```

Intermediate Graphics 321

If S is small, we can see each line being formed and cleared. But if S is fairly large (try 20), the line seems to move in somewhat "old-time movie" fashion. This is the way the illusion of motion is created on a TV set and in some of the popular video games.

Try this NEW program. It paints a dot on the displays and moves it down.

```
10 INPUT "HORIZONTAL START (0 TO 239)"; H
20 INPUT "VERTICAL START (1 TO 63)"; V
30 CLS
40 PRESET(H,V-1)
50 PSET(H,V)
60 V = V + 1
70 IF V < 64 GOTO 40
99 GOTO 99
```

Having problems spotting the dot? Don't worry, it isn't your eyes. They action is so fast that the pixel doesn't have a chance to turn fully on before PRESET turns it off. Add this delay Line to give PSET a chance to turn on the pixel:

```
65 FOR X = 1 TO 20 : NEXT X
```

The PRESET statement simply followed along behind and erased the dot from the last PSET.

What happens if we omit PRESET? When you try it, remember to change Line 70 to GOTO 50.

Details...Details

PRESET and PSET don't work with negative coordinates. Try changing Line 70 back to GOTO 40 and take a look at Line 40:

```
40 PRESET(H,V-1)
```

If you INPUT V equal to 0, then the V address really becomes V-1...-1. A no-no!

More of the Good Stuff
We can just as easily move a point to the right with by substituting these Lines:

```
10 INPUT "HORIZONTAL START (1 TO 239)"; H
20 INPUT "VERTICAL START (0 TO 63)"; V
30 CLS
40 PRESET(H-1,V)
50 PSET(H,V)
60 H = H + 1
65 FOR X = 1 TO 20 : NEXT X
70 IF H < 240 GOTO 40
99 GOTO 99
```

EXERCISE 30-1: Change the last two programs so that they move the dot up and to the left respectively.

Now, let's have the dot move down until it strikes a barrier. The NEW program will read:

```
10 V=15
20 CLS
30 FOR M = 90 TO 150
40  PSET(M,45)
50 NEXT M
60 PRESET(120,V-1)
70 PSET(120,V)
80 FOR X = 1 TO 20 : NEXT X
90 V = V + 1
100 IF V < 45 THEN 60
999 GOTO 999
```

The dot appears to strike the barrier and stick to it.

Now let's have the dot start in the middle and ricochet from both the top and the bottom:

```
NEW
10 CLS
20 FOR H = 90 TO 150
30   PSET(H,5)
40   PSET(H,60)
50 NEXT H
60 V = 14
70 D = 1
80 PRESET(120,V-D)
90 PSET(120,V)
100 FOR X=1 TO 20:NEXT X
110  V = V + D
120 IF V = 61 THEN 140
130 IF V <> 4 THEN 80
140 V = V - 2 * D
150 D = -D
160 GOTO 90
999 GOTO 999
```

You may want to adjust the Display control to make it easier to see the dot bounce. The change in direction of the moving dot is caused by:

```
150 D = -D.
```

Note that we must be careful not to accidentally erase part of the boundary. To do this, we move the dot back 2 steps with Line 140 (after moving it forward 1 in Line 110) but we also return to the PSET in 90, rather than to PRESET in 80. Tricky, tricky. You can kill the whole day messing around with this silly bouncing ball. Rather good resilience, eh?

SAVE this program for use in the next Chapter.

Real Moving Pictures

We can draw whatever figures we like. Let's try a stick man. First, his legs:

```
10 CLS
20 H = 64
30 FOR K = 0 TO 7
40   PSET(H+K,40+K)
50   PSET(H-K,40+K)
60 NEXT K
999 GOTO 999
```

...and RUN.

Then add his body and arms:

```
70 FOR K = 0 TO 5
80   PSET(H+K,34+K)
90   PSET(H,34+K)
100 PSET(H-K,34+K)
110 NEXT K
```

...and RUN.

And finally his head:

```
120 PSET(H,32)
130 PSET(H+1,33)
140 PSET(H-1,33)
```

...and RUN.

Now let's try and move him to the right. Add:

```
45   PRESET(H+K-1,40+K)
55   PRESET(H-K-1,40+K)
85   PRESET(H+K-1,34+K)
```

Chapter 30

```
 95  PRESET(H-1,34+K)
105   PRESET(H-K-1,34+K)
125  PRESET(H-1,32)
135  PRESET(H,33)
145  PRESET(H-2,33)
150  H = H + 1
160  GOTO 30
```

...and RUN.

Sure moves funny, doesn't he? Well, I'm no animator either, but you're beginning to get the idea.

Line Drawing With Line

We have been drawing lines (horizontal, vertical and diagonal) by using PSET. There is an easier and shorter method for drawing straight lines. Type in this NEW program:

```
10 CLS
20 LINE (170,0)-(120,50)
30 LINE - (220,50)
40 LINE - (170,0)
50 LIST
```

...and RUN.

WOW! Now that's fast. It only took 3 program Lines to draw 3 display lines. A similar program using PSET would require about five loops. By analyzing each Line we'll discover that LINE is actually similar to PSET. LINE and PSET use the same Horizontal and Vertical address numbers to spot the starting point on the display.

Nice. But what is it doing?

Line 10 clears the display

Line 20 *draws* a diagonal LINE by following the dots from coordinates 170 (horizontal) and 0 (vertical) to (−) 120 (horizontal) and 50 (vertical).

Line 30 draws the horizontal base line. The TO (−) and the destination coordinates are all that is included in this LINE statement. When the starting coordinates are omitted, the Model 100 uses the coordinates last used to PSET or LINE. In this example, the last pixel turned on in Line 20 was at (120,50). So, Line 30 really says "from the last coordinate (120,50), draw a LINE to (−) horizontal position 220 on vertical line 50.

Line 40 begins at the last pixel turned in by Line 30 and draws the third LINE up to the top of the triangle.

Line 50 then LISTs the program.

Zeroing Out the Line

Replace Line 50 in the resident program with:

```
50 LINE (145,50)-(195,50),0
```

...RUN

By selecting a portion of the horizontal LINE and adding ",0" to the end of the LINE statement, we made LINE act like PRESET. Do some experimenting on your own with LINEs before going on.

EXERCISE 30-2: Add two Lines to the LINE program that will draw this completed diagram:

Drawing Boxes

We can also draw boxes without topses. Try this NEW program:

```
10 CLS
20 LINE (5,5)-(234,58),1,B
99 GOTO 99
```

...and RUN.

Line 20 did all that? The first coordinate (5,5) established the top left hand corner of the box and (234,58) set the bottom right hand corner. Then B told LINE to connect these two points in the shape of a Box.

How about a box within a box? Add:

```
30 LINE (50,15)-(190,48),1,B
```

Now would't look neat to fill in the inside box. Suppose that requires several FOR-NEXT loops and a PSET. Wrong, just the letter F added to our LINE statement Fills in the Box. Change Line 20 to:

```
30 LINE (50,15)-(190,48),1,BF
```

...and RUN.

Just like that, the Box is Filled.

Do you suppose the are any more tricks left in the LINE statement? Well, there just happens to be one. We can remove an entire box the same way we removed a LINE. Let's add the finishing touches to this program by adding these Lines:

```
40 LINE (55,20)-(185,43),0,B
50 PRINT@137,"BURMA"
60 PRINT@177,"SHAVE"
```

This has been one long and active Chapter...and to think, all this with only the PSET, PRESET, and LINE statements. By simply exchanging PRESET for PSET or a 0 for a 1, in many cases we could have drawn the same pictures, with light on a dark background instead of dark on light. You might want to give it a try.

Because the ideas come so fast in the area of graphics, we have deliberately chosen to show a number of straightforward examples rather than get bogged down in elaborate programs. There is no substitute for lots of experimenting with graphics, and you now know the basics. Put in your time, study the examples, and soon you can apply for membership in the artists' guild.

Learned in Chapter 30

Statements

LINE

Miscellaneous

Diagonal lines
Broken lines
Animated graphics

Chapter 31

Display Formatting With PRINT@

Remember the bouncing dot? Wouldn't it be nifty if we could get the display to say "PING" each time the dot bounced off the barrier? Well I think it would be nifty, so we're going to do it. But first...

We learned all about PSET and PRESET earlier. Now we'll learn about PRINT@ (pronounced *print at*) -- a special type of PRINT statement especially useful in graphics.

I Thought You Printed On, Not Printed At

Learn something new every day. The PRINT@ statement allows us to *begin* printing AT a special numbered location. Example, type:

```
NEW
10 CLS
50 PRINT@ 170, "HELLO THERE #170."
```

...and RUN.

This is location #170? Back to the Video Display Worksheet in Chapter 29.

The PRINT@ numbers start at 0 in the upper-left hand corner and go through 39 -- in the *first line*. They then pick up on the second line with number 40 and continue through number 79. The third line starts with number 80, etc.

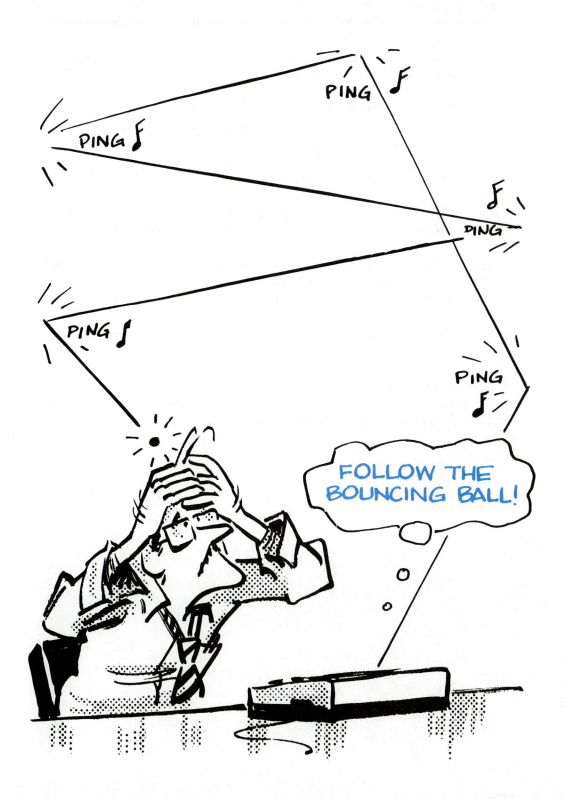

The width of PRINT@ divisions are really the same as those for TAB except PRINT@ does not start over again with zero on the second line. It keeps going right on through PRINT position number 319.

This perhaps strange sort of numbering is not so strange when you consider the problems we had very early in the graphics game with the fool carriage return scrolling our light right off the display.

> Remember what scrolling is? An upward line roll.

The PRINT@ statement does not trigger a scroll after it has done its printing, *except in the last line*, between print positions number 280 and number 319.

Further, PRINT@ can *directly* address any of the 319 printing locations (not pixel locations -- they are very different). Trailing semicolons are needed only after statements printed on that last or bottom line of the video "page".

We will soon see how valuable all this is.

Oh, It's That Time Already?

Let's create a 24-hour clock. (Why not...sounds like more fun than digging through all this obscure print statement logic.) Type:

```
NEW
10 CLS
20 PRINT@135,"H    M    S"
30 FOR H = 0 TO 23
40   FOR M = 0 TO 59
50     FOR S = 0 TO 59
60       PRINT@174,H; ":"; M; ":"; S
70       FOR N = 1 TO 330 : NEXT N
80     NEXT S
90   NEXT M
100 NEXT H
110 GOTO 10
```

...and RUN.

Nothing to it. Ahem!

"Hello? National Bureau of Standards?"

Of course the accuracy of this timer depends on how closely we calibrate it. We know that a Model 100 will execute somewhere around 330 simple FOR-NEXT loops per second when written as shown in Line 70 -- a multiple statement Line. If you really get carried away with this program, it can be calibrated against a precision timepiece, increasing or decreasing the "330" figure as needed. Over the short run, it is quite a good timer. Note that we are not triggering this with the power line frequency or a crystal oscillator, but relying solely on the amount of time required to execute FOR-NEXT loops. (It's not nearly as accurate as the Real Time Clock built into the Model 100).

Oh, Yes...The PRINT@

Anyway -- let's not lose sight of the forest for the trees (or is it trees for the forest). purpose of this little program is to demonstrate the PRINT@ statement.

We used it twice. By carefully squinting at the layout chart you can find address 135, with 174 neatly below it. With blazing speed, the HMS (no, no, not Her Majesty's Service -- it stands for Hours, Minutes and Seconds), are printed -- and the H, M and S updated each second.

NOTE: No carriage-return-suppressing semicolons follow the PRINT@ statements since they are not on the bottom line.

For the real clock nut, see Appendix H for an operational clock program. It only needs your closer calibration to be an acceptable sundial. Most expensive clock in the house!

That's How the Ball Bounces

Meanwhile, back with the bouncing ball. Let's CLOAD the program from Chapter 30. It reads:

```
10 CLS
20 FOR H = 90 TO 150
30   PSET(H,5)
40   PSET(H,60)
```

```
50 NEXT H
60 V = 14
70 D = 1
80 PRESET(120,V-D)
90 PSET(120,V)
100 FOR X=1 TO 20:NEXT X
110 V = V + D
120 IF V = 61 THEN 140
130 IF V <> 4 THEN 80
140 V = V - 2 * D
150 D = -D
160 GOTO 90
999 GOTO 999
```

Since we did not explain in detail how that fairly simple program worked, take time now to see if you can follow it through. Concentrate your thinking on the PSET and PRESET Lines, and the logic that gives them their numerical values. When you have it figured it out, tackle this exercise:

EXERCISE 31-1: Using PRINT@ statement(s), cause the word "PING" to appear near the ball each time it bounces off either the top or bottom boundary. A sample answer is in Appendix G.

Isn't it amazing how close we are building towards some of the video games that are all the rage -- and yet it's really so simple and logical.

Learned in Chapter 31

Statements

PRINT@

Chapter 32

Graphing Trig Functions

It is often helpful to graph mathematical functions to better understand what's happening. The Model 100 graphics are adequate for a non-precision examination of many mathematical functions, and the following short demo programs illustrate that capability.

Just imagine there is an X-Y coordinate system drawn on the display (or draw *your* own, either with the Computer or a china marker). The numbers in these demo programs are not magic, they just allow the graphs to be drawn large, but not so large they run off the display.

These programs are included to show how PRINT@ can be used in a supporting role to the Model 100 graphics. Experiment to get what you want for your own particular application.

A Single Sine Wave

```
1 CLS : PRINT@282,"SINE"
10 FOR X = 0 TO 255
20 Y = SIN(X/40)
30 PSET(X/2,30-Y*20)
40 PRINT@290,"X =";INT(X/2);
50 PRINT@300,"Y =";INT(20-Y*20);
```

```
60 NEXT X
70 GOTO 70
```

Cosine Waves

```
1  CLS: PRINT@282,"COSINE";
10 FOR X = 0 TO 765
20 Y = COS(X/40)
30 PSET(X/6,20-Y*20)
40 PRINT@290,"X =";INT(X/6);
50 PRINT@300,"Y =";INT(20-Y*20);
60 NEXT X
70 GOTO 70
```

Graph of the Tangent

```
1  CLS : PRINT@282,"TANGENT"
10 FOR X = 0 TO 126
20 Y = TAN(X/90)
30 PSET(X,47-Y*8)
40 PRINT@290,"X =";INT(X);
50 PRINT@300,"Y =";INT(47-Y*8);
60 NEXT X
70 GOTO 70
```

There is obviously quite an education to be had by careful study of the graphs. Look for such things as relative thickness of the line at different points, the rate at which blocks are lit relative to the other variable, etc. Sure beats the "early days" when we had to try and imagine these things on a blackboard.

Merely For Display Purposes

A good way to get a feel for PRINT@ (or any feature) is to look at a fairly simple program which illustrates its use. This NEW program lays out a graph format on the display. What you do with it beyond that point depends on your own needs and interests, but it is worth entering, studying and becoming comfortable with. Type:

```
10 CLS
20 PRINT@8,"G R A P H   H E A D I N G"
30 PRINT@48,"- - - - - - - - - - -"
40 REM * HORIZONTAL MARKERS *
50 FOR X = 1 TO 36
60   PRINT@243+X,".";
70 NEXT X
80 REM * HORIZONTAL NUMBERS *
90 FOR X = 0 TO 3
100   PRINT@283+10*X,X;
110 NEXT X
120 REM * VERTICAL MARKERS *
130 FOR Y = 1 TO 6
140   PRINT@Y*40+3,"-"
150 NEXT Y
160 REM * VERTICAL NUMBERS *
170 FOR Y = 1 TO 6
180   PRINT@Y*40,6-Y
190 NEXT Y
999 GOTO 999
```

One noteworthy procedure in this program is the use of trailing semicolons after PRINT@ statements. The reason, again, is that the printing is taking place in the last line on the display so the carriage return would activate a line feed scroll. We therefore have to suppress the carriage return with the semicolon.

Learned in Chapter 32

Miscellaneous

Graphing with PRINT@

Chapter 33

INKEY$

The INKEY$ (pronounced Inkey-string) function is a powerful one which enables us to INPUT information from the keyboard without having to use the ENTER key.

Enter this NEW program:

```
1 CLS
10 IF INKEY$="T" THEN 30
20 GOTO 10
30 PRINT "YOU HIT THE LETTER 'T'"
40 GOTO 10
```

...and RUN.

Press any key except T. The keyboard seems to be dead. Now hit the capital letter "T" key.

Aha! The test in Line 10 then passes, execution moves to Line 30 and a message is printed. Then the process starts over. Hit T again. Hold it down.

The way INKEY$ works is clever if somewhat subtle, so pay close attention.

The Model 100 keyboard is constantly scanned by the Computer, checking to see if any key is pressed. Any time a key is pressed while the Computer encounters an INKEY$ function, the character that key represents is stored in the INKEY$ storage, or buffer area. This buffer can hold only one character at a time so when a new key is pressed, that character replaces whatever preceded it in the buffer, if anything. INKEY$ automatically assumes the String Value of whatever character is in its buffer.

Since INKEY$ can only "photograph" one letter or number at a time, if we want to test for more than one character, we have to write the program to test for each one in sequence. In so doing, however, we must be careful or INKEY$ will trip us up.

Add these Lines to the program:

```
15 IF INKEY$="P" THEN 50
50 PRINT "YOU HIT THE LETTER 'P'"
60 GOTO 10
```

...and RUN, alternately pressing P and T.

Not terribly responsive, is it?

The Autopsy
BREAK the RUN and LIST the display so we can take a good look at the program.

Suppose that the operator presses the T key just as Line 15 begins execution. Where does that T go? Right into the INKEY$ buffer, of course.

In Line 15, the buffer's current value (T) is compared and tested for a match with the letter P. Since the two string values don't match, control passes to Line 20, then back to Line 10. In Line 10, an INKEY$ looks again, this time for a "T", but unless we just happened to hold the T key down, T is not to be found. What happened to the T?

Let's replay that last sequence and zoom in for a closeup on the INKEY$ buffer. When the operator hit the T key, T was stored in the buffer. After INKEY$ in Line 15 was executed, the buffer went blank, since each time INKEY$ is called, the buffer is cleared, whether INKEY$ found what it was looking for or not. (Conversely, the only way the INKEY$ buffer is cleared is by being read by INKEY$.) Do you understand the problem? If not, restudy the previous 3 paragraphs.

> (Non-believing readers who don't believe the above can write their own simple program to prove that the buffer goes blank after an INKEY$ read. Since the Model 100 keyboard keeps spitting letters into the buffer as quickly as it is cleared and as long as a key is held down, it is necessary to slow down program execution via a FOR-NEXT delay loop to prove the point.)

If we want to preserve the value of INKEY$ until it has gone through all the INKEY$ and any other tests, we'll need to store it in a temporary string variable so it can't be erased by the wrong INKEY$. It's all really very simple and straightforward.

Change Lines 10 and 15 to get:

```
1 CLS
10 A$=INKEY$ : IF A$="T" THEN 30
15 IF A$="P" THEN 50
20 GOTO 10
30 PRINT"YOU HIT THE LETTER'T'"
40 GOTO 10
50 PRINT"YOU HIT THE LETTER 'P'": GOTO 10
```

...and RUN alternately pressing P and T as quickly as you can.

Aha! Now we're getting somewhere.

By setting a "regular" string variable equal to INKEY$, and having T and P checked against the variable instead of against the INKEY$ buffer, we can store a value for as long as is needed, and process it much more efficiently and predictably.

Rapid Scanner

If INKEY$ scans the buffer and does not find a pressed key (the usual case), it is said to read a "null string". INKEY$ is a String Function, and null means *nothing*. A null string is represented by two separate quote marks with nothing between them, thus:

" "

The ASCII code for null is 0.

To see how fast INKEY$ scans the keyboard for input, try this NEW program:

```
10 K$ = INKEY$
20 IF K$="" THEN PRINT"NO KEYBOARD INPUT"
30 PRINT ,K$ : GOTO 10
```

...and RUN.

Type in some words and see them break the scan.

Get the general idea of how to use INKEY$? So simple, yet the possibilities are enormous. Only a lot of experimenting will make you comfortable with it, but INKEY$ will keep you awake nights staring at the ceiling thinking of exciting ways to put it to work.

Out of the Blue of the Western Sky...

While chasing the solitude needed to write Computer books, your author piloted a heavily loaded private plane, packed with computers, ham radio and other goodies, into a medium sized city airport. Transferring this freight to a rental car turned out to be a big deal since security wouldn't let a car on the apron to unload the plane. (You're supposed to drop it by parachute?)

After some cajoling (and a gratuity) it was agreed that my car could be driven up *near* the apron, and an "officially approved" car could haul the goodies from the plane to my car. It all seemed a bit officious, but elections were far away...

Anyway, to get my car thru the security fence it was necessary to drive to an electrically operated gate. A secret code was to be punched into a numeric keypad for some sort of computer to analyze, and it controlled the motorized gate. The secret code number was 1930.

Needless to say, as soon as the Computer was set up, I wrote a BASIC program to do everything but actually open the gate. It provides a good example of a real-life application of INKEY$, and is offered here for your amusement, amazement and study.

```
10 CLS:PRINT@170,"TYPE THE COMBINATION"
20 PRINT@210,"FOLLOWED BY A PERIOD"
30 PRINT@91,"THE GATE IS CLOSED"
40 K$ = INKEY$ : IF K$ = "" GOTO 40
```

```
50 READ D$ : IF D$ = "." GOTO 80
60 IF D$ = K$ GOTO 40
70 RESTORE : GOTO 40
80 CLS: PRINT@132,"YOU MAY ENTER NOW"
90 PRINT@168,"WAIT FOR THE GATE TO OPEN"
100 FOR T = 1 TO 1500 : NEXT T
110 RESTORE : GOTO 10
1000 DATA 1,9,3,0,.
```

The password (1930 followed by a period) is imbedded, a character at a time, in DATA Line #1000. The commas only separate the characters and should not be typed in to open the gate.

Line 40 holds the magic. It checks the INKEY$ buffer looking for something besides a null string. If it finds a key pressed, execution drops to Line 50.

Line 50 READs a piece of DATA. If it happens to be a period (which can only be READ from DATA after each of the other code characters have been READ), execution moves to Line 80, where the gate is OPENed, and then you are allowed to enter the premises.

If, however, the test in Line 50 does note find a period, execution defaults to the next test, in Line 60.

Line 60 checks to see if the keyboard character matches up with the character READ from DATA. If so, the first hurdle has been passed and execution returns back to Line 40 for INKEY$ to await another keyboard character. If the keyboard and DATA characters don't match, the test fails and execution drops to Line 70.

Line 70 RESTOREs the DATA pointer back to its beginning, and returns execution to Line 40 to start scanning all over again. The keyboard puncher sees none of this and has no idea if he is making progress towards cracking the code.

Line 100 merely allows the gate a brief time to open and close (and you to read the display), then

Line 110 RESTOREs the DATA and starts the program over again from the beginning.

The password can be changed to any combination of characters by changing Line 1000.

If you wanted it to be "MODEL 100" for example:

```
1000 DATA M,O,D,E,L,-,1,0,0,.
```

Or, 'OPENSESAME'

```
1000 DATA O,P,E,N,S,E,S,A,M,E,.
```

Don't forget that last piece of DATA, the period. By changing Line 50, of course, you could change that period to anything else you might want.

Happy gate crashing!

Learned in Chapter 33

Functions

INKEY$

Miscellaneous

INKEY$ buffer

Chapter 34

PRINT USING

Of all the ways we have to PRINT, the most powerful (but most confusing) is one called PRINT USING. The name PRINT USING itself implies that we *PRINT* something *USING* something else. That implication is correct.

As originally developed for use on large Computers, PRINT USING consists of two parts -- PRINT and USING. PRINT prints USING the Format (called the "image") found in *another* Line. The Model 100 PRINT USING is similar, but does not always require a second Line for the "image"...as we will see.

PRINT USING With Numbers
Type:

```
10 A = 123.456789
40 U$ = "###.##"
50 PRINT USING U$;A
90 PRINT : LIST
```

...and RUN.

The answer is PRINTed as

```
123.46
```

It was rounded up and PRINTed to an accuracy of 2 *decimal* places.

Add:

```
20 B = 1.6
60 PRINT USING U$;B
```

...and RUN.

The display shows

```
123.46
  1.60
```

The first thing to note is that we have called upon Line 40, or image Line, twice -- once in Line 50 and again in Line 60. Next, note that two answers appeared with their decimal points lined up. Last, see that a 0 has been added to the 1.6 to make it read 1.60. These latter two points are important if you're printing out business reports.

One more addition:

```
30 C = 9876.54321
70 PRINT USING U$;C
```

Produces:

```
123.46
  1.60
%9876.54
```

What gives???

Well, the % sign means we have overrun our image Lines capacity to print digits *left* of the decimal point, but it prints them anyway. Better to lose our decimal point lineup than important numbers, but it does call our attention to a programming problem. Let's add another # sign to make room for that extra digit. (We are adding another *element* to the *field* in the *image* Line. Got that?)

```
40 U$ = "####.##"
```

...and RUN.

```
     123.46
       1.60
    9876.54
```

That's better -- but the overrun message would appear again if we tried to print a number with more than 4 digits on the left.

So far, this PRINT USING business looks like it might have some potential, lining up decimal points like it does. We don't have any other reasonable, straightforward way to accomplish that, and it's essential for printing dollars and cents in business reports. Wonder how we can print a dollar sign?

Let's change our image Line to:

```
   40 U$ = "$####.##"
```
(count 'em carefully)

...and RUN.

Nice, eh? The dollar signs all Line up in a row:

```
   $ 123.46
   $   1.60
   $9876.54
```

But suppose we want the dollar signs to snug right up against each dollar amount? Make Line 40 read:

```
   40 U$ = "$$####.##"
```

...and RUN.

and we get:

```
     $123.46
       $1.60
   $9876.54
```

Not especially attractive in this format, but taken singly, as when writing checks, it's almost essential.

The lessons so far are:

1. PRINT USING with the # prints decimal points at the same place for every number printed, regardless of its size, within the limits of its Image Line.

2. It rounds off the cents (the numbers to the right of the decimal point) to the number of # signs there. It does not round off dollars (left of the decimal point), but sends up an error flag %, prints all dollars, and slips the decimal point to the right if the image field wasn't large enough.

3. If a single $ is added to the left in the Image Line, dollar signs will be printed and Lined up in a column like decimal points. This single $ does not expand the width of the field.

4. If two $ are placed on the left, one $ will be printed on each line and will be placed immediately in front of the first dollar digit. One $ can replace one # in the field, thereby not expanding it.

We've covered a lot with a very small program, but have a long way to go.

Printing Checks

When using a printer for writing checks, it's usually wise to take extra precautions against "alterations". This is easily accomplished by changing Line 40 to read:

```
40 U$ = "*****.##"
```
      (count 'em)

...and RUN.

The display now reads:

```
**123.46
****1.60
*9876.54
```

That's swell, it fills up the unused spaced alright, but we lost the dollar sign. Okay, let's replace the first # sign with a dollar sign, like so:

```
40 U$ = "**$##.##"
```
    (aren't you glad we have an Editor for all these changes?)

...and RUN.

See it Now:

```
 *$123.46
 ***$1.60
 $9876.54
```

just like they do it uptown!

If you want to really impress others with the size numbers your lemonade stand generates, add lots more # signs to the image Line, thus:

```
40 U$ = "**$##############.##"
```

and make your checks read:

```
**************$123.46
***************$1.60
*************$9876.54
```

...very impressive.

Since we're obviously big time operators having franchised the lemonade stands, it's getting hard to keep track of the big numbers. How about some commas to break them apart? (Knock out those extra *'s first. Too hard to count them.)

```
40 U$ = "**$,##,##"            (look closely)
```

...and RUN.

```
 **$123.46
 ****$1.60
 $9,876.54
```

Only one of our numbers has more than 3 digits, but a comma separated its 9 and 8 for easier readability. In the image field, the comma can be placed *anywhere*

between the $ and the decimal point, and only *one* comma is required to automatically insert commas to the left of every 3rd digit left of the decimal point.

You really big time operators who deal in the millions will find this next feature handy. Change Lines 30 and 40 to:

```
30 C = 123456789.01
40 U$ =    "$$###,######.##"
```

...and RUN.

There it is. $123,456,789.01. If we don't want to bother with the small change, we can use single precision variables. Make this change to Lines 30 and 70:

```
30 C! = 123456789.01
70 PRINT USING U$;C!
```

...and RUN

```
           $123.46
             $1.60
     $123,457,000.00
```

Sure enough, it rounds to $123,457,000.00. Notice that the image Line didn't have to change. All we did was use a technique learned in an earlier Chapter.

If the 16-place accuracy of double precision isn't adequate to keep track of the Krugerrands in your mattress, you and Scrooge McDuck can probably afford to spring for a bigger computer.

Profit, or Loss?

Was that last number this quarter's PROFIT from the lemonade stand, or was it a LOSS? We can make the image Line print either. Change Lines 30 and 70 back to double precision and add a + sign to read:

```
40 U$ =   "+$$###,######.##"
```

...and RUN.

Very nice. Wonder what would happen if C was a negative number?

```
30 C = -123456789.01
```

...and RUN.

So far, so good. Suppose we take the + out of the image Line. Wonder if it will print the negative number anyway? Use the Editor and take it out of Line 40.

Then RUN.

Oh, Phsaw! It goofed it up. The + sign adds an element to the image. Well, now we know.

Let's put the + sign back in, this time at the end of the image.

```
40 U$ = "$$###,######,###+"
```

...and RUN.

Mmmmm. That's nice. Now let's change C back to a positive number and see what happens.

```
30 C = 123456789.01
```

...and RUN.

Very nice. Looks better to have the signs at the end, not interfering with the dollar sign, don't you think?

Most printers don't print deficits in red. How can we tag them so we don't allow the project manager to slip them by us. (We'll just take all + numbers for granted.) Let's try changing the + to a minus and see what happens.

```
40 U$ = "$$###,######,##-"
```

...and RUN.

Seems normal. How about when it's hit with a negative number.

```
30 C = -123456789.01
```

...and RUN.

AHA! Sticks out on the printout like a sore thumb. Now about this little deficit here, Smythe...

Stringing It Out

Let's rework our resident program to show some other PRINT USING capabilities:

```
1 CLS : PRINT
10 A = 123.456789
20 B = 1.6
30 C = 9876.54321
40 U$ = "#####.##     #####.##     #####.##"
50 PRINT USING U$;A;B;C
```

Shorten Line 40 to read

```
40 U$ = "#####.##   #.#   ####.#"
```

...and RUN.

Each variable fits nicely in its own Field. Change it again to read

```
40 U$ = "#####.##"
```

...and RUN.

The effect is almost the same. PRINT USING will reuse the Fields in its Image Line over and over, in sequence, until all the values are printed.

Anyway, RUN it and see how the same numbers can be displayed vertically instead of horizontally. All depends on what we need at a given time.

Learned in Chapter 34

Statements

PRINT USING

Miscellaneous

Image Line
PRINT USING symbols:
#.$*,+ −

Chapter 35

PRINT USING
Round 2

USING With Strings

In the previous Chapter we learned almost everything needed to put PRINT USING to work with numbers. This Chapter covers use with Strings, Advanced Features, and a few other "tricks" that some readers might find helpful.

Type in this NEW program:

```
1 CLS : PRINT
10 A$ = "IT'S"
15 B$ = "HOWDY"
20 C$ = "DOODY"
25 D$ = "TIME"
40 U$ = "\\"         (press GRPH and − for \)
50 PRINT USING U$; A$
```

...and RUN.

The only thing unique about this program is in Line 40. \ is a symbol in Model 100 PRINT USING which is to strings something like what the # is to numbers.

We used two \, so we reserved two spaces for strings, and only IT was printed. Unlike # however, to reserve more spaces in the string field, we add blank spaces between the \ signs. Change Line 40 to

    `40 U$ ="\    \"`

…and RUN. 4 spaces are set aside and `IT'S` is printed without clipping.

Let's make room for printing another string on the same Line.

    `40 U$ = "\   \\      \"`

    `50 PRINT USING U$;A$,B$`

…and RUN.

Oops! We ran

    `IT'SHOWDY`

together.

To space them apart we have to put an actual space in the image field just as we did earlier with printing the numerics.

    `40 U$ = "\   \ \      \"`

…and RUN.

That's better.

Now it's your turn. Complete Lines 40 and 50 to print IT'S HOWDY DOODY TIME all on one line.

Answer:

    `40 U$ = "\   \ \    \ \    \ \   \"`

    `50 PRINT USING U$;A$,B$,C$,D$`

(If you have trouble with spacing in PRINT USING, add an adjacent "measuring" Line like this to help.)

    `39 PRINT"123456789012345678901 2345"`

It's time to quit doodling around and get down to business too! Let's change our

HOWDY DOODY to some typical report headings.

```
1 CLS : PRINT
10 A$ = "PART #"
15 B$ = "DATE PURCHASED"
20 C$ = "DESC."
25 D$ = "COST"
40 (you figure out this one yourself)
50 PRINT USING U$;A$,B$,C$,D$
```

Answer:

```
40 U$ = "\     \    \   (12 spaces)    \    \    \
     \    \"
```

(There should be 3 spaces between the \'s where we had to split the Line.)

More On Strings

There are three more PRINT USING characters that have real value. Like so many exotic "upgrades" of BASIC, they do nothing that can't be achieved using other BASIC words, but do it easier. Enter this NEW program:

```
1 CLS : PRINT
20 X$ = "ALEXANDER"
30 Y$ = "GRAHAM"
40 Z$ = "BELL"
50 A$ = "! ! \   \"
60 PRINT USING A$;X$,Y$,Z$
```

...and RUN.

Who should appear before our very eyes but:

```
A G BELL
```

The ! serves to reserve an element in the field for the *first letter* of the string assigned to it. Very handy when you want the initials and last names of a list of people to line up in a row on a printout.

Another Short Cut
An area of PRINT USING worthy of careful examination is the incorporation of the *image Line* into the PRINT USING Line. It requires some care, and has value primarily when only a few variables are to be PRINTed, or only PRINTed once. In most practical applications, the *image Line* is referenced many times during a RUN, frequently by different PRINT USING Lines.

Make a few changes in the resident program so it looks like this:

```
1 CLS : PRINT
20 X$ = "ALEXANDER"
30 Y$ = "GRAHAM"
40 Z$ = "BELL"
60 PRINT USING "! ! \   \";X$,Y$,Z$
```

...and RUN.

We simply did away with A$ and incorporated its elements into a built-in image Line, separated from the variables by a semicolon. It does save space, and for short and uncomplicated PRINT USING applications, has value. For the long and complicated ones, it's better to keep the Image and PRINT USING Lines separate.

INPUTting the Image
We move farther and farther into the woods as we seek to make BASIC's formatting capabilities resemble the superior (and far more complicated) ones of the FORTRAN language from which it was derived. We can even INPUT the *image Line*, since it is a string. An easy way to see this is by using our resident program, but add Line 50 and change Line 60 to read:

```
50 INPUT A$
60 PRINT USING A$;X$,Y$,Z$
```

...and RUN.

We now have to respond by typing in the image Line. (Seems like they're hard enough to create without INPUTting.) The safest one to use is old Line 50, so respond to the question mark with:

```
"!  !  \    \"
```

and see

```
A  G  BELL
```

appear again.

RUN again, this time responding with something like:

```
?  "\   \       \  \        \   \"
```

and we should see something like

```
ALEX     GRAH      BELL
```

Try some other INPUTs and see how fast you get into trouble with TM Errors. The down-to-earth value of this particular capability is a little elusive.

Deviant Forms of PRINT USING

Here's a full-blown weirdo. Even a contradiction in terms. Would you believe a double-precision number, clipped and expressed in double-precision Exponential notation, in PRINT USING? Even the technical types with mismatched socks and rope for a belt will cringe at that one. We aren't going to bore the business types with the gory details, except for a quick intro for those who like to explore the morbid (or is it moribund?).

Change or add these Lines:

```
10 A$ = "###################^^^^"
20 D = 1234567890987654321
22 D! = 1234567890987654321
30 PRINT USING A$;D
40 PRINT USING A$;D!
```

...and RUN.

WOULD YOU BELIEVE A DOUBLE-PRECISION NUMBER, CLIPPED and EXPRESSED IN DOUBLE-PRECISION EXPONENTIAL NOTATION, IN PRINT USING?...

```
123456789098770000E+01
123457000000000000E+01
```

What you see is what you get, both in double and single precision. Using the Editor, move the block of 4 up-arrows to the left, one position at a time, filling in with #'s. Have fun!

Bring on the Money Changers

Here is a straightforward user program which uses PRINT USING in a practical way. One would be hard pressed to get the same results in so short a program without USING it.

If you're not in the international currency biz, just type in the program, the first half-dozen or so DATA Lines, plus Line 1500 to get a feel for what PRINT USING can do. See how \ and # can be mixed with blank spaces on the same image Line?

```
10 REM  * INTERNATIONAL MONEY CHANGER *
20 REM  * RATES AS OF SEPTEMBER 1983 *
30 CLS
40 P$="\    (16 spaces)    \  ########.##"
50 RESTORE:PRINT"HOW MANY U.S. DOLLARS"
60 INPUT"DO YOU WISH TO EXCHANGE ";D
70 PRINT
80 PRINT "AT TODAYS RATE YOU WILL GET"
90 PRINT
100 READ A$,A : IF A$="END" THEN 50
110 PRINT USING P$;A$;D/A
120 C = C + 1 : IF C<7 THEN 100
130 FOR T=1 TO 500 : NEXT T
140 C = 0 : PRINT : GOTO 100
1000 DATA ARGENTINE PESO, .0776
1010 DATA AUSTRALIAN DOLLAR, .8971
```

```
1020 DATA AUSTRIAN SCHILLING, .0537
1030 DATA BELGIAN FRANC, .01892
1040 DATA BRAZILIAN CRUZEIRO, .00396
1050 DATA BRITISH POUND, 1.4960
1060 DATA CANADIAN DOLLAR, .8112
1070 DATA CHINESE YUAN, .5074
1080 DATA COLOMBIAN PESO, .0122
1090 DATA DANISH KRONER, .1047
1100 DATA ECUADORIAN SUCRE, .0118
1110 DATA FINNISH MARKKA, .1764
1120 DATA FRENCH FRANC, .1248
1130 DATA GREEK DRACHMA, .0108
1140 DATA DUTCH GUILDER, .3385
1150 DATA HONG KONG DOLLAR, .1235
1160 DATA INDIAN RUPEE, .0976
1170 DATA INDONISIAN RUPIAH, .001016
1180 DATA IRISH POUND, 1.1770
1190 DATA ISRAELI SHEKEL, .0159
1200 DATA ITALIAN LIRA, .000625
1210 DATA JAPANESE YEN, .004221
1220 DATA LEBANESE POUND, .2070
1230 DATA MALAYSIAN RINGGIT, .4274
1240 DATA MEXICAN PESO, .0067
1250 DATA NEW ZEALAND DOLLAR, .6560
1260 DATA NORWEGIAN KRONE, .1353
1270 DATA PAKISTANI RUPEE, .07575
1280 DATA PERUVIAN SOL, .000577
1290 DATA PHILIPPINE PESO, .0909
1300 DATA PORTUGUESE ESCUDO, .0081
```

```
1310 DATA SAUDI ARABIAN RIYAL, .2873
1320 DATA SINGAPORE DOLLAR, .4698
1330 DATA SOUTH AFRICAN RAND, .8965
1340 DATA SPANISH PESETA, .0067
1350 DATA SWEDISH KRONA, .1283
1360 DATA SWISS FRANC, .4657
1370 DATA TAIWANESE DOLLAR, .02501
1380 DATA THAI BAHT, .04346
1390 DATA URAGUAYAN NEW PESO, .02929
1400 DATA VENEZUELAN BOLIVAR, .23255
1410 DATA WEST GERMAN MARK, .3788
1500 DATA END, 0, END, 0
```

EXERCISE 35-1: Duplicate the following statement. Use PRINT USING for all but the column headings.

	CREDITS	TAX	TOTAL
Astral Computer	18.3	.7	19.0
Biofeedback adapter	1.8	.0	1.8
Personality module	7.2	.3	7.5
		DUE:	28.30

As you've seen, PRINT USING is the most complex of our PRINT statements but by far the most powerful. If you're a serious programmer you should master PRINT USING completely. Take these many simple learning examples and expand them into large, useful report routines.

Learned in Chapter 35

Miscellaneous

PRINT USING Symbols:
\ ! ^
Double precision PRINT USING

Chapter 36

Using A Printer

Ready to learn something that's very simple?

LPRINT and LLIST
These BASIC Commands/Statements are almost too simple.

We have learned a lot of ways to PRINT, but they have all been on the display screen. Now we'll learn how to PRINT-out on a Computer Printer. If you don't have a printer yet, at least skim this Chapter before proceeding.

Hook-up and turn on the printer and type this new one-Line program:

```
10 LPRINT "THE PRINTER WORKS!!!"
```

Notice that the first word is LPRINT -- not PRINT. RUN the program.

Did it print? If the printer did nothing, press **SHIFT BREAK** to regain control of the computer. Check the connections again. Make sure the printer is ON and ON-LINE. Try RUNning the one-Line program again.

NOTE: There is much widespread misuse of the language when it comes to naming printers. Here are some definitions:

    PRINTer = a device which converts Computer talk to "hard copy".

    Dot Matrix Printer = A printer such as the classic EPSON MX-80 printer which creates characters by printing clusters of dots which resemble letters and numbers.

Character Printer = A printer which, like most typewriters, prints complete characters on the paper.

Line Printer = A very large "hi-speed" printer which literally "sets" and then prints an entire *line* of type at one time.

There is much mislabeling of printers. Very few of them are "Line Printers", though many are sold under that title. True Line Printers are very expensive, and can print over 1000 LINES of type per minute.

It is from the Line Printer concept that the "L" in LPRINT was derived.

LLISTing the Program

LLIST is typed at the command level when we want to LIST a program to the PRINTer.

Both LLIST and LPRINT can be used either as statements or commands. If we want to PRINT both on the display and on paper, use duplicate program Lines, with PRINT in the one for the display, and LPRINT for the PRINTer.

Enter any program of your choice and convert it to LPRINT the results on your PRINTer. Make a "hard copy" LLISTing of it.

If we accidentally precede either PRINT or LIST with the letter L and don't have a PRINTer connected, there may be trouble. It's especially easy to have a simple LIST turn into LLIST. If there is no PRINTer hooked up or it's turned OFF, the Computer seems to go dead. This is termed "Hung up". Any time the system "hangs", use **SHIFT BREAK** to regain control. The Computer will respond with "?IO Error" (Input/Output Error). The same problem will arise if the printer *is* hooked up, but is Off Line.

LPRINT TAB

The TAB function can handle numbers up through 255. This has little value in displays PRINTed on the Computer, but on big PRINTers it is common to PRINT lines up to 132 characters long.

Formatting

Now, let's see how to LPRINT with a nice format. Erase the one-Line program and type:

```
10 FOR X=1 TO 6
20 LPRINT X,
30 NEXT X
```

RUN it.

See how the printer will format the PRINTing with proportional spacing. The comma with LPRINT works the same as it does with PRINT, except there may be a different number of columns on your printer. (The number of columns depends on which PRINTer we have.) The EPSON MX-Series printers are highly recommended.

Try using a semi-colon in Line 20 rather than a comma. Type:

```
20 LPRINT X;
```

and RUN. The semi-colon works the same on the PRINTer as it does on the display. Let's see how TAB works. Type NEW and then type in this program:

```
10 LPRINT TAB(25) "TELEPHONE LIST"
20 LPRINT
30 LPRINT TAB(15)"NAME";TAB(45)"NUMBER"
40 LPRINT
50 INPUT "NAME    :";A$
60 INPUT "NUMBER  :";B$
70 PRINT "THANK YOU"
80 LPRINT TAB(15)A$; TAB(45)B$
90 INPUT "ANOTHER ONE (Y/N)";Q$
100 IF Q$="Y" THEN 50
```

...RUN it.

If the paper size is smaller than 8 1/2 by 11 inches, you'll need to use different TAB settings.

LPRINT USING

In the last Chapter we saw how PRINT USING can be used in formatting our PRINT outputs on the display. Those same features can be applied to the printer by using LPRINT USING. To demonstrate this, let's incorporate LPRINT USING in one of the simple programs from the last Chapter.

```
10 X$ = "ALEXANDER"
20 Y$ = "GRAHAM"
30 Z$ = "BELL"
60 LPRINT USING "! ! \    \";X$;Y$;Z$
```

...and RUN.

More Soft Keys

We discovered earlier that the entire contents of the display can be *dumped* to a printer by pressing the **PRINT** key. This key also serves to LLIST our BASIC programs. Press **SHIFT** and **PRINT** and notice that llist appears on the display as our resident program is LLISTed to the printer.

To avoid pressing 2 keys to LLIST a program, a Soft Key can be programmed to do it in one step. Define Key 7 by typing:

```
KEY 7, "LLIST"+CHR$(13)
```

We learned earlier how to define Soft Keys, this time we added a new twist. Looking at the ASCII table in Appendix A, we see that ASCII 13 is a control code for **RETURN**. By adding this to LLIST, we are telling the Computer to **RETURN** (same as **ENTER** on our keyboard) after entering LLIST. Saves us yet another key stroke.

LCOPY

Another way to "dump" whatever is on the display to the PRINTER is with LCOPY. Type:

```
KEY LIST        ENTER
LCOPY           ENTER
```

We now have a PRINTout of all the defined function keys. Unfortunately, the printer will not recognize the special graphics characters. Printers have not been developed with a matching sets of graphics characters.

LCOPY and the **PRINT** key are handy tools for making quick hard-copy backups of charts and graphs we may be displaying.

Advanced LPRINT Capabilities

Six different ASCII codes are set aside for use with PRINTers. Since different PRINTers respond differently, we can only talk here in general terms, and learn how to test our own PRINTer to see how it responds. The 6 codes are:

7	buzzer
8	backspace
9	horizontal tabulation
10	Line feed and carriage return
12	roll paper to top of next sheet
13	Line feed and carriage return

To see what this all means, enter this program:

```
1 CLS : PRINT
10 INPUT "ENTER A CODE NUMBER ";N
20 LPRINT N;"IS ";CHR$(N);"TO A PRINTER"
30 GOTO 10
```

...and RUN.

Try each of the codes and see what happens. Some codes may do nothing. Your PRINTer's manual may have additional (or replacement) codes.

There are no universal rules. Keep your test program simple and be aware that LPRINT with CHR$ is not always predictable when mixed on the same program Line.

The "top of form" or "top of next sheet" feature is a necessary one for using the PRINTer to prepare PRINTed statements, or PRINTing information which must always start at the top of a page. Users with "continuous roll" PRINTers have little need for "top of form".

When your Computer is turned on, if it's going to do any PRINTing, it automatically assumes it will be PRINTing 6 lines per inch on sheets of paper 11 inches long, 66 lines per page.

With a little experimenting, we will have your big PRINTer doing what we paid to have it do.

Learned in Chapter 36

Statements	**Commands**	**Miscellaneous**
LPRINT	LLIST	Trailing semicolon
LPRINT USING	LCOPY	Print codes

"The way we control and keep track of that many variables is by printing them in an *array*."

Part 6

Arrays

Chapter 37

Arrays

We know we can use combinations of the 26 letters of the alphabet and digits 0-9 to create names for variables. We've also discovered that very few of our programs so far have required anywhere near that many variables. There are times, however, when we need more variables -- sometimes *hundreds* or even *thousands* of them.

The way we control and keep track of that many variables is by printing them in an *array*. Array is just another word for "lineup", "arrangement" or "series of things".

Let's organize a collection, arrangement or lineup (array) of autos, each of which has a different I.D. (address) number.

We line up 10 cars, as in an *array*. They are all the same except for their engine size -- and each has a different I.D. number. Let's say the I.D. numbers range from 1 to 10, and we want to use the Computer to quickly spit out the engine size when we identify a car by its I.D. numbers. This might not seem like a real heavyweight problem -- but, as before, we discover the full potential of these things by learning them little steps at a time. We'll establish the I.D. numbers and engine sizes as follows:

CAR #	ENG SIZE
1	300
2	200
3	500
4	300
5	200
6	300
7	400
8	400
9	300
10	500

Now, we could give each car's engine size different letter name using the variables A through J, but that would be a waste of variable names -- and what would we do when we have a thousand cars, not just ten?

Setting Up Arrays

Model 100 BASIC allows any valid variable name to be used as an array name. An *Array* named "A" is not the same as the *numeric* variable "A", and neither is it the same as the "A" used in the *string* variable A$. (Nor is it the same as A!, A# or A% used to specify levels of precision). It is a totally separate "A" used to identify a *numeric array*. We call it A-sub(something), and it can only hold numbers. We will name the cars A(1) through A(10), pronounced A sub-1 through A sub-10. Get the idea?

What's that -- you're not sure you believe a single letter such as A can designate three different storage places? OK, here we go again -- type:

```
A = 12
A$ = "(YOUR NAME)"
A(1) = 999
```

then:

```
PRINT A; A$; A(1)
```

Arrays

Does that make you a believer?

Next, let's store the car engine sizes in a Line or two of DATA statements.

Type in:

```
100 DATA 300,200,500,300,200
110 DATA 300,400,400,300,500
```

Notice how carefully we kept the DATA elements in order from 1 to 10 so the first car's engine size is found in the first DATA Location, and the 10th one's in the 10th location?

We now have to "spin up" an array inside the Computer's memory to make these data elements *immediately addressable*.

> Big words meaning "so we can find a car fast!"

Think how difficult it would be to try to address the 7th engine (or the 7 thousandth!) for example, using only what we've learned so far. It *can* be done using only DATA, READ and RESTORE statements but that would be very messy and slow.

The easy way to create the array is as follows...Type in:

```
50 FOR L = 1 TO 10
55   READ A(L)
60 NEXT L
```

...and RUN.

Nothing happen? Yes, it did. We simply didn't display what happened.

The FOR-NEXT loop READs 10 pieces of DATA, and named the elements (or "cells") in which they're stored, A(1) through A(10). To PRINT out the values in those array elements. Type:

```
200 FOR N = 1 TO 10
210   PRINT A(N),
220 NEXT N
```

...and RUN.

Aha! It works, but how? We READ the DATA elements into an array called A(L), but PRINTed them out of an array called A(N). Why the difference? Nothing significant.

The array's *name* is "A". The *location* of each data element within that array is identified by the number which we place inside the parentheses. We can bring that number inside the parentheses by using any of our numeric variables, and can even do some simple arithmetic inside the parentheses if we wish. We arbitrarily used N to READ them in, and L to PRINT them out.

Remember, the array we are using is named "A". Its elements are numbered, and called A-sub(number).

> Some pure mathematicians might insist on calling A(N) -- A "OF" N. We don't need that added confusion? Best that you know, just in case.

Let's work some more on the program.

Type:

```
170 PRINT
180 PRINT "CAR #","ENGINE SIZE"
210 PRINT N,A(N)
```

...and RUN.

Now that's more like it. We have every I.D. number, every engine size, and are not "using up" any of the "regular" alphabetic variables. Having demonstrated that point, erase Lines 200, 210 and 220, and type:

```
1 CLS
10 PRINT "WHICH CAR'S ENGINE SIZE ";
20 INPUT "DO YOU WANT";W
210 PRINT W,A(W)
```

...and RUN.

Get the idea? Can you see the beginning of a simple inventory system for a small business?

Let's go one small step (for mankind) further. Suppose we know the color of each of the 10 cars, and for simplicity, suppose the colors are coded 1, 2, 3 and 4. might then have a master chart that looks like this:

CAR #	ENG SIZE	COLOR
1	300	3
2	200	1
3	500	4
4	300	3
5	200	2
6	300	4
7	400	3
8	400	2
9	300	1
10	500	3

In the language of professional computer types, this is called a *matrix*. A *matrix* is just an array that has more than one dimension. (Our first array had the dimension of 1 by 10...1 *column* by 10 *rows*.) This new array has a horizontal dimension of 2 and a vertical dimension of 10. If we wanted to be terribly inefficient about the matter, we *could* say that this is a 3 by 10 array, counting the I.D. number. If so, our first one would have been a 2 by 10 array -- but who needs it? As long as we keep our I.D. numbers in a simple 1 to 10 FOR-NEXT loop, and our DATA in proper sequence, we can keep our arrays simpler and easier to handle.

> Since we do not store the license number in the computer, it is only a "pointer" or an "index". That's why we don't consider it as another "DIMension" to our Matrix.

How then can we label this 2 by 10 *matrix?* We have already used up our A array elements numbered 1 through 10. Oh, you want to know how many elements we have to work with? Very good!

Let's just arbitrarily assign array locations 101 through 110 to hold the color code. information has to be stored in the program in a DATA statement. From the table, type:

```
300 DATA 3,1,4,3,2,4,3,2,1,3
```

and

```
80 FOR S = 101 TO 110
85   READ A(S)
90 NEXT S
```

These last Lines load the color code DATA into the array. Array element numbers 11 through 100 are not used, nor are those from 111 to the end of memory since they have not been formally assigned any values.

...RUN it and select any I.D. number.

Awwk!! What is this ?BS Error business? (Bad Subscript or Subscript out of range.) Well, since arrays take up a lot of memory space, the Model 100 automatically allows us to use up to only 11 array elements without question. (They can be numbered from 0 to 10.) Then our credit runs out. We earlier used elements numbered from 1 to 10 without any problem.

To use array elements numbered beyond 10 in the array called "A", we have to "reDIMension" the available array space. Our highest number in Array "A" needs to be 110, so we'll add a program Line:

```
5 DIM A(110)
```

...and RUN again.

That's better, but we are not printing out the color code. To display all the information, change these Lines:

```
10 PRINT "WHICH CAR'S ENGINE & COLOR ";
180 PRINT "CAR #","ENG SIZE      COLOR"
210 PRINT W,A(W);"            ";A(W+100)
```

...then RUN.

Check your answers against the earlier master matrix chart. Adjust the blank spaces in Lines 180 and 210 for a well-aligned display.

Let your imagination go. Can you envision entire charts and "look-up" tables stored this way? Entire inventory lists? How about trying to *find* the car which has a certain size engine *and* a certain color? Hmmm. We will come back to the Logic needed for that last one.

EXERCISE 37-1: Assume that your inventory of 10 cars includes 3 different body styles, coded 10, 20 and 30, as follows:

CAR #	STYLE
1	20
2	20
3	10
4	20
5	30
6	20
7	30
8	10
9	20
10	20

Modify the resident program to PRINT the body style information along with the rest when the car is identified by license number.

A Smith & Wesson Beats 4 Aces

If we want to create a computerized card game (they make good examples to show so many things), how can we set it up so we draw the 52 or so (watch the dealer at all times) cards in a totally random way? **Answer:** Spin up the deck into a single-dimension array, pick array elements using a random number generator, as each card is "drawn" set its array element value equal to zero, then test each card drawn to be sure it isn't zero. Now that is *really* simple! (Let's read that once again, more slowly).

We will now, a step at a time, write a program which will draw, at random, all 52 cards numbered from 1 through 52, and PRINT the card numbers on the display as they are drawn. No card will be drawn more than once. When all cards have been drawn, it will PRINT "END OF DECK".

You do a step first, then check against my example. Then change yours to match mine -- otherwise we might not end up at the same place at the same time.

Step 1: Spin up all 52 cards into an array.

```
20 DIM A(52)
30 FOR C=1 TO 52 : READ A(C) : NEXT C
```

```
40 DATA 1,2,3,4,5,6,7,8,9,10,11,12,13
50 DATA 14,15,16,17,18,19,20,21,22,23
60 DATA 24,25,26,27,28,29,30,31,32,33
70 DATA 34,35,36,37,38,39,40,41,42,43
80 DATA 44,45,46,47,48,49,50,51,52
```

At this point, all we can tell when RUNning is that it is taking some processing time since the Ok doesn't come back right away.

> Shhhh! I know there's a shorter way to program this special case, but it doesn't teach what's needed.

Step 2: Draw 52 cards at random, PRINTing their values.

```
90  FOR N = 1 TO 52
100   V = INT(52*RND(1)+1)
110 PRINT A(V);
120 NEXT N
```

…and RUN.

True, 52 card values are PRINTed on the display, but if you look carefully, the same number appears more than once. This means that some "cells" are not being READ and some READ more than once.

Step 3: When a card is drawn, set its array value equal to zero. Test each card drawn to be sure it is not 0. When 52 non-0 cards have been drawn and PRINTed, type END OF DECK.

```
90 P = 52
105 IF A(V) = 0 GOTO 100
```

```
120 A(V) = 0
130 P = P - 1
140 IF P<> 0 GOTO 100
150 PRINT "END OF DECK!"
```

Line 120 sets the value in cell A(V) equal to 0 only if Line 105 finds it *not* equal to zero already, letting the program pointer fall through.

When a "fall through" occurs:

1. The card's value is PRINTed (Line 110)

2. The number stored in that cell is set to 0 (Line 120)

3. Line 130 counts down the number of cards PRINTed. Line 90 initialized the number of PRINTs at 52.

4. The number of PRINTs is tested (Line 140). When there are no more PRINTs to go, END OF DECK! is PRINTed (Line 150).

Pretty slick -- and you don't have to watch the dealer (just the programmer).

But how do we really know that every card has been dealt? Write a quick addition to the program to "interrogate" each array cell and PRINT its contents.

```
200 FOR T = 1 TO 52
210   PRINT A(T);
220 NEXT T
```

RUN...and every cell comes up zero.

If you don't really trust all this, change Line 90 to read:

```
90 P = 50
```

RUN and see what happens.

AHA! It flushed out those 2 cards up the sleeve, didn't it?

Did you notice that each time the deck is dealt the cards come out in the same order? It's the old Random Generator problem.

Let's also add two new Lines to reseed the generator:

```
5 R = VAL(RIGHT$(TIME$,2))
10 FOR X = 1 TO R : Z = RND(1) : NEXT X
```

Change P back to 52 in Line 90, eliminate test program Lines 200, 210, and 220, and end up with a good card-drawing routine. You might want to clean it up to your satisfaction and save for future projects.

Question: Why does the PRINTing of card numbers slow down to a near halt as those last few cards are being drawn. Is the dealer reluctant?

Answer: The random number generator has to keep drawing numbers until it hits one that is the array address of an element which has not been set to 0. Near the end of the deck, almost all elements have been set to 0. The random number generator has to keep drawing numbers as fast as it can to find a "live" one.

Look again at the card numbers PRINTed. There will not be any duplication. No stray aces.

> **EXERCISE 37-2:** Change the program so the original array can be loaded with the card numbers without having to READ them in from DATA Lines.

New Dimensions

As we saw earlier, DIM is to arrays what CLEAR is to strings. When we have a string *array* we have to do the same thing.

Suppose we have a program like this: (Type it in)

```
10 FOR N = 1 TO 16
20 READ A$(N)
30 PRINT A$(N),
40 NEXT N
100 DATA ALPHA,BRAVO,CHARLIE,DELTA,ECHO
110 DATA FOXTROT,GOLF,HOTEL,INDIA
```

```
120 DATA JULIETT,KILO,LIMA,MIKE
130 DATA NOVEMBER,OSCAR,PAPA
```

...and RUN.

Oops. There's that same problem. ?BS Error means "not enough space set aside for an array". You'll recall that only 11 elements *per array* (from 0-10) are set aside on power-up. We are trying to read in 16 of them, starting with 1. The solution:

```
5 DIM A$(16)
```

...and RUN.

That's better. DIMensioning a string array is just like dimensioning a numeric one -- call it by its name. In this case, its name is A$. You "high speed" types will want to know that to do "dynamic redimensioning" (that's doing it while a program is running), the program must encounter a CLEAR first. Oh.

Array Names

```
A(N)
BC(N)
D3(N)
E4$(N)
XY$(N)
```

are examples of legal array names. The last 2 are for "string arrays."

EXERCISE 37-3: Study the User Programs in Appendix H to better understand the use of arrays for storage and access purposes. Time spent studying programs written by others is wisely invested.

Learned in Chapter 37

Statements

DIM

Miscellaneous

Arrays

Chapter 38

Search and Sort

One of the Computer's most powerful features is its ability to *search* through a pile of DATA and *sort* the findings into some order. Alphabetical, reverse alphabetic, numerical from smallest to largest, or the reverse, are all common sorts. This feature is so important we are going to spend an entire Chapter learning how to use it.

Typical applications of *search* and *sort* include:

1. Arranging a list of customers' or prospects' names in *alphabetical* order.

2. Sorting names in *zip-code* order for lower-cost mailing.

3. Sorting the names of clients in telephone *area code* order.

While not really all that complicated, the sorting process is sufficiently rigorous that we are going to take it *very slowly* and examine each step. Once we get the hang of it, the Computer can blaze away without our considering the staggering number of steps it's going through.

A Problem of Sorts

Let's start with a problem. We have the names of 10 customers (if that doesn't grab you, make it 10 million -- the process is identical). We need to arrange them in alphabetical order.

Start by storing their names in DATA Lines. Type in:

```
1000 DATA BRAVO,XRAY,ALPHA,ZULU,FOXTROT
1010 DATA TANGO,HOTEL,SIERRA,MIKE,DELTA
```

Since we are sorting by *name* rather than by number, we have to use *string* variables, *string* arrays, etc. They work equally well with numbers such as zip codes, but numeric variables and arrays work *only* with numbers.

The backbone of a sort routine is the array. Each name has to be READ from DATA into an array. So add:

```
10 REM * ALPHA STRING SORT FROM DATA *
20 CLS
30 FOR D=1 TO 10:READ A$(D):N=N+1:NEXT D
```

Line 10 is of course just the title.

Line 20 clears the display, then

Line 30 "loads the array" by READing the 10 names into storage slots A$(1) to A$(10). N is simply a "counter" which will follow through the rest of the program. In this simple program we could have made N=10, since we know how many names we have. In the next sample program we won't know how many names there are, so let's leave N the way it's usually used.

Important to the sort routine are 2 nested FOR-NEXT loops.

1. The first one, F, controls the First name.

2. S, the Second one, will control the name to be compared against the first one.

Names and words are compared as we learned in the Chapter on the ASCII set, remember?

Let's establish our loops first, and fill in the guts later:

```
40 FOR F = 1 TO N-1      (F=First word to be compared)
50 FOR S = F+1 TO N      (S=Second word to be compared)
```

```
100    NEXT S      (Makes 9 passes)
110    NEXT F      (Makes 9 passes)
```

It may seem puzzling that F and S only have to make 9 passes when there are 10 names. Think of it this way. Whatever word *isn't* smaller than the rest, just ends up last. No need to test again to prove that.

The F loop READs array elements 1 through 9 (N-1 = 9). The S loop READs array elements 2 through 10. This always provides us with *different* array elements to compare against each other.

Now let's jump to the end of our program and prepare it to PRINT out what we are about to do. Type:

```
120 FOR D=1 TO N: PRINT A$(D), :NEXT D
```

When the sorting is done, the *contents* of A$(1) to A$(10) will be the same as READ from DATA, but will be in *alphabetical* order. We'll PRINT the array contents on the display.

Now for the routine itself. Type:

```
60      IF A$(F) <= A$(S) THEN 100
```
                                                                          (Test for smaller ASCII#)

```
70      T$ = A$(F)       (Temporary storage for first word)
80      A$(F) = A$(S)    (Copy second word to first place)
90      A$(S) = T$       (Switch first word to second place)
```

And there is the biggie! If you can follow those last 4 Lines the rest is duck soup.

Line 60 says "If the First word is smaller than (or equal to) the Second word, leave well enough alone and bail out of this routine by going to Line 100, which will end this pass and READ another word to compare against F. If not, drop to the next Line.

Line 70 says, "Oh, they weren't in the right order, eh? We'll just store the First word in a temporary storage location called T$ and hold it there for future use. I'm sure we'll need it again."

Line 80 copies the name held in the second cell into the first array cell. If the Second one had an earlier starting letter than the First one, we do want to do this, don't we?

Line 90 completes the switch by copying the name temporarily held in T$ into the Second array cell. A$(1) and A$(2) contents have now been exchanged with the aid of the temporary holding pen, T$.

Us simple country boys find this one easy: There are two brahma bulls in separate pens, A$(1) & A$(2), and we want to switch them around. Ain't no way we're going to put them in the same pen at the same time. (Not with me in there anyway. Already broken too many 2 by 4's between their horns, and have some scars in the wrong end from escapes that were a hair too slow.) That's why we built a temporary holding pen called T$. Got it?

If we did everything right, the program should:

RUN.

and in a flash the names appear on the display in alphabetical order:

```
ALPHA          BRAVO
DELTA          FOXTROT
HOTEL          MIKE
SIERRA         TANGO
XRAY           ZULU
```

RUN it to your heart's delight. It's one of the most powerful things a Computer can do, and it does it so well. The identical procedure is used to sort a very long list of names (or zip codes, or whatever) but we would, of course, have to reDIMension for a larger array.

To get a really good look at what's happening, it's necessary to slow the beast *way* down, and insert a few extra PRINT Lines. They allow us to peer inside the program by watching the display.

Aw c'mon Horse -- Whoa!

Add these temporaries:

```
55      PRINT F;A$(F);TAB(20)S;A$(S)
57      FOR Z = 1 TO 500 : NEXT Z
65      PRINT "         <<--<< SWITCHEROO"
95      PRINT F;A$(F);TAB(20)S;A$(S)
```

...and RUN.

If this isn't slow enough, change Line 57 so there is time for you to completely think it through. Use the **BREAK** key to freeze execution for as much study as you need to completely understand the process. Pretend you're the Computer and have to make the decision that Line 60 has to make. The whole idea is to rearrange the words so the smallest (lowest ASCII #) word is first, and the largest (ASCII #) is last, and the inbetweens are in ascending sequence. Take it from the top -- very slowly!

The Diagnosis

   1 BRAVO   2 XRAY

Means "in cell #1 is the word BRAVO. In cell #2 is the word XRAY" (just as they came from the DATA Line). Of the two words, BRAVO is the "smallest" (ASCII#), so it stays in number 1 place. Onto the next pass of S.

   1 BRAVO   3 ALPHA

Oops. BRAVO is in #1 and ALPHA is in #3, but ALPHA is smaller than BRAVO. We better switch them around. So

          <<--<< SWITCHEROO

   1 ALPHA   3 BRAVO

Don't worry too much about what is happening in the second column. S is scanning through the array and its contents are always changing, testing against what's in the first column. It's what *ends up* in the *first* column that counts -- and the list must be in increasing alphabetical order.

As the program keeps RUNning, watch the new words appear in S, the second loop and column, and compare them against what's in F, the first column. Try to guess what the Computer's going to do. Also keep an eye on the increasing numbers on the left. The *final word* assigned to a given number in the first column is what will appear in the final PRINTout.

RUN the program as many times as it takes (and at as many sessions as it takes) to completely understand what's happening. It's awfully clever, awfully important, and awfully fundamental. We can carry this principle over to many useful programs in the future, but only if we *really* understand it.

When you feel it's under control, add one more little item to the display. What

T$ is holding while all this *sorting* is going on is interesting. Add and change these Lines so they read:

```
55       PRINT F;A$(F),,S;A$(S);
56       PRINT TAB(30)"T$= ";T$
95       PRINT F;A$(F),,S;A$(S);
97       PRINT TAB(28)"T$= ";T$
```

...and RUN.

"T$= " starts off empty since there is nothing in the holding pen. As BRAVO is replaced by ALPHA in the switching process, however, T$ holds it. When BRAVO replaces XRAY for the #2 position, T$ holds XRAY, etc.

On a clear head it's very easy to follow what's happening. If you're tired, it's hopeless. SAVE this program and review it as often as necessary for a deep understanding of the process.

Sorting from the Outside

We don't really have to keep all our names, numbers or other information in DATA Lines. They can be INPUT from the keyboard or from cassette tape. The following program is quite similar to the resident one, and the logic is identical. Change and add these program Lines:

```
5  REM * ALPHA SORT OF NAMES VIA INPUT *
10 INPUT"NEXT NAME";N$
20 IF N$ = "END" GOTO 40
30 N=N+1 : A$(N)=N$ : GOTO 10
```

Delete Lines 1000 and 1010.

...and RUN.

Enter 6 or 8 random names, and when finished, enter the word "END". The process displayed will be identical to what we saw before.

Erase Line 57 to let the computer RUN at full speed in BASIC. For still higher speeds, erase all unnecessary PRINT Lines.

Can you see the potential for all this?

EXERCISE 38-1: Change Line 60 of the SORT program to list the names in reverse alphabetical order.

Learned in Chapter 38

Miscellaneous

Sorting

Chapter 39

Multi-Dimension Arrays

We have learned that an array is nothing more than a temporary parking area for lots of numbers, or characters, or both. We also learned how to compare string contents outside the matrix (or array) with those inside it.

An array which only has one DIMension, that is, just one long line-up of parking places is sometimes called a *vector*. We can take that same one-dimensional array and cut it into perhaps four equal chunks, and position those chunks side by side. We then call it a two-dimensional array -- since the parking places are lined up in *rows* and *columns* (or *streets* and *avenues*). Its data holding or processing abilities are not changed. Only the addresses of the parking places (or elements or memory cells) have changed.

Type this NEW program:

```
10 DIM M(24)
20 FOR V = 1 TO 24
30   PRINT V,M(V)
40 NEXT V
```

Remember, any array with more than 11 elements (counting 0) must be DIMensioned.

...and RUN.

The RUN simply shows us the contents of 24 storage positions and their addresses (numbers). Since they are all lined up in a single row, it is a vector array.

Why are the cell contents always 0. Because every cell value is initialized at 0 upon entering BASIC, or whenever we RUN, just like all the other numeric or string variables. It's easy to find the *address* and *contents* of each memory cell.

Side by Side

Let's cut our 24 cell array into 4 equal strips, and line them up side by side. That would make 6 *rows* each containing 4 cells…right? Or 4 *columns* containing 6 cells. Multi-dimensional arrays always have *rows* and *columns*.

Let's start over with this NEW program:

```
10 DIM M(6,4)     (that's 6 rows by 4 columns)
20 FOR R = 1 TO 6
30   FOR C = 1 TO 4
40     PRINT R;",";C;TAB(C*9);
50   NEXT C : PRINT
60 NEXT R
```

…and RUN.

The *addresses* of all 24 cells are displayed at the same time, but not the contents. Again, nothing has changed from the earlier vector array containing the same 24 cells. We just rearranged the furniture and gave the pieces different addresses. They read:

```
1 , 1
4 , 3
```

etc.

To view the *contents* of each of these cells, change Line 40:

```
40     PRINT M(R,C);TAB(C*9);
```

…and RUN.

See, the contents remain unchanged. They are still at their initialized value of

0, since we have made no arrangement to store information in them. (The *addresses* are not displayed). Isn't this easy (...so far)?

Memory cells, like any other variables have to be "loaded" with values to be useful. This can be done by READing in DATA from DATA Lines, by INPUTting it via the keyboard, or from a previously recorded DATA disk or tape. We will load our Matrix from DATA Lines imbedded in the program.

Add these Lines:

```
100 DATA 1,2,3,4,5,6,7,8,9,10,11,12,13
110 DATA 14,15,16,17,18,19,20,21,22,23,24
```

and this Line to READ the DATA into matrix cells:

```
35  READ M(R,C)
```

...and RUN.

The DATA is nicely arranged in the matrix, and each matrix position has its original specific address. Again, that address is not displayed -- just the contents. Let's stay in the command mode for a minute and "poll" or "interrogate" several matrix positions and see what they are holding. Ask:

```
PRINT M(2,3)
```

write down 7, the answer. (We'll RUN the program again later to check it.)

```
PRINT M(5,2)
```

it reports that cell (5,2) in array M holds the number 18

```
PRINT M(3,5)
```

?BS Error? Why did we get that? Oh, there is no column 5. No wonder.

RUN the program again and check the display, counting down the Rows and over the Columns to see if our answers match up.

Mine did -- how about yours?

```
Row 2 Col. 3 = 7
Row 5 Col. 2 = 18
```

As an aside, type

    CLEAR

then, at the command level, check any matrix memory spot again.

    PRINT M(2,2)

and get 0. CLEAR re-initialized *all cells* to zero, along with *all other* variables. We can of course reload them by RUNning again:

RUN

    PRINT M(2,2)   Row 2 Col. 2 = 6

Okay, Now What Do We Do With It?
Good question. Everything we learned in the earlier Chapters on Arrays applies. We've only rearranged the deck chairs on this Titanic -- the end result is unaffected.

So far, what we've learned works best for calling up and loading relatively unchanging DATA. It is loaded into a matrix where it can be accessed and compared, processed or otherwise put to work. Typical applications are:

   1. Technical Tables: Instead of looking up information in tables, store the tables in DATA Lines and let the Computer look them up and, do any needed calculations. Time saved can quickly pay for the Computer.

   2. Price Quotes: I saw this approach used by a lumber yard to furnish fast quotes on materials, and by a printing shop for fast quoting of all sorts of printed materials. The program was written so simply that the customers just bellied up to the counter, answered the computer's questions, and got their quote right on the screen.

   The latest prices on paper products and printing costs were held in DATA Lines and "spun up" into the Matrix at the beginning of the day. The customers responded to a "menu" on the screen, and answered some questions. The quote was calculated, and PRINTed on the screen, and (optionally) on a printer.

When DATA is loaded in externally, either via the keyboard, disk or tape, we obviously don't want to have to go through *that* loading process each time we want an answer. It's important therefore, to never let execution END. Always have it come back to a screen "Menu" of choices, or at least to a simple INPUT statement. If an END is hit, the matrix crashes and the program must be reRUN to reload it.

String Matrices

So far we have concentrated mainly on *numeric* arrays. We can also use them to hold letters or words, using the same rules we learned earlier in Chapters on strings, and on CLEARing enough space for the strings.

String matrices need string names. Make these subtle changes in the resident program.

```
10 DIM M$(6,4)
35   READ M$(R,C)
40   PRINT M$(R,C);TAB(C*9);
```

...and RUN.

Absolutely no difference! We changed a string matrix but the data is all numeric. Strings handle numbers as well as letters, but not vice-versa.

Let's change our DATA to words and try it again. Change:

```
100 DATA ALPHA,BRAVO,CHARLIE,DELTA,ECHO
110 DATA FOXTROT,GOLF,HOTEL,INDIA
120 DATA JULIETT,KILO,LIMA,MIKE
130 DATA NOVEMBER,OSCAR,PAPA,QUEBEC
140 DATA ROMEO,SIERRA,TANGO,UNIFORM
150 DATA VICTOR,WHISKEY,XRAY
```

...and RUN.

Really no difference between the string matrix and the numeric ones before, except it handles words.

Stop for a moment and contemplate the string-comparing and string-handling techniques you learned a few Chapters ago. Your mind should be running flat out at this point, considering the possibilities.

How About Mixing Strings and Numerics?

Oh! Funny you should ask. That's why we ran all numbers in a string matrix, then all words with that same program. They mix very well, as long as the mixer is a string matrix and not a numeric one.

We have one final program. It is designed for demonstration only, but could be expanded to INPUT the DATA from tape and be quite usable. It demonstrates some important possibilities and programming techniques.

The Objective

The objective of this demo program is to allow a church treasurer to keep track of who gave what, when. Could use the same program with a service club, bowling league, or any organization that has a membership and dues. We want to be able to access every member's record by name, and get a readout on his payment status.

Let's start the program with the DATA. Type this in the NEW program:

```
1000 REM * DATA FILE *
1010 DATA 07.0184, JONES, 15
1020 DATA 07.0184, SMITH, 87
1030 DATA 07.0184, BROWN, 24
1040 DATA 07.0184, JOHNSON, 53
1050 DATA 07.0184, ANDERSON, 42
```

The first number in each DATA Line employs "data compression", that is, "encoding" several pieces of information into one number. This number contains the month, date and year in one 6 digit number. (Using string techniques, we could easily strip them apart again if we wished, for special reports.) Single precision will hold the 6 digits accurately.

The second thing we've done with this first number is protect the leading 0. Since months below October are identified by only one digit, the leading 0 would be lost on these months and the overall number changed to only 5 digits. There are other ways to get around that problem, but we will throw in a decimal point just to act as an unmovable reference.

The second element in each DATA Line is the *name*. We could put in the full name, but if we used a comma we'd of course have to enclose the name in quotes.

The third element of each DATA Line holds the amount of money given on that date.

Obviously, a full DATA set would contain many entries for each week, and many weeks in a row. We don't need to enter that much DATA to demonstrate the principles so will keep it short and to the point.

This DATA must now be READ into a string matrix (displaying it as we go). Add:

```
5 CLS
10 FOR E=1 TO 5:PRINT E; 'TODAY'S ENTRY
20   FOR D=1 TO 3
30     REM ENTRY DATA : DATE, NAME, TITHE$
40     READ R$(E,D)
50     PRINT TAB(D*11);R$(E,D);
60   NEXT D
70   PRINT
80 NEXT E
100 PRINT"ENTRY        DATE        NAME";
110 PRINT TAB(32);"TITHE$"
```

...and RUN.

Very good. The Matrix is loaded, and confirmed on the display. We see the first 5 bookkeeping entries from July 1, 1984.

Now that we know it loads OK, we can remove some of the software. Change these Lines:

```
10 FOR E = 1 TO 5      'TODAYS ENTRY
```

and Delete Line 50

...and RUN.

Good. We still get the heading, but the display is gone. Now, how can we interrogate the Matrix to pull an individual member's record? Guess we first have to ask a question. Type:

```
90 INPUT"WHOSE REVIEW DO YOU NEED";N$
```

...and RUN.

Seems to work OK. We will just answer the question with any member's name as it appears in the DATA Lines. Then we have to scan the matrix and compare N$, the name we INPUT, with each element, R$(E,D), until we find a match. This means setting up the FOR-NEXT loops again and scanning every element. Add:

```
95 CLS
120 FOR E = 1 TO 5
130  IF R$(E,2) = N$ THEN 160
140 NEXT E
150 PRINT"NOT IN THE FILE":BEEP:GOTO 90
160 PRINT E;TAB(11);R$(E,1);TAB(22);
170 PRINT R$(E,2);TAB(33);R$(E,3)
180 PRINT : GOTO 90
```

Try names that are in the DATA Lines, and those that are not. Lines 150 and 180 have built-in defaults back to the question.

Notice the new function we slipped into Line 150. Each time BEEP is encountered, the Computer BEEPs for about a half second. Handy thing to keep around for times like this when we need to wake up the operator. We'll study BEEP in more detail later.

The key Lines are 160 and 170. They PRINT 4 things:

    E Obviously the entry number on that date

    R$(E,1) not so obviously, the contents of the memory cell just *preceding* the one containing the member's name.

    R$(E,2) the cell containing the name

    R$(E,3) the cell following it

Chapter 39

If you have trouble visualizing what Lines 160 and 170 are doing, add these temporary Lines. They PRINT the *address* of each DATA element just below it, and is very helpful:

```
175 PRINT E;TAB(12);E;1;TAB(22);E;2;
178 PRINT TAB(31);E;3
```

...and RUN.

Implications

Again, the preceding program was not written to be a model of programming style and efficiency -- but to be a learning program. You should now sit by the bank of the creek and think through how you would modify it to load in say, 1000 Lines of DATA from cassette tape via an INPUT statement. Then, add more DATA each week and shoot that updated DATA back out to tape for reuse the following week, or inbetween as needed. It *is* possible, and marginally practical to use your Model 100 for this application.

EXERCISE 39-1: Write a program that fills a two dimension string array with:

JONES,C.	10439	100.00
ROTH,J.	10023	87.24
BAKER,H.	12936	398.34
HARMON,D.	10422	23.17

EXERCISE 39-2: Sort the names of the array in Exercise 39-1 alphabetically. Don't forget to keep the rest of the information on each row with the original name. This exercise will be a challenge. Think it through carefully.

EXERCISE 39-3: If you survived Exercise 39-2, try sorting column 3 in the array in increasing numeric value.

Learned in Chapter 39

Commands

BEEP

Miscellaneous

Multi-Dimension Arrays
String Arrays

Chapter 40

Advanced Graphics

Special Graphic Characters

The uses of PRINT go well beyond the simple display formatting we have tried so far. Used in conjunction with the CHR$ function, PRINT can speed up our graphic displays by a factor of 30 in some applications. That's right, 30 times as fast as PSET.

How can that be? Remember the set of ASCII characters discussed in Chapter 21? If not, better take a brief glance to refresh your own memory cells. The codes from 128 to 255 represent graphics and foreign characters. Those between 225 and 255 are known as *graphic blocks*. Let's check out these characters with this NEW program:

```
10 CLS
20 FOR I = 225 TO 255
30   IF I = 5*INT(I/5) THEN PRINT
40   PRINT I;CHR$(I)" ";
50 NEXT I
60 GOTO 60
```

...and RUN.

The characters are made up of the very same PSET pixels we used before. By PRINTing the complete characters, we can light as many as six pixels with one statement. It would take many PSET statements to do the same thing. The gain in speed is considerable.

Skeptical? Bring out your stop watch and we'll do the same thing 2 different ways. First the PSET approach:

```
10 CLS
20 FOR Y=0 TO 32 : FOR X=0 TO 239
30   PSET(X,Y)
40 NEXT X : NEXT Y
50 GOTO 50
```

...and RUN.

It fills up half the display in about 50 seconds. Contrast that with using the PRINT statement and graphic character 239:

```
10 CLS
20 FOR P=0 TO 159
30   PRINT CHR$(239);
40 NEXT P
50 GOTO 50
```

...and RUN.

Ahhhh. About 1 1/2 seconds. The message is clear: PRINTing graphic characters is *a lot* faster than PSETting them.

EXERCISE 40-1: Rewrite the program to fill the entire display using CHR$(239). Hint: 320 PRINT positions must be filled.

Dilemma

This puts us on the horns of a real dilemma. We've seen how convenient PSET is for jobs like plotting math functions, yet see just how slow PSET is compared to PRINTing graphic characters. Which method should we use?

Before making a hasty decision, let's zoom in for a closer look at graphic characters.

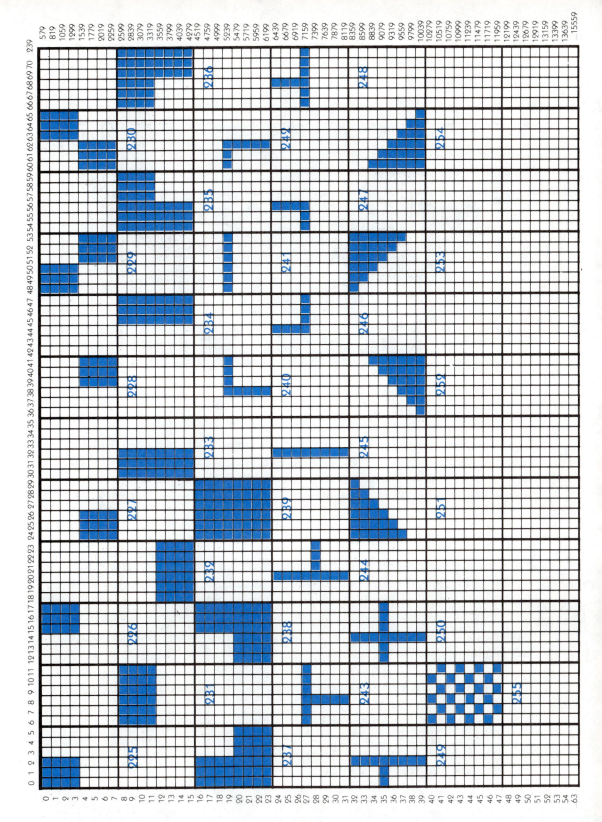

Figure A

Starting with the character we need to store, develop a program which will display it almost instantly.

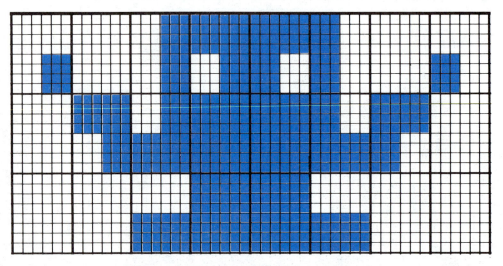

Figure B

Sound impossible? Just pay attention.

To achieve this kind of speed, we must store the entire figure in a single variable using string concatenation. (Yes, we covered concatenation earlier. See Chapter 23). If successful, we can then PRINT the entire figure *instantaneously* anywhere on the display with a PRINT statement.

Graphic Codes

Check each block that makes up the graphic figure and find its matching ASCII number in Figure A. Each of these numbers placed in a DATA statement to be READ by the NEW program.

Nothing to it! Once we recognize the pattern, it's easy to find the number for any graphics character.

Try translating a few characters from Figure B before peeking at the program.

For those who don't need the practice, the top row is composed of codes:

    228 224 234 236 235 233 224 227
    224 236 238 239 239 237 235 224
    224 224 232 239 239 232 224 224

Building the String

The next task is to combine these code numbers into a single string variable. At first blush, we might be tempted to use a brute force method like:

```
10 PRINT X$= CHR$(228) + CHR$(224) +
CHR$(228) + . . .
```

But why not place the numbers in DATA statements and READ them into the program? Enter this NEW program:

```
10 CLS : CLEAR 400
40 FOR I=1 TO 8
50   READ N : X$ = X$ + CHR$(N)
60 NEXT I
110 DATA 228,224,234,236,235,233,224,227
220 PRINT@96,X$
```

...and RUN.

Line 10 CLearS the display and, reserves some extra string space.

In Line 50, each code number is READ into N. It is then converted to a graphics character via the CHR$ function and added to the end of the string variable X$.

Line 110 holds the DATA, and

Line 220 PRINTs X$.

Does your program look like the top row of Figure B?

Cursor Control Codes

Add the second and third rows with:

```
30 FOR L=1 TO 3
80 NEXT L
120 DATA 224,236,238,239,239,237,235,224
130 DATA 224,224,232,239,239,232,224,224
```

...and RUN.

Oops! The figure calls for three rows, one on top of the other, but our string PRINTs everything in one row. How can we position the second and third rows directly under the first without using three separate strings? Everyone look back to the ASCII chart in Appendix A. Pay particular attention to codes 8 and 10. By adding the appropriate cursor motion codes into X$ after each row, the second and third row of characters will PRINT where they belong.

After each row is PRINTed, we need to move the cursor down once, then left eight spaces. Add:

```
70 X$ = X$ + CHR$(10) + STRING$(8,8)
```

That should do the trick. RUN to make sure we are on the right track.

Voila! Our very own creature.

Notice how quickly the figure is displayed once the string is assembled in memory. We have just unlocked the secret of high speed graphics using BASIC.

But Can It Fly?

Some people don't know when to quit. I suppose you want the figure to flap its wings! OK.

The Rationale

Before we start this adventure, be aware that we are working with a *slow* computer language. BASIC is very easy to use, but its simple nature makes it the sloth of computer languages. Unfortunately, animation requires speed.

Our alternatives:

    1) Use assembly language---ARRRGGH.

    2) Work only with PSET and PRESET and a single bouncing dot.

    3) Continue with the "string packing" technique used above.

The latter technique requires extra programming effort, but it is the only way to generate reasonably fast graphics in BASIC. So much for the rationale.

To achieve the animation, we will create several packed string variables identical to the first one, except the wings will be in slightly different positions. By displaying these strings in rapid fire succession, the illusion of motion will be created. This idea is not new. It is the same process used to create animated cartoons.

The other two figures (or frames) needed are shown in Figure C.

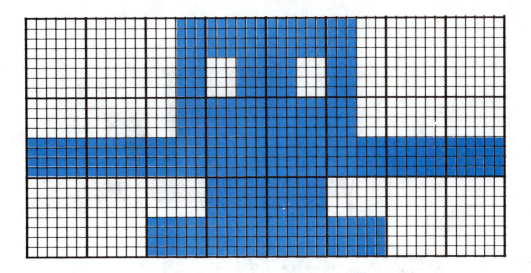

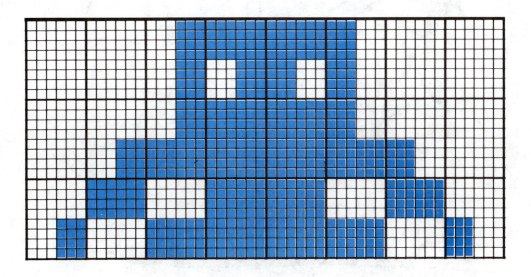

Figure C

Loading an Array

Instead of storing these figures in separate variable names, let's turn X$ into a string array. Change the program to read:

```
40      FOR I=1 TO 8
50        READ N : X$(F)=X$(F) + CHR$(N)
60      NEXT I
```

Now we can add the looping instructions to READ in DATA for all three strings:

```
20 FOR F=1 TO 3
90 NEXT F : X$(4)=X$(2)
```

and the DATA:

```
140 REM * SECOND FIGURE *
150 DATA 224,224,234,236,235,233,224,224
160 DATA 232,232,238,239,239,237,232,232
170 DATA 224,224,232,239,239,232,224,224
180 REM * THIRD FIGURE *
190 DATA 224,224,234,236,235,233,224,224
200 DATA 224,228,238,239,239,237,227,224
210 DATA 228,231,232,239,239,232,231,227
```

and finally, instructions to display the figure:

```
220 FOR F=1 TO 4:PRINT@96,X$(F);
230 FOR I=1 TO 30:NEXT I:NEXT F
310 GOTO 220
```

The complete program should now look like this:

```
10 CLS : CLEAR 400
20 FOR F=1 TO 3
30   FOR L=1 TO 3
```

```
40      FOR I=1 TO 8
50        READ N : X$(F)=X$(F) + CHR$(N)
60      NEXT I
70      X$(F) = X$(F)+CHR$(10)+STRING$(8,8)
80    NEXT L
90 NEXT F : X$(4)=X$(2)
100 REM * FIRST FIGURE *
110 DATA 228,224,234,236,235,233,224,227
120 DATA 224,236,238,239,239,237,235,224
130 DATA 224,224,232,239,239,232,224,224
140 REM * SECOND FIGURE *
150 DATA 224,224,234,236,235,233,224,224
160 DATA 232,232,238,239,239,237,232,232
170 DATA 224,224,232,239,239,232,224,224
180 REM * THIRD FIGURE *
190 DATA 224,224,234,236,235,233,224,224
200 DATA 224,228,238,239,239,237,227,224
210 DATA 228,231,232,239,239,232,231,227
220 FOR F=1 TO 4:PRINT@96,X$(F);
230 FOR I=1 TO 30:NEXT I:NEXT F
310 GOTO 220
```

...and RUN

Up, up, and away. The computer acts like a series of flash cards.

Line 230 adds a delay to control the speed of animation. By playing with the delay, and changing flap speed, it can be made to look like a rooster trying to take off.

Save this program as BIRD. We'll use it again in a later Chapter.

EXERCISE 40-2: List the graphic codes that make up the following figure, then pretend it is a snail:

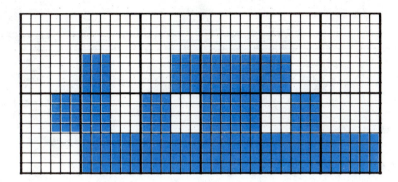

Learned in Chapter 40

Techniques

String packing
Animation
Array Loading

Miscellaneous

Graphics character code pattern
code pattern
Cursor control codes

Chapter 41

Graphic INKEY$

The implications of instantaneous (well, nearly instantaneous) input are not limited to the applications shown thus far. INKEY$ adds a new dimension to games and animation programming. Using INKEY$, we can write game programs with "real time" response to keyboard input.

CLOAD "BIRD", the wing flapping monstrosity from the last Chapter. Here is the listing:

```
10 CLS : CLEAR 400
20 FOR F=1 TO 3
30    FOR L=1 TO 3
40       FOR I=1 TO 8
50          READ N : X$(F)=X$(F) + CHR$(N)
60       NEXT I
70    X$(F) = X$(F)+CHR$(10)+STRING$(8,8)
80    NEXT L
90 NEXT F : X$(4)=X$(2)
100 REM * FIRST FIGURE *
110 DATA 228,224,234,236,235,233,224,227
120 DATA 224,236,238,239,239,237,235,224
130 DATA 224,224,232,239,239,232,224,224
```

```
140 REM * SECOND FIGURE *
150 DATA 224,224,234,236,235,233,224,224
160 DATA 232,232,238,239,239,237,232,232
170 DATA 224,224,232,239,239,232,224,224
180 REM * THIRD FIGURE *
190 DATA 224,224,234,236,235,233,224,224
200 DATA 224,228,238,239,239,237,227,224
210 DATA 228,231,232,239,239,232,231,227
220 FOR F=1 TO 4:PRINT@96,X$(F);
230 FOR I=1 TO 30:NEXT I:NEXT F
310 GOTO 220
```

We will use INKEY$ along with the 4 arrow keys on the keyboard to move the figure around the display. The first step is to change the PRINT position in Line 220 into a variable. Change:

```
10 CLS : CLEAR 400 : P=96
220 FOR F=1 TO 4:PRINT@P,X$(F);
```

...and RUN.

Because of the way the PRINT locations are layed out, changes in the position variable, P, will have to be made according to:

Right $P = P + 1$
Left $P = P - 1$
Up $P = P - 40$
Down $P = P + 40$

Horizontal positions on the display differ by 1. Vertical positions differ by 40. Make sure this is clear before proceeding.

Since we want to direct the movement from the keyboard, we need to associate the above changes in P with the correct keys. A bit of experimenting shows that the arrow keys return the following ASCII values:

Right	28
Left	29
Up	30
Down	31

So, the proper matchups are:

Right	28:	$P=P+1$
Left	29:	$P=P-1$
Up	30:	$P=P-40$
Down	31:	$P=P+40$

Add this information to the BASIC program as follows:

```
215 P=P+K
240 X$=INKEY$:IF X$="" THEN 290
250 K=0:V=ASC(X$):IF V=28 THEN K=K+1
260 IF V=29 THEN K=K-1
270 IF V=30 THEN K=K-40
280 IF V=31 THEN K=K+40
310 GOTO 215
```

Don't RUN yet.

In Line 230, keyboard input is stored in the string variable X$. In Line 250, V is set to the ASCII value of X$. This value is compared to the ASCII numbers returned by each of the four arrow keys in Lines 240 through 280, and K is changed accordingly. Then back in Line 215, the display position variable P is adjusted by K.

I'll bet you forgot about testing for the figure floating off the edge of the display. Stick with us kid, we wouldn't steer you wrong. (Moooo...)

Add:

```
290 IF P+K > 191 THEN P=P-K:GOTO 220
300 IF P+K < 0 THEN P=P-K:GOTO 220
```

"WHAT'S WITH THE BROOM?"

"JUST CLEANIN' UP AFTER OUR FLYIN' FRIEND!"

Now RUN it. Press the arrow keys to move the figure around the display.

Argggg! Forgot one tiny little detail. Can't leave a messy trail behind our flying friend, can we?

Add Line 218:

```
218 CLS
```

and change Lines 290 and 300 to:

```
290 IF P+K < 191 THEN P=P-K:GOTO 218
300 IF P+K < 0 THEN P=P-K:GOTO 218
```

...and RUN.

There it is: A flying creature that would give King Kong fits. All due to the INKEY$ function and some elementary programming.

So much for weird birds.

Learned in Chapter 41

Miscellaneous

Real time input

"Fortunately, our use of sound isn't limited to the single tone of the BEEP statement. The full range of frequencies usable by most human ears is available to create concertos with."

Part 7

Sound

Chapter 42

A Cheap Buzz

Type:

    `BEEP`   **ENTER**

Sorry if that scared the dog! Just couldn't resist it. It is widely incorporated in programs as an alarm to indicate something.

Sure . . . do it again. We'll wait.

Since our computer has a "Real Time Clock", we can use it as a "time is up" alarm. Just include BEEP in the program. It also makes a great audio prompter, telling the operator it's time to do something. The applications are virtually endless.

BEEP is just a simplified form of

    `PRINT CHR$(7)`   **ENTER**

Try it.

Technically, what we heard is called The BELL, and ASCII 7 makes it ring. Buzzers have pretty well replaced bells, so we'll usually refer to it as a buzzer, alarm, or something more contemporary.

Type in this NEW program:

    `10 CLS`

```
20 INPUT "TYPE ANY NUMBER";N
30 IF N <> 0 THEN 60
40 BEEP : PRINT "I CAN'T DIVIDE BY ZERO!"
50 GOTO 20
60 PRINT "100 DIVIDED BY";N;"=";100/N
70 GOTO 20
```

...and RUN.

Enter some familiar numbers, then try 0. The computer tells all. The noise can be interpreted as a chastisement for trying to divide by 0. Your imagination can take it from there.

The point of this is that the BEEP statement is used mostly to alert the user about something. It may tell us to do something, or alert us we've made an error or just Zapped a Klingon.

Sound Statement

Fortunately, our use of sound isn't limited to the single tone of the BEEP statement. The full range of frequencies usable by most human ears is available to create concertos with. Move over Beethoven!

For example type:

```
SOUND 2793,50        ENTER
```

and hear a perfect concert pitch A of 440 cycles per second, for about 1 second. (Can't you just see the concertmaster rising with a Model 100 . . .)

In the last Chapter we used BEEP as a prompt. Now type:

```
SOUND 2434,6
```

Sound familiar? It is the frequency used by the BEEP statement, and sounded for 6 internal "clock ticks", or about 6/50 = .12 seconds.

The SOUND statement plays a specific note for a specific duration, and we do the specifying. The first number is a number which relates to a note. The second number is the duration in clock ticks. The clock ticks about 18 times per second.

We must use the chart below to determine the frequency of the note we want to play. Let's listen to the range of sounds we can do. Type in this program:

```
10 CLS': PRINT "FIRST LOOP"
20 FOR X = 100 TO 2000 STEP 30
30  SOUND X, 5
40 NEXT X
50 PRINT "SECOND LOOP"
60 FOR X = 2000 TO 16383 STEP 200
70  SOUND X,5
80 NEXT X
```

...and RUN.

Note	Octave				
	1	2	3	4	5
G	12538	6269	3134	1567	783
G#	11836	5918	2959	1479	739
A	11172	5586	2793	1396	698
A#	10544	5272	2636	1318	659
B	9952	4976	2488	1244	622
C	9394	4697	2348	1174	587
C#	8866	4433	2216	1108	554
D	8368	4184	2092	1046	523
D#	7900	3950	1975	987	493
E	7456	3728	1864	932	466
F	7032	3516	1758	879	439
F#	6642	3321	1660	830	415

It sounds terrible because we're going down the musical scale without regard to musical "intervals". We must choose the notes more "chromatically". Try this NEW program:

```
10 SOUND 2348,30
```

```
20 SOUND 1396,30
30 SOUND 1758,30
```

...and RUN.

We could use a different statement for each note, as above, but we're into advanced stuff now so let's cut down the programming by using READ-DATA statements. Type NEW and then we'll start over again:

```
10 CLS
20 READ N,L
30 IF N = 0 THEN END
50 SOUND N,L
60 GOTO 20
500 DATA 2348,20,2348,20,1567,20,1567
510 DATA 20,1396,20,1396,20,1567,50
699 DATA 0,0
```

Yes, yes, I'm sick of Twinkle Twinkle too, but now that we have it started, we might as well finish, and CSAVE it:

```
520 DATA 1758,20,1758,20,1864,20,1864
530 DATA 20,2092,20,2092,20,2348,50
540 DATA 1567,20,1567,20,1758,20,1758
550 DATA 20,1864,20,1864,20,2092,50
560 DATA 1567,20,1567,20,1758,20,1758
570 DATA 20,1864,20,1864,20,2092,50
580 DATA 2348,20,2348,20,1567,20,1567
590 DATA 20,1396,20,1396,20,1567,50
600 DATA 1758,20,1758,20,1864,20,1864
610 DATA 20,2092,20,2092,20,2348,50
```

...and RUN.

We simply READ in a pair of numbers, the frequency and duration, and PLAY them in Line 50.

To view the numbers as they are READ, add this Line:

```
40 PRINT N;L,
```

Notice the variation this places on the tune once the display is full? The computer bogs down when the display scrolls up to fit in another line.

Now let's try for a song with a little more programming built in. Since we don't normally think in terms of clock ticks, let's use timing numbers that make more sense, and let the program do the converting for us. How about 1 divided by the actual note length. Quarter notes will be 4, eighth notes will be 8, and whole notes will be 1.

Delete Lines 500-610 and change Line 50 to:

```
50 SOUND N,(1/L)*50
```

and put in some DATA:

```
500 DATA 3718,1,4148,4,4697,8,3718,4
510 DATA 4184,8,4697,2,2348,2,2793,4
520 DATA 2348,1
```

...and RUN.

Hey, that doesn't SOUND too bad. Since this phrase is repeated, we can use the same DATA Line. We could retype them, but why not use the EDITor and PASTE then in...etc.

Now add these three Lines:

```
530 DATA 3134,1,3718,2,4697,2,4184,,5
580 DATA 3134,2,3718,4,4697,8,4148,2
590 DATA 4148,2,4697,1
```

...and RUN

(Hey Tony, where's the gig?)

One finishing touch. Add:

```
540 SOUND 1,2
```

...and RUN.

That's better. It puts a half note rest between the two phrases. By selecting 1 as the frequency, the SOUND is out of the audible range, giving a note that only the dog will enjoy.

Sound Control

The SOUND statement can also turn ON or OFF the computer's speaker. It will not prevent the speaker from beeping with the SOUND statement or when we make an illegal entry, but it will stop the noise we hear while LOADing data from cassette or while listening to the dial tone in TELCOM.

This is convenient while trying to load tapes during a meeting, in a quiet library, or in a class.

Connect the cassette recorder to the computer and insert a program tape. Set the recorder to PLAY then type:

```
SOUND OFF        ENTER
```

Then type:

```
CLOAD            ENTER
```

Watch the display. After it reports that it found a program, it continues loading without a SOUND. It remains silent even if we turn it off and on. It needs SOUND ON to turn on the speaker. After the tape stops, type:

```
SOUND ON         ENTER
```

And repeat the CLOAD procedure. There it is again, that wretched noise.

Learned in Chapter 42

Statements	**Commands**	**Miscellaneous**
SOUND	BEEP	Speaker control

"It's generally good programming practice to CLOSE all files soon after reading or writing data. There's always the possibility of wiping out files that have been left OPEN."

Part 8

Miscellaneous

Chapter 43

PEEK and POKE

PEEK and POKE are BASIC words that allow us to do non-BASIC things. They provide the means whereby we can PEEK into the innards of the Computer's memory and, if we wish, POKE in new information.

It is not our purpose here to become an expert in machine language programming, nor on how the Computer works. We have to approach this and related topics a little gingerly, lest we fall over the edge into a computer abyss (or is it an abysmal computer?).

We do know, however, that computers do their thing entirely by the manipulation of numbers. Therefore, when we PEEK at the contents of memory, guess what we'll find? Numbers? Very good! (Ummmyaas).

The Memory Map on the next page shows that large chunks of the Computer's memory are reserved or "mapped" for very specific uses. The BASIC ROM, for example, uses byte addresses 0 through 32767. The RAM (which holds our programs and where execution takes place) is assigned addresses 32768-65535. (All numbers we talk about here are decimals, not hex, octal, binary or Sanskrit.)

Type in this NEW program:

```
20 N=0
40 PRINT N;PEEK(N), CHR$(PEEK(N))
50 N=N+1
60 GOTO 40
```

Memory Map

Decimal Address	Hex Address	Function
65535	FFFF	END OF STANDARD "8K" SYSTEMS
57344	E000	START OF STANDARD "8K" RAM
57343	DFFF	END OF OPTIONAL "8K" SYSTEMS
32768	8000	START OF OPTIONAL RAM
32767	7FFF	END OF READ ONLY MEMORY
:	:	:
:	:	BANK SWITCHED WITH "32K"
:	:	OPTIONAL ROM
:	:	:
255	00FF	INPUT/OUTPUT PORTS
:	:	:
0	0000	START OF SYSTEM ROM

Figure A

Let's analyze the program before RUNning it.

Line 20 sets the beginning address where we want to start PEEKing. As Figure A shows, there are lots of good places to go spelunking, and we can change Line 20 to start wherever we want.

Line 40 PRINTs three things:

　　1. The address -- that is, the number of the byte, the contents of which we are PEEKing.

　　2. The contents of that byte, expressed as a decimal number between 0 and 255.

　　3. The contents of that address converted to its ASCII character. (Many of the ASCII characters are not PRINTable. Go back to the Chapter on ASCII if your memory has grown dim.)

Okay, now RUN the program, being ready to freeze it with **PAUSE** if you see something interesting. You have to be able to read vertically as the letters swish by. It can also be stopped at any time with **SHIFT BREAK**, and restarted with CONT without having to start all over again with N at 0. Refer to the chart in Figure A to see where in memory you're looking.

Change N to start at different places in memory and PEEK to your heart's delight. You can't goof up anything by just PEEKing. It's indiscriminate POKEing that gets people into trouble.

The command level is very handy for resetting the starting address. We can change the value of N by just typing:

```
N=25000
```

for example, then:

```
CONT
```

instead of RUN.

Didn't see anything interesting? What did you find starting at address 32768?

When done PEEKing, and having seen far more information than can possibly be absorbed, rework Line 40 to read simply:

```
40 PRINT CHR$(PEEK(N));
```

It PRINTs only the ASCII characters, horizontally, and is the ideal program to RUN when friends visit. If you have a TEXT file or other program SAVEd, it may appear on the display. If not, just act casual about the whole display and avoid any direct questions. Makes a great background piece for a science fiction movie.

When you find an interesting spot, hit **SHIFT BREAK**, then:

```
PRINT N
```

at the command level to find out where in memory you are PEEKing. (Don't you wish we could explore the corners of our minds as easily?)

CONTinue on when ready.

Having degenerated from PEEKing to leering, we are ready to see what else we can do.

Careless POKEing Can Leave Holes...

Before POKEing, we'd better see that we're not POKEing a stick into a hornets' nest. It's with the greatest of ease that we destroy a program in memory by POKEing around where we shouldn't.

Obviously there is no use POKEing the ROM area since ROM stands for Read Only Memory. It's not changeable. Anything above 32767 should be RAM (Random Access) Memory, unless taken up with our BASIC program or required for processing. With such a short program as ours we surely can't goof anything up? Can we?

Let's PEEK around 57344 and see if anything is going on there. Change these two program Lines to:

```
20 N = 57344
40 PRINT N; PEEK(N),
```

...and RUN.

```
57344  0        57345  0
57346  0        57347  0
57348  0        57349  0
57350  0        57351  0
57352  0        57353  0
57354  0        57355  0
57356  0        57357  0
57358  0        57359  0
```

What we see are the address numbers and their contents, in easy-to-read parallel rows. Unless you've been messing around with other programs, we should just see nice rows of 0's. The memory at these locations has not been used.

Let's change our program and POKE in some information and do something with it. Make it read:

```
10 REM * POKE PROGRAM *
20 N = 57344
30 READ D
40 POKE N,D
50 N = N + 1
```

```
60 IF N = 57354 THEN END
70 GOTO 30
100 DATA 80,69,69,75,45,65,45,66,79,79
```

Before RUNning, let's analyze it.

Line 20 initializes the starting address at 57344.

Line 30 READs a number from the DATA Line.

Line 40 POKEs the DATA "D" into address "N".

Line 50 increments the address number by one.

Line 60 ENDs execution when we have POKEd in all 10 pieces of DATA.

Line 70 sends us back for more DATA.

Line 100 stores the DATA we are going to POKE into memory.

...now RUN.

Well, that was sure fast. I wonder what it did? How can we find out? Should we PEEK at it? Yes, but let's leave the old program in and just start a new one at 200.

```
200 REM * PEEK PROGRAM *
210 FOR N=57344 TO 57353
220 PRINT N, PEEK(N)
230 NEXT N
```

..and RUN 200.

```
57344    80
57345    69
57346    69
57347    75
57348    45
```

```
57349    65
57350    45
57351    66
57352    79
57353    79
```

How about that? We really did change the contents of those memory locations. We shot the numbers from our DATA Line right into memory. Now if we only knew what those numbers stood for. Wonder…if we changed them to ASCII characters, would they tell us anything?

Add:

```
205 CLS
220 PRINT CHR$(PEEK(N));
```

…and RUN 200

And that's how PEEK and POKE work.

Learned in Chapter 43

Statements	**Functions**	**Miscellaneous**
POKE	PEEK	Memory map

Chapter 44

Logical Operators

In classical mathematics (fancy words for simple ideas), there exist what are known as the "logical AND", the "logical OR", and the "logical NOT".

So The One Cow Said to the Other Cow...

In Figure A, if gate A AND gate B AND gate C are open, the cow can move from pasture #1 to pasture #2. If any gate is closed, the cow's path is blocked.

By the way, the cow's name is Bessie.

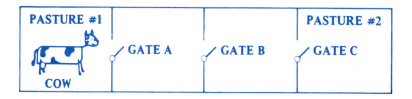

Figure A

The principle is called "logical AND".

In Figure B, if gate X OR gate Y OR gate Z are open, then old Bess can move from pasture #3 to #4. That principle is called "logical OR". These ideas are both pretty logical. If the cow can figure them out surely we can!

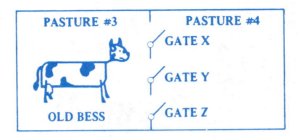

Figure B

Using these ideas is very simple. Type this NEW program:

```
10 INPUT "IS GATE 'A' OPEN"; A$
20 INPUT "IS GATE 'B' OPEN"; B$
30 INPUT "IS GATE 'C' OPEN"; C$
40 PRINT
50 IF A$="Y" AND B$="Y" AND C$="Y" THEN 80
60 PRINT "OLD BESSIE IS SECURE."
70 END
80 PRINT "ALL GATES ARE OPEN."
90 PRINT "OLD BESSIE IS FREE TO ROAM."
```

...and RUN.

Answer (Y/N) the questions differently during different RUNs to see how the logical AND works in Line 50.

Where Is the Logic in All This?

You should by now understand every part in the program, except perhaps Line 50.

> Lines 10, 20, and 30 INPUT the gate positions as *open* (which we defined as equal to "Y"), or *closed* (defined as "N"). We could have defined them the other way around and rewritten Line 50 to match, if we'd wanted to.

> Line 50 is the key. It reads, literally, "If gate A is *open*, AND gate B is *open*, AND gate C is *open*, then go to Line 80. If any one gate is closed, report that fact by defaulting to Line 60.

Imagine how this simple logic could be used to create a super-simple "computer" consisting of only an electric switch on each gate. Add a battery and put a light bulb in the farmer's house. The bulb could indicate whether the gates are all open. Such a "gate-checking" computer would have only three memory cells -- the switches.

> Hmm. It would do the job a lot cheaper than a Model 100...but would be awfully hard to play *Invaders* with.

EXERCISE 44-1: Using the above program as a model, and the "OR logic" seen in Figure B, write a program which will report Bess' status as determined by the position of Gates X, Y and Z.

Teacher's Pet

Here is a simple program which uses > instead of the equals sign in a logical test. student passes if he has a final grade over 60 OR a midterm grade over 70 AND a homework grade over 75. Enter this NEW program, RUN it a few times, and see how efficiently the logical OR and logical AND tests work in the same program Line (40).

```
10 INPUT "FINAL GRADE"; F
20 INPUT "MIDTERM GRADE"; M
30 INPUT "HOMEWORK GRADE"; H
40 IF (F>60 OR M>70) AND H>75 THEN 70
50 PRINT "FAILED"
60 END
70 PRINT "PASSED"
```

Does this give some idea of the power and convenience of logical math? The actual "cut off" numbers could, of course, be set at any level.

Logical Variations

This next program example mixes equals, greater-than and less-than signs in the same program. It determines and reports whether the two numbers we INPUT are both positive, both negative, or have different signs.

Analyze the program. Note the parentheses. Although they are not necessary, they tell us to shift our thinking to "logical". Type it in and RUN.

```
10 INPUT "FIRST NUMBER IS"; X
20 INPUT "SECOND NUMBER IS"; Y
30 IF (X>=0) AND (Y>=0) THEN 70
40 IF (X<0) AND (Y<0) THEN 90
50 PRINT "OPPOSITE SIGNS"
60 END
70 PRINT "BOTH POSITIVE OR ZERO"
80 END
90 PRINT "BOTH NEGATIVE"
```

With Graphics Too, Yet

Yes, the logical symbols also work along with the graphic statements. See if you can figure out the surprise which will be caused by the logical AND in Line 40. Type this NEW program in, and RUN.

```
10 CLS
20 FOR X = 106 TO 132
30   FOR Y = 14 TO 56
40     IF (X>=119) AND (Y>=35) THEN 60
50     PSET(X,Y)
60   NEXT Y
70 NEXT X
99 GOTO 99
```

Use **SHIFT BREAK** to exit the program's endless loop.

What happens if we replace the AND in Line 40 with an OR? After you think you have it figured out, do it and see the result.

Did you guess right?

There's More?

Oh, yes -- the only limit is your imagination. See how easily the logical notation makes the drawing of lines? Change Line 40 to read:

```
40    IF (X=119) OR (Y=35) THEN 60
```

What happens to the program if we replace OR with AND? Sketch your estimated result, then change Line 40 and try it.

Hope you got it right. If not, it really sneaked up, didn't it!

Using the INT function we can create an elaborate checkerboard. The reasoning is:

In the *horizontal* dimension:

The INT(X/15)*15-X will equal 0 when X equals 0,15,30,45,60,75,90 and 105.

In the *vertical* dimension:

The INT(Y/8)*8-Y will equal 0 when Y equals 0,8,16,24,32,40,48 and 56.

Oh come on, it's very simple if you take the time and think it through!

Replace the old Line 40 with:

```
40    IF INT(X/7)*7-X=0 OR INT(Y/7)*7-Y=0
      THEN 60
```

and you will create an elaborate four-by-six checkerboard.

And on and on it goes...

NOT

In addition to the logical AND and OR functions, we have what is called logical NOT. Here is how it can be used:

```
1 CLS : PRINT
10 INPUT "ENTER A NUMBER";N
```

```
20 L = NOT(N>5)
30 IF L = 0 GOTO 60
40 PRINT "N WAS NOT GREATER THAN 5"
50 END
60 PRINT "N WAS GREATER THAN 5"
```

...and RUN.

Line 20 is obviously the key one, containing NOT. If the statement in Line 20 is *true* (namely, that N is NOT larger than 5), the Computer makes the value of L=-1. The test in Line 30 then fails.

If, on the other hand, N IS larger than 5, the statement is *false* and the Computer makes the value of L = 0.

True = -1 and False = 0. (Time for the primal scream, again. All together, now...)

Order of Operations

When trying to figure out which gets calculated first in the thick of a "humongous" equation, here's the pecking order:

Those operations buried deepest inside the parentheses get resolved first. The idea is to clear the parentheses as quickly as possible. When it all becomes a big tie, here's the order:

1. Exponentation -- a number raised to a power.

2. Negation, that is, a number having its sign changed. Typically, a number multiplied times -1.

3. Multiplication and division -- from left to right.

4. Addition and subtraction -- from left to right.

5. Less than, greater than, equals, less or equal to, greater or equal to, not equal to -- from left to right.

6. The logical NOT.

7. The logical AND.

8. The logical OR.

More Logical Operators

As if these 3 *logical* operators weren't enough, the Model 100 Computer allows use of 3 more "Logical" words. They are (in order of appearance):

EQV, XOR, and IMP.

To help see how these things work, let's write a "testbed" program into which we can install them.

```
10 CLS
20 INPUT "ENTER A VALUE FOR X";X
30 INPUT "ENTER A VALUE FOR Y";Y
40 IF (X<10) AND (Y>10) THEN 70
50 PRINT : PRINT"CONDITION WAS FALSE"
60 END
70 PRINT:BEEP:PRINT"CONDITION WAS TRUE"
```

...and RUN.

INPUT the number 5 for X and 15 for Y. No big deal. Both comparisons were true, which made the AND condition true.

OR

Replace the AND in Line 40 with OR and RUN. Try different numbers to get a feel for the program.

EQV

There are several more "advanced" logical operators. EQV stands for EQuiValence. Replace the OR in Line 40 with the word EQV.

```
40 IF (X<10) EQV (Y>10) THEN 70
```

The condition in Line 40 will be true only if both arithmetical comparisons are the same. Only if X is less than 10 AND Y is greater than 10, OR if X is *not* less than 10 AND Y is *not* greater than 10.

Try the number 5 for X and 15 for Y. Both tests pass so the overall condition is true.

Try 15 for X and 5 for Y. Both conditions are false, but since they are *both* the same (false in this case) the overall condition is true and execution jumps to Line 70.

XOR

XOR stands for eXclusive OR. This means that if one *and only one* test passed, the overall condition will be true and the Computer will BEEP at us.

Replace the EQV in Line 40 with the word XOR. RUN with different numbers. Try 5 for X and 15 for Y. Execution falls through to Line 50 because *both* tests pass. Remember if we were using the regular OR, the overall condition would be true.

IMP

Our final operator is IMP which stands for IMPlication. This is probably the hardest to understand. The IMP condition will be *true* for all conditions except when the first test is *true* and the second test is *false*. The *overall condition* is then *false*. Replace the XOR with an IMP:

```
40 IF (X<10) IMP (Y>10) THEN 70
```

...and RUN.

Try 5 for both X and Y. These numbers give us a *false* condition. All other conditions are *true*.

And In Conclusion

Logical math is worth the hassle. As one last fun program, enter and RUN this "Midnight Inspection." Line 100 checks each response for a NO answer (instead of a YES). Using logical OR, it branches to the "no-go" statement (Line 120) if any one of the tests is negative ("N").

```
10 CLS
20 PRINT "ANSWER WITH 'Y' OR 'N'."
```

```
30 PRINT
40 INPUT "HAS THE CAT BEEN PUT OUT";A$
50 INPUT "PORCH LIGHT TURNED OFF";B$
60 INPUT "ALL DOORS/WINDOWS LOCKED";C$
70 INPUT "IS THE T.V. TURNED OFF";D$
80 INPUT "THERMOSTAT TURNED DOWN";E$
90 PRINT:PRINT
100 IF A$="N" OR B$="N" OR C$="N" OR D$=
"N" OR E$="N" THEN 120
110 PRINT "          GOODNIGHT":END
120 PRINT "SOMETHING HAS NOT BEEN DONE."
130 PRINT "DO NOT GO TO BED"
140 PRINT "UNTIL YOU FIND THE PROBLEM!"
150 GOTO 30
```

In most cases, AND and OR statements are interchangeable if other parts of a program are rewritten to accommodate the switch.

Learned in Chapter 44

Miscellaneous

Logical AND
Logical OR
Logical NOT
Logical EQV
Logical XOR
Logical IMP
Order of Operations

Chapter 45

Advanced Saving & Merging of BASIC Programs

Everyone type in this NEW program:

```
10 REM LINE 10
20 REM LINE 20
40 REM LINE 40
```

We know the above program is not destined for fame, but let's SAVE (**F3**) it into the Computer's memory or RAM (Random Access Memory). Each program SAVEd to RAM becomes a FILE. Like any file, it is labeled with a file name. We will call this program FIRST. Type:

```
SAVE "RAM:FIRST"
```
(Remember to use the **F3** key)

Using RAM: to specify RAM storage is optional. The Model 100 defaults storage to RAM if just written as SAVE "FIRST".

BASIC programs can be SAVEd to RAM, Cassette, Modem, RS-232 port, Line Printer or to the Model 100 display. Programs SAVEd to RAM and Cassette can be in either of 2 "formats". Unless we specify otherwise, the so-called "compressed format" is used.

1) In the compressed format, everything that can be abbreviated is stored in a shortened form. All numbers except those enclosed in

452

quotes are stored in the minimum number of bytes, with BASIC keywords like PRINT and GOTO stored under special shorthand "codes". This is the format usually used, and is fine for most purposes since it conserves memory and cassette space. This entire process is "invisible" to the user.

2) There are times when we will sacrifice a little space for the luxury of SAVEing a program or data "character for character" in what's known as the "ASCII format". Programs or files sent to a Modem, RS-232 port, Printer or to the Model 100 display can be sent in the ASCII format only.

Files *must* be SAVEd in the ASCII format so they can be MERGEd with other files -- either to hook them end-to-end, overlay one on top of the other, or intermesh their Line numbers. By SAVEing a program in ASCII format, we can MERGE it into other programs without having to retype it.

Merging Files

Let's try a MERGEr right now. Type this NEW program:

```
30 REM THIS LINE GOES BEFORE LINE 40
40 GOTO 10 'THIS LINE OVERLAYS LINE 40
50 REM THIS LINE GOES AFTER LINE 40
```

and SAVE it:

```
SAVE "SECOND",A
```

The ",A" causes it to be SAVEd in ASCII format.

Now we can MERGE the two programs. LOAD the original program back into memory with:

```
LOAD "FIRST"
```
(Use the **F2** key)

then:

```
LIST
```

to be sure only the FIRST program is in memory. Bring in the next program by typing:

```
MERGE "SECOND"
```

LIST the program to verify that we combined both programs into one.

```
10 REM LINE 10
20 REM LINE 20
30 REM THIS LINE GOES BEFORE LINE 40
40 GOTO 10 'THIS LINE OVERLAYS LINE 40
50 REM THIS LINE GOES AFTER LINE 40
```

Of course it worked! Look very carefully. We have new Lines 30 and 50, and the original Line 40 was replaced by Line 40 from the incoming file.

Observe that the *first* program did not have to be in ASCII format, only the one drawn in for MERGEr. If we wish to MERGE 2 programs and their Line numbers conflict, we can easily renumber them first with the EDITor.

The combined programs are now stored in memory under FIRST.BA. This can be verified by pressing **F1** to pull a list of Files. Notice that the program saved in ASCII is filed as SECOND.DO, the same .DO extension we see with TEXT files, since they are automatically saved in ASCII for PATCHing and EDITing.

Try repeating the MERGE process except this time save the first program in ASCII format by typing:

```
SAVE "SECOND.DO"
```

It still MERGEs. Any file SAVEd as a .DO file is automatically stored in the ASCII format.

Now that we have a MERGEd program, let's SAVE it under a new file name. Type:

```
SAVE "MERGE1.BA"
```

Hummm! The Computer reports an FC Error (Illegal Function Call). Since the BASIC file is already named FIRST.BA, it refuses to generate a backup file. There is a way around the problem. Simply SAVE it as a new TEXT file by typing:

```
SAVE "MERGE1.DO"
```

A quick check of the files shows that we are no longer working on a program listed in the Main Menu. We can now SAVE this same program as a BASIC file by typing:

```
SAVE "MERGE1"
```

A file check now shows that we have a new BASIC file called MERGE1.BA along with the ASCII file MERGE1.DO. Clever, if a bit elusive the first time around.

Cassette Merging

SAVEing and MERGEing from cassette is very similar to what we did in RAM. We'll go through the MERGE procedure a little quicker this time since you already know the fundamentals.

Type:

```
LOAD "SECOND"
```

and check the LISTing.

```
30 REM THIS LINE GOES BEFORE LINE 40
40 GOTO 10 'THIS LINE OVERLAYS LINE 40
50 REM THIS LINE GOES AFTER LINE 40
```

Connect the cassette to the Computer and set it up for RECORD. Type:

```
SAVE "CAS:SECOND",A
```

Our program is now SAVEd on cassette in the ASCII format. Best to make sure we have a good copy on cassette, so SAVE it again.

Reenter the first program by typing NEW and:

```
10 REM LINE 10
20 REM LINE 20
40 REM LINE 40
```

Now rewind the tape and set the recorder for PLAY. Type:

```
MERGE "CAS:SECOND"
```

If the SECOND program was SAVED on a tape with other programs, the Computer will skip those and find the one SAVEd in the ASCII format. When when MERGE is complete, pull a LISTing to verify that we have MERGEd the cassette file with our resident program.

Merging With RS-232 and Modem

The last two devices that can be used to MERGE files are COM and MDM.

When merging with COM, we must specify a five character configuration string. For example:

```
MERGE "COM:38N1D"
```

This will MERGE a file entering the RS-232C port with the resident program. The system configuration in this example is:

3	300 baud
8	8 bit word length
N	No parity
1	1 stop bit
D	Disable XON/XOFF

To MERGE a file from the internal modem with the resident program, we need only specify Word length, Parity, Stop bits and line (XON/XOFF) status. For example:

```
MERGE "MDM:7O1E"
```

tells the Computer to MERGE information entering the PHONE jack via the internal MoDeM using

7	Bit word length
O	Odd parity
1	1 stop bit
E	Enable XON/XOFF status

If you're rusty in this area, go back and read the TELCOM section.

Advanced SAVEing

We can tell the Computer where to SAVE a BASIC program, not just onto cassette or into RAM. As with MERGE, we must specify the device name: RAM, CAS, COM, or MDM.

For example:

```
SAVE "CAS:BOOKS"
```

saves the BASIC program "BOOKS" to the cassette recorder (the same as CSAVE "BOOKS").

```
SAVE "COM:37N1E"
```

sends the BASIC program out through the RS-232C port with the five character string configuration code.

```
SAVE "MDM:7I1D"
```

sends the BASIC program out through the Modem with the four character configuration code. BASIC sets the BAUD rate to 300.

```
SAVE "LPT:"
```

sends the current program LISTing to the printer (same as LLIST).

```
SAVE "LCD:"
```

sends the current program LISTing to the LCD display (same as LIST).

Learned in Chapter 45

Statements

MERGE

Miscellaneous

Advanced SAVEing techniques

Chapter 46

File Handling

MAXFILES

The MAXFILES statement reports or sets the maximum number of files that the Model 100 can OPEN. For example:

```
PRINT MAXFILES
```

If you haven't set MAXFILES to a different value, the Model 100 will report its default value of 1.

```
10 MAXFILES = 3
```

in a BASIC program or at command level reserves space in memory to store 3 data files. As we specify more files, less memory is available for programs.

OPEN

The OPEN statement is used to OPEN data files for the transfer of information for BASIC programs. For example:

```
OPEN "RAM:TEST.DO" FOR OUTPUT AS 2
```

This statement Line OPENs a file in the Computer's memory (RAM) and assigns TEST.DO as its file name. FOR OUTPUT tells the Computer to OUTPUT the data sequentially from the program to memory. Buffer number 2 has been assigned AS the buffer to transfer the data to memory. Since a second buffer is used, there must be at least 2 files assigned with the MAXFILES statement.

In our example we used OPEN to OUTPUT data to RAM. We can also use it to INPUT or APPEND data to the following devices:

    RAM   Model 100 memory
    CAS   Cassette tape
    COM   RS-232C port
    LCD   Model 100 Liquid Crystal Display
    LPT   Printer
    MDM   Model 100 internal modem

An example of how OPEN might be used in a program is:

```
10 OPEN "RAM:TEST1.DO" FOR APPEND AS 1
20 OPEN "CAS:TEST2" FOR INPUT AS 2
30 OPEN "COM:58N1D" FOR INPUT AS 3
40 OPEN "MDM:7I1D" FOR OUTPUT AS 4
50 OPEN "LPT:" FOR OUTPUT AS 5
```

Line 10 OPENs a RAM file named TEST1.DO. DATA sent from the BASIC program will be APPENDed to any information currently contained within TEST1. Output is directed through file buffer #1.

Line 20 reads DATA from a cassette file named TEST2, using buffer #2.

Line 30 reads DATA from the RS-232C port with the configuration of 1200 baud, 8 bit words, No parity, 1 stop bit and line status disabled. Input is through buffer #3.

Line 40 outputs DATA through the internal modem with the following configuration: 7 bit word length, Ignore parity, one stop bit and line Disabled. Buffer #4 is allocated to handle the DATA.

Line 50 OPENs buffer #5 for output to the printer.

Of course, to get this program to work we would have had to include this line:

```
5 MAXFILES = 5
```

All files OUTput to RAM are automatically assigned the .DO extension on the file name.

Attaching extensions on file names is optional when SAVEing to CASsette. INPUT and OUTPUT are the only modes available.

COM files must have a five character configuration code instead of a file name (Rate, Word Length, Parity, Stop Bits, Line Status).

MDM files need a four character configuration code in place of a file name (Word Length, Parity, Stop Bits, Line Status).

CLOSE

An OPEN file must be CLOSEd when we are finished reading and writing data to and from it.

```
CLOSE X
```

CLOSEs file X. If more than one file is OPEN, we can CLOSE them all with:

```
CLOSE
```

or more specifically with:

```
CLOSE 1,3,5,6,,,etc,
```

It's generally good programming practice to CLOSE all files soon after reading or writing data. There's always the possiblility of wiping out files that have been left OPEN.

PRINT

The PRINT # statement is used to "write" information to an OPENed file. Type in this NEW program:

```
10 OPEN "RAM:TEST" FOR OUTPUT AS 1
20 A$ = "WOW! IT WORKED PERFECTLY!"
30 PRINT #1, A$
40 CLOSE 1
```

...and RUN.

Nothing appears to have happened. Press **F8** to return to the Main Menu. Call up the new file in the directory called TEST.DO. There it is again,

```
WOW! IT WORKED PERFECTLY!
```

We have just created a TEXT file from BASIC! Press **F8** to RETURN to the MENU, and go back into BASIC.

INPUT

Since we now know we can create files of TEXT, we now learn how to READ them from BASIC using a NEW form of the INPUT statement.

Press **F5** to list the resident program then add these Lines:

```
45 END
50 OPEN "RAM:TEST" FOR INPUT AS 1
60 INPUT #1, A$
70 CLOSE 1
80 PRINT "THE TEST FILE CONTAINS:"
90 PRINT A$
```

...RUN.

Again, nothings happens. The program hits the END in Line 45 and ENDs. Now type:

```
RUN 50
```

Aha!!! There it is! The same message we found in the TEST.DO file when viewed from the TEXT program. This is exciting stuff!

APPENDing FILES

Let's modify the resident program to make the Computer APPEND information to the TEST.DO file.

Change Lines 10 and 30 to:

```
10 OPEN "RAM:TEST" FOR APPEND AS 1
30 FOR I=1 TO 3 : PRINT #1,A$ : NEXT I
```

...now RUN.

Ok, what did it write this time?

Line 10 told the Computer to APPEND the data PRINTed to file #1 to the end of what ever may already be there.

Line 30 PRINTs the contents of A$ to file TEST.DO 3 times. The original data remains intact and the 3 new lines are APPENDed to the end for a total file length of 4 Lines.

To make the Computer READ the file and PRINT its contents, let's use the routine starting at Line 50. Type:

```
RUN 50
```

Hmmm. It only displayed "WOW! IT WORKED PERFECTLY!" once. The Computer was told to INPUT 1 string from file TEST.DO. We have to make it loop 4 times to READ all the strings. Change these Lines:

```
60 FOR I=1 TO 4: INPUT #1,A$(I): NEXT I
90 PRINT:FOR I=1 TO 4:PRINT A$(I):NEXT I
```

...RUN 50.

Great! It PRINTed all 4 lines (just for fun, go to the Main Menu and look at the TEST.DO file again to see if it's the same).

End Of Files

As files continue to grow, it becomes important to know where they end. We knew that TEST.DO had 4 lines after we APPENDed the last 3. If we RUN the entire program again, 3 more lines will be APPENDed for a total of 7 lines. To READ them all would require changing the INPUT loop in Line 70. This is getting awfully complicated.

Delete Line 45. Change and add these Lines:

```
60 IF EOF(1) THEN 70
65 N=N+1: INPUT #1,A$(N):GOTO 60
90 PRINT:FOR I=1 TO N:PRINT A$(I):NEXT I
```

...and RUN.

Line 60 tests for the **End Of File** in buffer 1. If the End Of File has not been reached, the EOF test fails and execution defaults to Line 65.

Line 65 counts the number of times that the file is INPUT and stores the INPUTted string in A$. Control then returns to Line 60 where the EOF is again tested. Once the Computer detects the End Of File, the tests passes in Line 60 and execution branches to Line 70 where the file is CLOSEd.

Each time the program is RUN, 3 more lines are APPENDed to TEST.DO. After the program is RUN a few times a ?BS Error is reported in Line 65. Array variable A$() can only hold 10 elements before we must add a Line to CLEAR some more string space and DIM A$() at a higher value. By adding:

```
5 CLEAR 500 : DIM A$(50)
```

we have allowed enough space for several more RUNs. Isn't this a lot easier? No more guessing or changing looping values.

INPUT$ ()
The INPUT$ statement can be used with files very similar to how we have used it to INPUT data from the keyboard. Change Line 65 in the resident program to:

```
65 N=N+1: A$(N)=INPUT$(27,1):GOTO 60
```

Line 65 will INPUT 27 characters form file #1 and store them in A$(). It takes a little practice to match the character number with the data in the file to pull out the desired information.

LINE INPUT From Files
It is sometimes necessary to read data from files that contain commas. By using the LINE INPUT statement any characters placed in a file can be INPUT. Otherwise, the Computer will only READ up to the end of the line or to a comma. as we saw with the INPUT$ statement, there are many similarities between how we use LINE INPUT with files and how we use it to INPUT data from the keyboard.

We can also use PRINT USING when writing out to a file to insure neat formatting. Example:

```
100 PRINT #3, USING "$###.##",M
```

In this example, we "PRINT" the data in the file just as it would appear had we PRINTed it on a printer. Review a few of the PRINT USING techniques we studied in Chapter 34 and use them to PRINT data to our TEST.DO file. Remember to check the data in the file by looking at it in the TEXT mode.

Learned in Chapter 46

Statements	Commands	Functions
PRINT#	OPEN	MAXFILES
INPUT$	CLOSE	EOF( )
INPUT#	APPEND	

Chapter 47

A Study of Obscurities

Model 100 BASIC has advanced features that are not used by most beginning programmers. Their use requires special applications and knowledge which is really beyond the scope of this book. In the interest of completeness, abbreviated descriptions of what they are and how they are used are included in this Chapter.

CALL
The CALL function has a variety of uses, most of them having little to do with BASIC. It allows us to "call" or "gosub" a program written in assembly language, and "return" back to our BASIC program when it's finished. The benefit of CALL is that the "wordy" type programming requiring PRINT, etc. can be done in BASIC, while complex mathematical programming which takes a lot of computer time to execute in BASIC can be done in ASSEMBLER, which executes very quickly. To make much sense of CALL you'll need ASSEMBLY language skills -- not a part of this book.

A typical CALL statement might look like this:

```
CALL 58000
```

It tells the Computer to execute the program beginning at memory address 58000.

Without getting out too deep in the water, two storage areas (registers) can have values inserted with CALL.

```
CALL 58000,150,62500
```

tells the Computer to execute the program beginning at address 58000 and place the value 150 in register A and 62500 in register HL. The value placed in the A register must be between 0 and 255 while the value placed in register must be between -32768 and 65535. The use of these two values is optional.

To see CALL in action, type:

```
CALL 21117
```

Recognize this mode? That's right, by CALLing the program starting at address 21117 we executed the TERM program. Press **F8** and return to BASIC.

Machine and Assembly language programming books are readily available for that small percentage of readers who want to pursue the subject. You at least have a sufficient introduction to nod your head and smile knowingly when others try to impress you with their knowledge of these things.

SAVEing and LOADing Machine Code

If you've been daring enough to write a machine language program (perhaps through POKEing), it can SAVEd to Memory or Cassette.

```
SAVEM "name", start address, end address, entry point
```

This may look like the SAVE command used to SAVE BASIC programs, but the letter M specifies that we are saving a Machine language program to memory. The machine language program is found in memory between the *start* and *end* addresses. The file *name* can be any name we would assign a TEXT file or a BASIC program. If an extension isn't added to the file name, the Computer adds .CO. The *entry point* is optional. That tells the Computer where to start program execution.

By adding CAS: to the file name,

```
SAVEM "CAS:name", start address, end address, entry point
```

the Model 100 SAVEs the machine program on cassette tape.

CSAVEM "name" can be used in place of SAVEM "CAS:name".

LOADing is just as easy, use:

```
LOADM "name"
```

to LOAD from memory, or

```
LOADM "CAS:name"
```

to LOAD from cassette tape.

To LOAD and RUN a machine language program from memory, type:

```
RUNM "name"
```

or `RUNM "CAS:name"`

to LOAD and RUN for cassette tape.

INP

The Model 100 has 256 "ports" or channels of communication with the "outside world". They are numbered from 0 to 255. Because this subject itself is worthy of an entire book, we will only learn enough to get an elementary "feel" for it.

```
PRINT INP(255)
```

PRINTs the value found at INput Port 255.

OUT

The opposite of INP is OUT.

```
OUT 255,7
```

sends the value 7 to OUTput port 255. Any value from 0 to 255 can be sent to any of the 256 ports.

VARPTR

While VARPTR (short for VARiable PoinTeR) is found in Model 100 BASIC, it's about as far from main-line BASIC as anything we have.

Take a Deep Breath

If a variable is numeric, VARPTR tells us the memory location of the first byte of the number stored in that variable.

If it's a string variable, VARPTR tells us where in memory the *index* to a given variable is located. Read that last line carefully. Don't want anyone getting lost. VARPTR doesn't have the common decency to point to the contents of a string variable in memory. Instead, it points to a three byte "index" to that variable. The three bytes contain:

1. The *length* of the string.

2. The least significant byte of the *starting location* of the string.

3. The most significant byte of the *starting location* of the string.

To actually find the contents of the string variable, we have to calculate the location using bytes two and three of the index to that variable. Sound complicated? Well, it is a bit tricky, but an example should clarify matters nicely.

Enter this NEW program:

```
10 REM * STRING VARIABLE LOCATER *
20 CLS
30 A$ = "123456"
40 X = VARPTR(A$)
45 PRINT "INDEX TO A$ IS AT ";X
```

...and RUN.

Line 40 uses VARPTR to store the location of the index to A$ in X. Then Line 45 PRINTs it.

If the address is displayed as a negative number, this simply means the address was larger than 32767. VARPTR handles numbers as integers so it must display values starting with 32768 as a negative value continuing in descending order.

We haven't found the contents of A$ yet, just the index. Hang in there. Add:

```
50 L = PEEK(X+1) + 256*PEEK(X+2)
```

```
55 PRINT "A$ IS HIDING AT LOCATION";L
```

...and RUN.

So that's where the little rascal is. Line 50 uses some fancy footwork to convert bytes two and three of the index into the actual location of A$. Line 55, of course, PRINTs its value.

How could we prove that we have found the correct location? Sure. PEEK at the contents of A$ and compare it with "123456". Add:

```
60  FOR I=L TO L+5
70  PRINT CHR$(PEEK(I));
80  NEXT I : PRINT
```

...and RUN.

Satisfied?

Now, knowing where a variable is located in memory may not seem too useful at first blush, but it has some surprising consequences. Once we have found the location of a string variable, we can modify its contents. Try this one on for size:

```
70 READ N : POKE I,N
80 NEXT I : PRINT A$ : PRINT
90 DATA 228,232,238,237,239,231
```

...and RUN.

Surprise! We have just poked graphic codes into an unsuspecting "normal" string variable and transformed it into a pictorial masterpiece.

Type:

```
PRINT A$
```

to be sure you aren't dreaming. Yes, it really happened. We have actually modified the contents of A$. These computers can be down right fun once you get to know them.

Now type:

```
LIST
```

Did we do that to Line 30? Afraid so.

Leave with this thought. We packed a "dummy" string with only six graphic codes. A string variable can hold up to 255 characters (nearly the entire video display). Just imagine what we could do with a single string packed with up to 255 cursor control codes, graphic codes, and special character sets! If that doesn't push your cardiovascular system to overload, might as well trade the 100 in for a calculator.

CSRLIN

CSRLIN (pronounced "CurSoR LINe") tells which row (verticle position) the cursor is sitting on when CSRLIN is executed. CLS the display and type:

```
PRINT CSRLIN        ENTER
```

The Computer reports a 2. Try it again and we get 5.

LPOS

This command works a lot like POS. Where POS found the POSition of the cursor on the display, LPOS finds the POSition of the print head on the Line printer. Connect the printer (assuming you have one) and place it ON-LINE, type:

```
LPRINT "PRINTER POSITION IS:";LPOS(0)
```

The dummy number within the parentheses can be any value.

LPRINT USING

Bet you didn't know we could use PRINT USING with the printer. Well, we can! The action is exactly the same, except output goes to the printer. Look back at a few examples in Chapter 34 and try them with your printer. Simply change all PRINT USINGs to LPRINT USING.

SCREEN

SCREEN allows us to turn the LABEL line on or off.

```
SCREEN 0,0        turns LABEL line OFF
SCREEN 0,1        turns LABEL line ON
```

LINE INPUT

The LINE INPUT statement is similar to the regular INPUT statement except by adding LINE, it is now possible to enter commas, leading blanks and quotation marks which are then stored in a string variable. The question mark prompt is not displayed.

Type in this NEW program:

```
10 LINE INPUT"ENTER ANYTHING AT ALL ";A$
20 PRINT "YOU ENTERED ";A$
```

...and RUN.

MAXRAM and HIMEM

MAXRAM tells us the highest address number in memory the Computer can use. This is a fixed value that will not change as we use up memory space. The advantage to having MAXRAM is its use with CLEAR. To CLEAR the MAXimum amount of MEMory for program use, we can tell the Computer to:

```
CLEAR 0,MAXRAM
```

This tells the Computer reserve 0 bytes of memory for strings and use the entire RAM memory space for programs.

If we wanted to reserve space for strings and reserve some space in the top of memory for machine language programs, we would have to CLEAR some room. For example, type:

```
CLEAR 1000,62000
```

We have set aside 1000 bytes in memory for string storage and protected memory addresses above 62000 for machine language programs. Now type:

```
PRINT HIMEM,MAXRAM          ENTER
```

The HIMEM value is less than MAXRAM because of the space reserved between the HIgh point in MEMory for program use and the MAXimum RAM memory address available in our computer.

Enabling and Disabling Function Keys

If we press a Function Key during the execution of a BASIC program, the computer will usually ignore it. But if we wanted our program to do something special when a Function Key has been pressed, there are two things we must know.

We have learned how to branch to other areas of programs by using ON-GOTO and ON-GOSUB. With ON KEY GOSUB, we can branch within a program when any of the 8 Soft Keys are pressed. This makes it possible to use Function Keys as additional inputs from the keyboard, but does not affect their normal operation.

Before the Computer can recognize the Function keys, we must first turn them ON with KEY ON. Type and RUN this NEW program to demonstrate both features:

```
10 KEY ON
20 PRINT "PRESS A FUNCTION KEY"
30 ON KEY GOSUB 100,200,300,400,500,600,700,800
40 GOTO 30
100 PRINT "YOU PRESSED F1":RETURN
200 PRINT "YOU PRESSED F2":RETURN
300 PRINT "YOU PRESSED F3":RETURN
400 PRINT "YOU PRESSED F4":RETURN
500 PRINT "YOU PRESSED F5":RETURN
600 PRINT "YOU PRESSED F6":RETURN
700 PRINT "YOU PRESSED F7":RETURN
800 PRINT "YOU PRESSED F8":RETURN
```

Line 10 enables all 8 Function keys for inputting.

Line 30 acts similar to ON - GOSUB in that it branches to a Line number corresponding to the function key pressed. If a key is not pressed, execution defaults to Line 40 to continue the loop.

Change Line 10 to:

```
10 KEY (8) ON
```

...and RUN.

Key 8 is the only key that responds when pressed. By inserting a number in parentheses following KEY, we can specify one key for inputting.

Similarly, we can selectively turn OFF specific Function Keys. Make these changes to our resident program:

```
10 KEY ON
100 PRINT "YOU PRESSED F1"
110 KEY (1) OFF : RETURN
```

...and RUN.

After **F1** is pressed, Line 110 turns OFF key 1 before RETURNing to the ON KEY GOSUB Line. We can turn OFF each of the 8 keys individually or turn them all off at once with:

```
KEY OFF
```

If we want to temporarily STOP the Computer from recognizing all Function Keys, we can type:

```
KEY STOP
```

The Computer remembers the Function key pressed, but it won't branch till KEYed ON.

Learning how to manipulate around the Soft Keys is easy. The challenge is coming up with good uses for this function within a program.

ON TIME$ GOSUB

We can also make the Computer branch, at a specified time, to a routine in a program. The procedure resembles that of the Function Key routine. We enable ON TIME$ by typing:

```
TIME$ ON
```

or disable it with:

```
TIME$ OFF
```

Enter and RUN this typical program to show how it works:

```
10 TIME$ ON
```

```
20 ON TIME$= "12:00:00" GOSUB 50
30 IF T=1 THEN END
40 PRINT@ 0,TIME$: GOTO 30
50 PRINT "IT'S LUNCH TIME!": T=1
60 BEEP : RETURN
```

A space can not be placed between TIME$ and the = sign. The fussy Model 100 will give us a syntax error report.

When the internal clock reaches high noon, the program branches from wherever it is to the ON TIME$ subroutine. It then RETURNs to wherever it was when interrupted.

ON COM/MDM GOSUB

As with all other "ON device GOSUB" routines, ON COM GOSUB and ON MDM GOSUB must first be turned on with COM ON or MDM ON. And just as easily, we can tell the Model 100 to ignore then by using "device OFF".

If we have an external device connected to the RS-232C port, we can have our program branch to a BASIC routine when DATA begins to enter the COM port. For example, type:

```
10 COM ON
20 ON COM GOSUB 5000
     :
     :
5000 REM ROUTINE TO ACT ON THE INTERRUPT
GOES HERE
```

The same can be done for a modem interrupt:

```
10 MDM ON
20 ON MDM GOSUB 2500
     :
     :
2500 REM MODEM INTERRUPT ROUTINE GOES HERE
```

The "ON device GOSUB" statement is usually placed at the beginning of a program. Once the Computer has READ the statement, it will perform the rest of the BASIC program with its usual reliability. But, as soon as it encounters DATA through the device, it branches from wherever it is within the program to the specified Line number in the ON device GOSUB statement. A RETURN at the end of the subroutine sends execution back to the Line where the interrupt occurred.

Each device branching statement can be turned OFF or temporarily STOPped with COM OFF, COM STOP, MDM OFF or MDM STOP.

IPL

Tired of seeing the MENU each time the Computer is turned on? If you have a special program that you would like to automatically RUN everytime you turn on the Computer, then IPL is for you.

    IPL "name.BA"

Each time the Computer comes on, "name.BA" will automatically RUN. Here's the catch, the Computer must be in BASIC with the resident program the same as that used in IPL when the Computer is turned off.

To "CLEAR out" the IPL function, type:

    IPL ""

The previous IPL program is left intact in memory, although the Computer will display the Main Menu when turned ON.

We can also tell the Computer to automatically RUN BASIC, TEXT, TELCOM, ADDRSS, or SCHEDL files from the MENU by using (for example:)

    IPL "TELCOM"

The Computer will now enter TELCOM when we Power-Up. Remember, the Computer must be Turned OFF while in BASIC to activate IPL.

MOTOR

If we want to advance a some extra tape in the cassette recorder between SAVEs, we can turn on the recorder's motor with the Computer by typing:

    `MOTOR ON`

and

    `MOTOR OFF`

Make sure the PLAY (and RECORD if SAVEing) buttons are pressed before trying MOTOR ON.

POWER

The Model 100 is initially set to stay on for 10 minutes without interruption until it shuts off by itself. We can regulate its automatic shut off time by using the POWER command.

    `POWER CONT`

keeps the power on CONTinuously until the power switch is turned off. Not recommended when using batteries.

    `POWER 150`

Allows the Computer to stay on 15 uninterrupted minutes before shut down. A little math tells us that each number is worth 6 seconds. Therefore, the default time of 10 minutes can be reset by typing:

    `POWER 100`   (100 * 6 sec = 600 sec or 10 min.)

The POWER ON value can range from 10 to 255.

Learned in Chapter 47

Statements	Commands	Functions	Miscellaneous
LPRINT USING	CALL	INP	Enable/Disable
LINE INPUT	SCREEN	OUT	Function keys
ON TIME$ GOSUB	IPL	VARPTR	Saving/Loading
ON COM/MDM GOSUB	MOTOR	CSRLIN	machine codes
	POWER	LPOS	
		MAXRAM	
		HIMEM	

"How do we find the problem? The answer is simple -- *be very systematic*. Even experienced programmers make lots of silly mistakes..."

Part 9

Program Control

Chapter 48
Flowcharting

Most of the programs we wrote in this book were simple; but, they met fairly simple needs. Suppose we want to write a program to play chess or bridge, evaluate complicated investment alternatives, keep records for a bowling league or a small business, or do stress calculations for a new building? How would we go about writing such a complex program?

Answer: We break down the big program into a group of individual programs. This is called *modular programming* and the individual programs are called *modules*. But how are the modules related -- and how do we write them, anyway?

Module is just a 75-cent word for "section" or "building block".

One way to plan a program is to make a picture displaying its logic. Remember, a picture is worth a thousand words (or is it the other way around?). The picture that programmers use is called a *flowchart*. Flowcharts are so widely used that programmers have devised standard symbols. There are many specialized symbols in use, but we will only examine the most common ones.

BEGIN or END

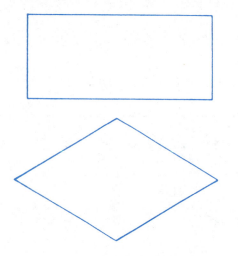

PROCESSING BLOCK
(encloses something the Computer does without making any decisions)

DECISION DIAMOND
(it branches off in different directions, depending on the decision it makes.)

Each decision point asks a question such as *"Is A larger than B?"* or *"Have all the cards been dealt?"* The different branches are marked by *yes* or *no*.

Another useful symbol is:

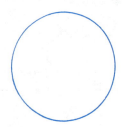

CONTINUATION

The circle usually has a number inside it which corresponds to a number on another page if the flowchart is too large for a single sheet.

CONNECTOR ARROWS

Arrows indicate the direction in which program execution proceeds.

Flowcharts are most helpful in designing programs when they are kept simple. A cluttered flowchart is hard to read and usually isn't much more helpful than an ordinary written program LISTing. A good flowchart is also helpful for "documentation", to give us (or others) a picture of how the program works -- for later on, when we've forgotten.

There are no hard-and-fast rules about what goes into a flowchart and what doesn't. A flowchart is supposed to help, not be more work than it's worth. It helps us plan the *logic* of the program. When it stops helping and makes us feel like we're back in arts and crafts designing mosaics, then we've gone as far as the flowchart will take us or more typically, it's already passed its point of usefulness.

Let's look at some examples. Suppose we want to grade a 5-question test by comparing each of the *students'* answers with the *correct* answer. We will put the correct answers in a DATA statement in the program, enter a student's answers through the keyboard, compare (grade) them, then PRINT the % of correct answers. This procedure will be repeated until all the students' papers are graded.

The flowchart might look like this:

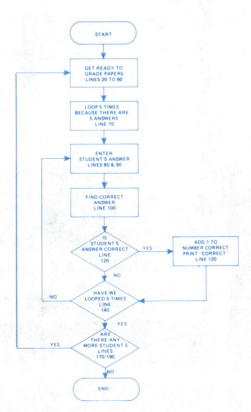

This flowchart has three decision diamonds. In the first, the Computer determines if an answer is correct. In the second, the Computer determines if all the questions in a single student's paper have been graded. The third one terminates execution when all the tests have been graded.

EXERCISE 48-1: Using the flowchart as a guide, write a program that grades a test having five question.

For more complicated problems, we may want to subdivide the flowchart into larger modules. A *master flowchart* will then show the relationship between the flowcharts of individual programs.

For example, let's say we want to write a program that calculates the return on various investments. The options might be:

1 - CERTIFICATE OF DEPOSIT
2 - BANK SAVINGS ACCOUNT
3 - CREDIT UNION
4 - MONEY MARKET FUND

The main (or Control) program will select one of these 4 options using an INPUT question, execute the correct subprogram, and PRINT the answer. Its flowchart might be as shown on next page.

We can now flowchart each of the individual programs in the blocks separately. The Certificate of Deposit program would, for example, have to contain the rate of return, size of deposit, and number of years in which the certificate matures. The order in which that program INPUTs data and performs the calculations would be specified in its own flowchart.

EXERCISE 48-2: Write the master program as flowcharted, with a branch to a program to calculate the return on a Bank Savings Account paying simple interest.

EXERCISE 48-3: Choose a program from an early Chapter and design your own flowchart.

Learned in Chapter 48

Miscellaneous

Flowcharting

Chapter 48

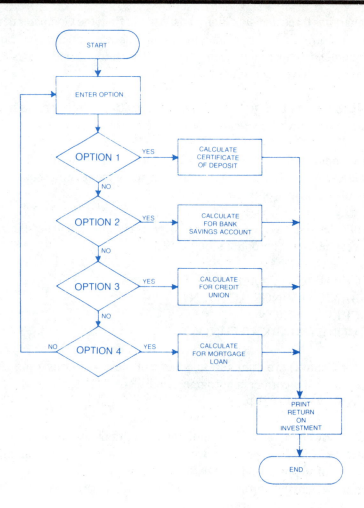

Chapter 49

Debugging Programs

Quick -- The Raid!
Throughout this book the Computer has given us plenty of nasty messages. We knew something was wrong, but it wasn't always obvious exactly where, or why.

How do we find the problem? The answer is simple -- *be very systematic*. Even experienced programmers make lots of silly mistakes...but the experience *can* teach how to locate mistakes quickly.

Hardware, Cockpit or Software?
The first step in the "debugging" process is to isolate the problem as being either:

1. A hardware problem,

2. An operator problem, or

3. A software problem.

Is It Farther To Ft. Worth or By Bus?
Starting with the least likely possibility -- is the Computer itself working improperly? Chances are very high that the Computer is working perfectly. There are several fast ways to find out.

A. Type:

```
PRINT FRE(0)
```

The answer should be slightly less than the number of free bytes shown in the Main Menu. If the answer is considerably more or less than the Main Menu there may be trouble.

Possible Solution

In either of the above cases, turn the Computer off. Let it sit for a full minute before turning it on again. After turning it back on, enter BASIC and type NEW. Try the PRINT FRE(0) test again. If the results are the same, it's time to try a complete restart. (Or, as they say in the big time, *"Take it all the way down."*) This step will erase any files you placed in memory, but at this point they're probably shot anyway. You could try to SAVE them to cassette if it makes you feel any better.

Press **CTRL PAUSE** while pressing the RESET button on the back of the Computer. Or, you can press **CTRL PAUSE** while turning the Computer ON.

Turn the Computer back ON, enter BASIC and try the PRINT FRE(0) test again. If the results are the same, there is probably a chip failure that will require professional troubleshooting and replacement.

Liquid Crystal Display Problems?

The Display may need to be adjusted for the best contrast at the angle it is viewed. adjusting the DISP control on the right side fails to give the desired display, there may be a hardware problem.

Idiot Here -- What's Your Excuse?

Of course, *you* don't make silly mistakes!

Now that's settled,

    1. Is everything plugged in? Correctly? Firmly?

    2. Are the Computer and recorder batteries fresh (if you're using batteries)?

    3. Is the recorder volume level properly set?

4. Is the recorder tone switch on "high" (if yours has one)?

5. Are you using "legal" commands?

IF so...

Go walk the dog, then check it all over again.

If...Then

If the trouble was not found in the cockpit or with the hardware, there is probably something wrong with your program. Dump out the troublesome program. Load in one that is known to work and RUN it as a final hardware and operator check.

Common Errors

Let's look at some of the common sources of "computer-detected errors".

1. Assume the error is in a PRINT, or INPUT statement. Did you:

    a. Forget one of the needed pair of quotation marks?

EXAMPLE:

```
10 PRINT "ANSWER IS, X : GOTO 5
```

ERROR: No ending quotation mark after IS.

Yes, we know it's OK if the missing quote is the last character in the Line.

---

b. Use an illegal variable name?

EXAMPLE:

```
10 INPUT 6G
```

ERROR: Must be recognizable by the Computer.

c. Forget a semicolon or comma separating variables or text, or bury the semicolon or comma inside quotation marks?

EXAMPLE:

```
10 PRINT "THE VALUE IS "V X
```

ERROR: A semicolon is missing between V and X (so the variables are not properly separated.)

    d. Forget the Line Number, accidentally mix a letter in with the number, or use a Line number larger than 65529?

EXAMPLE:

```
72B3 PRINT "BAD LINE NUMBER."
```

ERROR

    e. Accidentally have a double quotation mark in your text?

EXAMPLE:

```
10 PRINT "HE SAID "HELLO THERE.""
```

    f. Type a Line more than 255 characters long?

    g. Misspell PRINT or INPUT (It happens!)?

    h. Accidentally type a stray character in the Line, especially an extra comma or semicolon?

2. If the error is in a READ statement, almost all the previous possibilities apply, plus:

    a. Is there really a DATA statement for the Computer to read? Remember, it will only READ a piece of DATA once unless it is RESTOREd.

EXAMPLE:

```
10 READ X,Y,Z
20 DATA 2,5
```

ERROR: There are only two numbers for the Computer to READ.

If you mean for Z to be zero, you must say so.

```
20 DATA 2,5,0
```

3. If the trouble area is a FOR-NEXT loop, most of the previous possibilities also apply, plus:

    a. Do you have a NEXT statement to match the FOR?

EXAMPLE:

```
10 FOR A=1 TO N
```

ERROR: Where's the NEXT A?

Some of these FOR-NEXT loop errors won't cause actual error messages; instead the program may wind up in endless loops, requiring the use of the **BREAK** key.

    b. Do you have all the requirements for a loop -- a starting point, an ending point, a variable name, and a STEP size if it's not 1?

EXAMPLE:

```
10 A=1 TO N
```

ERROR: Must have a FOR and a NEXT.

    c. Did you accidentally nest two loops using the same variable in both loops?

Example:

```
10 FOR X=1 TO 5
20  FOR X=1 TO 3
30   PRINT X
40  NEXT X
50 NEXT X
```

ERROR: The nested loops must have different variables.

d. Does a variable in a loop have the same letter as the loop counter?

EXAMPLE:
```
10 A=22
20 FOR R=1 TO 5
30   R=18
40   Y=R*A
50    PRINT Y
60 NEXT R
```

ERROR: The value of R was changed by another R inside the loop, and NEXT R was overrun, since 18 is larger than 5.

e. Did we nest loops incorrectly with one not completely inside the other?

Example:
```
10 FOR X=1 TO 6
20   FOR Y=1 TO 8
30    PSET (X,Y)
40   NEXT X
50 NEXT Y
```

4. If the goofed-up statement is an IF-THEN or GOTO:

a. Does the Line number specified by the THEN or GOTO really exist? Be especially careful of this error when we eliminate a Line in the process of "improving" or "cleaning up" a program.

5. The ERROR comes back as ?OM (Out of Memory) but the PRINT FRE(0) indicates there is room left in memory. If we get an ?OM and are using an array, extra room (up to hundreds of bytes) has to be left for processing. We have probably overrun the amount of available memory.

6. The ERROR comes back as ?BS (Bad Subscript).

a. Did we exceed the limits of an array?

7. Did we tell the Computer to divide by zero? (The Computer isn't about to let us get away with that one!)

To find out whether we did any of these things, PRINT (in immediate mode) the values for all the variables used in the offending Line. If we still don't see the error, try carrying out the operations indicated on the Line. For example, the error may occur during a multiplication of two very large numbers.

PRINT in calculator mode (no Line number).

These certainly aren't all the possible errors one can make, but at least they give us some idea where to look first. Since we can't completely avoid silly errors, it's necessary to be able to recover from them as quickly as possible.

By the way...a one-semester course in beginning typing can do wonders for programming speed and typing accuracy.

From the Ridiculous to the Sublime:

All the Computer can tell us is that we have (or have not) followed all of its rules. we have followed all the rules, the Computer will not ask "questions" -- even if we're asking it to do something that's quite silly and isn't at all what we intended. It will dutifully put out garbage all day long if we feed it garbage -- even though we follow its rules. Remember GIGO? If the program has no obvious errors, what might be the matter?

GIGO stands for Garbage In, Garbage Out.

Typical "unreported" errors are:

1. Accidentally reinitializing a variable -- particularly easy when using loops.
EXAMPLE:

```
10 FOR N=1 TO 3
20    READ A
30    PRINT A
40    RESTORE
```

```
50 NEXT N
60 DATA 1,2,3
```

2. Reversing conditions, (i.e. using "=" when we mean "<>", or "greater than" when we mean "less than").

3. Accidentally including "equals", as in "less than or equals", when we really mean only "less than."

4. Confusing similarly-named variables, particularly the variable A, the string A$, and the array A(X). *They are not at all related.*

5. Forgetting the order of program execution -- from left to right on each Line, but multiplications and divisions always having priority before additions and subtractions. And intrinsic functions (INT, RND, ABS, etc.) having priority over everything else.

6. Counting incorrectly in loops. `FOR I=0 TO 7` causes the loop to be executed eight, not seven, times.

7. Using the same variable accidentally in two different places. This is okay if we don't need the old variable any more, but disastrous if we do. Be especially careful when combining programs or using the special subroutines.

But how do we spot these errors if the Computer doesn't point them out? Use common sense and let the Model 100 help you. The rules to follow are:

1. Isolate the error. Insert temporary "flags". Add STOP, END, and extra PRINT statements until we can track the error down to 1 or 2 Lines.

Examples of useful flags:
```
299 PRINT "    Line #299"
399 IF X<0 THEN PRINT "X<0 in #399":STOP
```

Line 299 will help us check whether the Line immediately following Line 299 is executed. This helps us follow program flow. Line 399 might be used to locate the point where X goes out of range.

---

2. Keep the "tests" as simple as possible. Don't make the program more complicated until *after* we've found the error.

3. Check simple cases by hand to test the logic, but let the Computer do the hard work. Don't try to wade through complex calculations with pencil and paper. We'll introduce more new mistakes than we'll find. Use the calculator mode, or a separate hand calculator to do that work.

4. Remember that we can force the Computer to start a program at any Line number we choose. Just type:

`GOTO ###`

(where ### represents the desired Line number). This is a useful tool for working back through a program. Give the variables acceptable values using calculator-mode statements, then GOTO some point midway through the program flow using a GOTO statement. If the answers are what we expect, then the error is before the "test point" we've created. Otherwise, the error is after the test point.

Although the details would be different for our program, these techniques can be applied easily.

5. Remember also that it's not necessary to LIST the entire program just to get a look at the one section of it. Just type:

`LIST ###-###`

(where ### tells the Computer on which Lines we'd like to start and end the LIST).

6. Practice "defensive programming". Just because a program "works okay", don't assume it's dependable. Programs that accept INPUT data and process it can be especially deceptive. Make a point of checking a new program at its critical edges.

EXAMPLES: A square root program should be checked for INPUTs less than or equal to 0. Math functions we have programmed should be checked at points where the function is undefined, such as TAN(90°).

Beware of Creeping Elegance

Programs grow and become more elegant with the ego reinforcement of the programmer. This "creeping elegance" increases the chance of silly errors. It's fun to let our mind wander and add on some program here, and some more there, but it's easy to lose sight of the program's *purpose*. At times like this the flow chart is ignored and trouble begins.   Nuff said.

We'll leave some space to make notes on our own debugging and troubleshooting ideas…

Share them with us too…especially if we come up with some really neat ones.

Learned in Chapter 49

Miscellaneous

Defensive programming
Common Errors
Flags
Hardware check-out procedures

Chapter 50

Chasing the ERRORs

MODEL 100 BASIC contains 31 different ERROR messages to help us troubleshoot program or operator problems. There are so many we need a separate Chapter plus an Appendix just to understand what they mean.

Let's quietly tiptoe into the hall of ERRORs by typing this little test program:

```
1 CLS
10 REM * TESTING ERROR CODES *
20 INPUT"WHAT ERROR CODE NUMBER SHALL WE CHECK";N
30 ERROR N
```

RUN the program a number of times (entering numbers between 1 and 255), forcing the Computer to PRINT out the message for various types of ERRORs. Don't waste time trying to understand them now. You can study them in detail in Appendix E.

The only new BASIC word above is in Line 30. ERROR has little real use in life except as above, PRINTing the error message abbreviation from its code number.

Error Report Codes

Code	Message	Meaning
1	NF	NEXT without FOR.
2	SN	Syntax Error.
3	RG	RETURN without GOSUB.
4	OD	Out of Data.
5	FC	Illegal function call.
6	OV	Overflow.
7	OM	Out of Memory.
8	UL	Undefined line.
9	BS	Bad Subscript.
10	DD	Double Dimensioned Array.
11	/0	Division by Zero.
12	ID	Illegal Direct.
13	TM	Type Mismatch.
14	OS	Out of String Space.
15	LS	String Too Long.
16	ST	String Formula Too Complex.
17	CN	Can't Continue.
18	IO	Error.
19	NR	No RESUME.
20	RW	RESUME Without Error.
21	UE	Undefined Error.
22	MO	Missing Operand.
23-49	UE	Undefined Error.
50	IE	Undefined Error.
51	BN	Bad File Number.
52	FF	File Not Found.
53	AO	Already Open.
54	EF	Input Past End of File.

Code	Message	Meaning
55	NM	Bad File Name.
56	DS	Direct Statement in File.
57	FL	Undefined Error.
58	CF	File Not Open.
59-255	UE	Undefined Error.

ERROR Trapping

The ON ERROR GOTO statement is of more value, and we should use it when we think we're on the trail of a specific type of ERROR, but are not sure.

Suppose we suspect that some place in the program there is an accidental division by zero, and it's goofing up the results. Type in this NEW test program:

```
10 ON ERROR GOTO 70
20 PRINT
30 INPUT"WHAT NUMBER SHALL WE DIVIDE 100 BY";N
40 A = 100/N
50 PRINT"100 DIVIDED BY";N;"=";A
60 GOTO 10
70 PRINT "DIVISION BY ZERO IS ILLEGAL"
80 PRINT " - MAYBE EVEN IMPOSSIBLE!"
99 END
```

...and RUN.

Try positive and negative values, then try a 0.

ON ERROR GOTO is acting much as our old friend ON X GOTO did, so there are no big surprises here.

Change Line 10 to a REM line and try assorted values, ending with 0. Again, no big surprise. An error message was delivered, pinpointing both the nature and location of the ERROR, and execution was terminated with a READY.

Change Line 10 back to:

    10 ON ERROR GOTO 70

and add:

    80 RESUME 20

...and RUN with various values, including 0.

Notice that even though the Computer was forced to operate with an error (division by zero), execution did not terminate. The ERROR message was delivered and the Computer kept on going, thanks to RESUME. This is the essence of good ERROR trapping -- identifying the ERROR without "crashing" the program. There may be several interrelated ERRORs that can be found easily only by continuing the RUN.

Change Line 80 to:

    80 RESUME NEXT

...and RUN.

Although the results are similar to those with RESUME 20, there is a subtle difference.

RESUME NEXT causes execution to resume at the NEXT line immediately following the line which made the ERROR. Thus Line 50 is PRINTed, even though (in this case) it gives a wrong answer. RESUME 20 directed execution to a very specific line. With a little head-scratching you can quickly see how both features can be used in difficult debugging situations.

Next, change Line 80 to simply:

    80 RESUME

...and RUN.

RESUME by itself (or RESUME 0) sends execution back to the Line in which the ERROR is being made.)

Chapter 50

More Variations on the Theme

Change Line 80 back to:

```
80 RESUME 20
```

and add Line 75:

```
75 PRINT"ERROR IS IN LINE #";ERL
```

...and RUN.

ERL is a "reserved" word that PRINTs the *Line number* in which the ERROR occurs. For my money, this little jewel in combination with ON ERROR GOTO to snag 'em, and RESUME NEXT (or RESUME Line number) to keep the program from crashing, makes this whole hassle worthwhile.

ERR

A final esoteric touch may be obtained by adding the ERR (not ERL) statement. ERR produces the code number of the last error that our computer encountered.

Add Line 77:

```
77 PRINT"AND ERROR CODE IS";ERR
```

...and RUN.

Finally, to complete this loop begun several pages ago, add:

```
78 PRINT"WHICH STANDS FOR" : ERROR ERR
```

...and RUN.

Which brings us back to Do, a deer, a female deer...(it must be time to STOP this book -- getting too silly!)

A very useful application of the ERROR traps we've learned allows the program to automatically LIST itself if there is an ERROR. It requires the addition of two temporary program lines using all three ERROR statements.

From Appendix E (which covers the ERROR messages) comes the example of what happens when there is an ERROR in the FOR-NEXT loop. Type in:

```
10 FOR A = 1 TO 5
20 PRINT "THERE IS NO 'NEXT A'"
30 NEXT Z
```

...and RUN.

In this simple program the Computer responds with:

```
?NF ERROR IN 30.
```

There is a FOR-NEXT ERROR in Line 30. By adding the following lines we can approximate the same result, plus cause an automatic program LISTing:

```
5 ON ERROR GOTO 100
```

to "set" the error trap,

```
99 END
```

to END execution if all is well,

```
100 PRINT ERL,ERR : LIST ERL
```

to print the line # with the ERROR, the ERROR code (which can be found in Appendix E) and LIST the program (or LIST##-##).

Try this routine. If all is well in the program, nothing will seem different. If there is an ERROR, it will be trapped as you can see on the screen.

EXERCISE 50-1: Enter the following NEW program:

```
20 CLS
30 FOR I=1 TO 10
40 X = RND(21)-1 : F = X-10/X
50 PRINT I, "X=" X, "F(X)=" F;
60 IF F<0 THEN PUNT ELSE PRINT
70 NEXT I
```

```
80 INPUT "PRESS ENTER TO CONTINUE"; Z :
GOTO 20
```

Write an error trapping routine that recovers from both ERRORs and PRINTs:

```
ATTEMPTED DIVISION BY ZERO IN LINE ##
```

or

```
SYNTAX ERROR IN LINE ##
```

as appropriate.

HINT -- Syntax ERROR is code 2, and Division by Zero is code 11.

Learned in Chapter 50

Statements	Functions	Miscellaneous
ERROR	ERL	Error Codes
ON ERROR GOTO	ERR	
RESUME		

Appendices

Appendix A
ASCII Chart

Decimal	Hex	Character	Key
0	00		CTRL @
1	01		CTRL A
2	02		CTRL B
3	03		CTRL C
4	04		CTRL D
5	05		CTRL E
6	06		CTRL F
7	07		CTRL G
8	08		CTRL H
9	09		CTRL I
10	0A		CTRL J
11	0B		CTRL K
12	0C		CTRL L
13	0D		CTRL M
14	0E		CTRL N
15	0F		CTRL O
16	10		CTRL P
17	11		CTRL Q
18	12		CTRL R
19	13		CTRL S
20	14		CTRL T
21	15		CTRL U
22	16		CTRL V
23	17		CTRL W
24	18		CTRL X
25	19		CTRL Y
26	1A		CTRL Z
27	1B		ESC
28	1C		→
29	1D		←
30	1E		↑
31	1F		↓

Decimal	Hex	Character	Key
32	20		SPACEBAR
33	21	!	!
34	22	"	"
35	23	#	#
36	24	$	$
37	25	%	%
38	26	&	&
39	27	'	'
40	28	(	(
41	29	)	)
42	2A	*	*
43	2B	+	+
44	2C	,	,
45	2D	-	-
46	2E	.	.
47	2F	/	/
48	30	0	0
49	31	1	1
50	32	2	2
51	33	3	3
52	34	4	4
53	35	5	5
54	36	6	6
55	37	7	7
56	38	8	8
57	39	9	9
58	3A	:	:
59	3B	;	;
60	3C	<	<
61	3D	=	=
62	3E	>	>
63	3F	?	?

ASCII Chart

Decimal	Hex	Character	Key
64	40	@	@
65	41	A	A
66	42	B	B
67	43	C	C
68	44	D	D
69	45	E	E
70	46	F	F
71	47	G	G
72	48	H	H
73	49	I	I
74	4A	J	J
75	4B	K	K
76	4C	L	L
77	4D	M	M
78	4E	N	N
79	4F	O	O
80	50	P	P
81	51	Q	Q
82	52	R	R
83	53	S	S
84	54	T	T
85	55	U	U
86	56	V	V
87	57	W	W
88	58	X	X
89	59	Y	Y
90	5A	Z	Z
91	5B	[	[
92	5C	\	GRPH -
93	5D	]	]
94	5E	^	^
95	5F	_	_

Appendix A

Decimal	Hex	Character	Key
96	60	`	GRPH [
97	61	a	A
98	62	b	B
99	63	c	C
100	64	d	D
101	65	e	E
102	66	f	F
103	67	g	G
104	68	h	H
105	69	i	I
106	6A	j	J
107	6B	k	K
108	6C	l	L
109	6D	m	M
110	6E	n	N
111	6F	o	O
112	70	p	P
113	71	q	Q
114	72	r	R
115	73	s	S
116	74	t	T
117	75	u	U
118	76	v	V
119	77	w	W
120	78	x	X
121	79	y	Y
122	7A	z	Z
123	7B	{	GRPH 9
124	7C	|	GRPH —
125	7D	}	GRPH 0
126	7E	~	GRPH]
127	7F		DEL
128	80		GRPH p

ASCII Chart

Decimal	Hex	Character	Key
129	81		GRPH m
130	82		GRPH f
131	83		GRPH x
132	84		GRPH c
133	85		GRPH a
134	86		GRPH h
135	87		GRPH t
136	88		GRPH 1
137	89		GRPH r
138	8A	≠	GRPH /
139	8B	Σ	GRPH s
140	8C		GRPH '
141	8D	±	GRPH =
142	8E	∫	GRPH i
143	8F		GRPH e
144	90		GRPH y
145	91		GRPH u
146	92		GRPH ;
147	93		GRPH q
148	94		GRPH w
149	95		GRPH b
150	96		GRPH n
151	97		GRPH .
152	98	↑	GRPH o
153	99	↓	GRPH ,
154	9A	→	GRPH l
155	9B	←	GRPH k
156	9C		GRPH 2
157	9D		GRPH 3
158	9E		GRPH 4
159	9F		GRPH 5
160	A0		CODE '
161	A1		CODE x

Appendix A

Decimal	Hex	Character	Key
162	A2	¢	CODE c
163	A3	£	GRPH 8
164	A4	˙	CODE "
165	A5	μ	CODE M
166	A6	∴	CODE)
167	A7	⊤	CODE −
168	A8	†	CODE +
169	A9	§	CODE s
170	AA	▯	CODE R
171	AB	▯	CODE C
172	AC	¼	CODE p
173	AD	½	CODE ;
174	AE	¾	CODE /
175	AF	¶	CODE 0
176	B0	¥	GRPH 7
177	B1	Ä	CODE A
178	B2	Ö	CODE O
179	B3	Ü	CODE U
180	B4	¤	GRPH 6
181	B5	¨	CODE [
182	B6	ä	CODE a
183	B7	ö	CODE o
184	B8	ü	CODE u
185	B9	ß	CODE S
186	BA	™	CODE T
187	BB	é	CODE d
188	BC	ù	CODE ,
189	BD	è	CODE v
190	BE	¨	CODE =
191	BF	ƒ	CODE F
192	C0	ã	CODE 1
193	C1	ê	CODE 3

ASCII Chart

Decimal	Hex	Character	Key
194	C2	î	CODE 8
195	C3	ê	CODE 9
196	C4	ü	CODE 7
197	C5	ʌ	CODE -
198	C6	ē	CODE e
199	C7	ï	CODE i
200	C8	ą	CODE q
201	C9	í	CODE k
202	CA	ó	CODE l
203	CB	ú	CODE j
204	CC	ý	CODE y
205	CD	ñ	CODE n
206	CE	ɜ	CODE z
207	CF	ö	CODE .
208	D0	Ä	CODE !
209	D1	Ê	CODE #
210	D2	Î	CODE *
211	D3	Ö	CODE (
212	D4	Ü	CODE &
213	D5	Ï	CODE l
214	D6	Ë	CODE E
215	D7	É	CODE D
216	D8	Á	CODE Q
217	D9	Í	CODE K
218	DA	Ó	CODE L
219	DB	Ú	CODE J
220	DC	⋄	CODE Y
221	DD	Ù	CODE <
222	DE	È	CODE V
223	DF	À	CODE X
224	E0		GRPH Z
225	E1	▦ (upper left)	GRPH !

Appendix A

Decimal	Hex	Character	Key
226	E2	(upper right)	GRPH @
227	E3	(lower left)	GRPH #
228	E4	(lower right)	GRPH $
229	E5		GRPH %
230	E6		GRPH ^
231	E7	(upper)	GRPH Q
232	E8	(lower)	GRPH W
233	E9	(left)	GRPH E
234	EA	(right)	GRPH R
235	EB		GRPH A
236	EC		GRPH S
237	ED		GRPH D
238	EE		GRPH F
239	EF		GRPH X
240	F0	┌	GRPH U
241	F1	─	GRPH P
242	F2	┐	GRPH O
243	F3	┬	GRPH I
244	F4	├	GRPH J
245	F5	│	GRPH :
246	F6	└	GRPH M
247	F7	┘	GRPH >
248	F8	┴	GRPH <
249	F9	┤	GRPH L
250	FA	┼	GRPH K
251	FB		GRPH H
252	FC		GRPH T
253	FD		GRPH G
254	FE		GRPH Y
255	FF		GRPH C

Appendix B

Control Codes

Control Code	Operation Performed
CTRL A	Moves the Cursor from current position to the beginning of the first word to the left.
CTRL B	Moves the Cursor from current position to the bottom of the Display.
CTRL C	Cancels a SELECT, SAVE, LOAD, FIND, or PRINT function.
CTRL D	Moves the Cursor one character to the right.
CTRL E	Moves the Cursor up one line from current line.
CTRL F	Moves the Cursor to the beginning of the next word to the right.
CTRL G	Saves a file or a program.
CTRL H	Deletes previous character.
CTRL I	TAB.
CTRL L	Same as SELECT Function Key.
CTRL M	Carriage Return and Line Feed.
CTRL N	Same as FIND Function Key.
CTRL O	Same as COPY Function Key.
CTRL Q	Moves the Cursor to the left-most position of the current line.
CTRL R	Moves the Cursor to the right-most position of the current line.
CTRL S	Moves the Cursor one character to the left.
CTRL T	Moves the Cursor to the top of the Display in the current column.
CTRL U	Same as CUT Function Key.
CTRL V	Same as LOAD Function Key.
CTRL W	Moves the Cursor to the beginning of the current file.
CTRL X	Moves the Cursor down one line from its current position.
CTRL Y	Prints the entire file.
CTRL Z	Moves the Cursor to the end of the current file.

Handwritten note: CTRL J = LINE FEED

CTRL P Allows embedding print codes in TEXT mode.

CTRL P allows control codes to be sent to the printer using the `SAVE TO:LPT:` format. This is only available in TEXT mode. When the text is printed using **SHIFT BREAK**, the control code is printed as an actual character and is not used as a control code.

For example, by placing **CTRL P CTRL O** in the text, and then sending the text to the printer with:

`Save to:LPT:` **ENTER**

the computer sends Control code 15 to the printer. On the Daisy Wheel II this turns on the underlining mode while it places the EPSON Graftrax plus printer into Compressed mode. Refer to your printer manual to determine the applicable control codes.

Appendix C

Reserved Words

@	FIX	NOT
ABS	FOR	ON
AND	FORMAT	OPEN
ASC	FRE	OR
ATN	FREE	OUT
AUTO	GOSUB	PEEK
BEEP	GOTO	POKE
CALL	HIMEM	POS
CDBL	IF	POSN
CHR$	INKEY$	POWER
CINT	INPUT$	PRESET
CLEAR	INSTR	PRINT
CLOAD	INT	PSET
CLOCK	IPL	RANDOM
CLOSE	KEY	READ
CLS	KEY LIST	REM
COM	KILL	RENAME
CONT	LCOPY	RESTORE
COS	LEFT$	RESUME
CSAVE	LEN	RIGHT$
CSAVEM	LET	RND
CSNG	LINE	RUN
CSRLIN	LIST	RUNM
DATA	LLIST	SAVE
DATE$	LINE INPUT#	SCREEN
DAY$	LOAD	SGN
DEFDBL	LOADM	SIN
DEFINT	LOC	SOUND
DEFSNG	LOF	SPACE$
DEFSTR	LOG	SQR
DEFUSR	LPOS	STEP
DELETE	LPRINT	STOP
DIM	MAXFILES	STR$
EDIT	MAXRAM	STRING$
ELSE	MDM	TAB
END	MENU	TAN
EOF	MERGE	THEN
ERL	MID$	TIME$
ERR	MOTOR	USING
ERROR	NAME	VAL
EXP	NEW	VARPTR
FILES	NEXT	VERIFY

Appendix D

Communication Parameters

Model 100 Communications Parameters		
	You Type:	For:
Baud Rate	M	Internal Modem (300 baud only)
	1	75 baud (RS-232C port only)
	2	110 baud "
	3	300 baud "
	4	600 baud "
	5	1200 baud "
	6	2400 baud "
	7	4800 baud "
	8	9600 baud "
	9	19200 baud "
Word Length	6	6 bits
	7	7 bits
	8	8 bits
Parity	I	Ignore parity
	O	Odd parity
	E	Even parity
	N	No parity
Stop Bit	1	1 stop bit
	2	2 stop bit
Line Status	E*	Enable XON/XOFF
	D*	Disable XON/XOFF
Pulse Rate	10	10pps
	20	20pps

*Note: **CTRL Q** sends XON, **CTRL S** sends XOFF.

Appendix E

Error Report Codes

Code	Message	Meaning
1	NF	NEXT without FOR.
2	SN	Syntax Error.
3	RG	RETURN without GOSUB.
4	OD	Out of Data.
5	FC	Illegal function call.
6	OV	Overflow.
7	OM	Out of Memory.
8	UL	Undefined line.
9	BS	Bad Subscript.
10	DD	Double Dimensioned Array.
11	/0	Division by Zero.
12	ID	Illegal Direct.
13	TM	Type Mismatch.
14	OS	Out of String Space.
15	LS	String Too Long.
16	ST	String Formula Too Complex.
17	CN	Can't Continue.
18	IO	Error.
19	NR	No RESUME.
20	RW	RESUME Without Error.
21	UE	Undefined Error.
22	MO	Missing Operand.
23-49	UE	Undefined Error.
50	IE	Undefined Error.
51	BN	Bad File Number.
52	FF	File Not Found.

Code	Message	Meaning
53	AO	Already Open.
54	EF	Input Past End of File.
55	NM	Bad File Name.
56	DS	Direct Statement in File.
57	FL	Undefined Error.
58	CF	File Not Open.
59-255	UE	Undefined Error.

Appendix F

Hex-to-Decimal Conversion Chart

HEX CODE	Most Significant Bytes		Least Significant Bytes	
	IV	III	II	I
0	0	0	0	0
1	4096	256	16	1
2	8192	512	32	2
3	12288	768	48	3
4	16384	1024	64	4
5	20480	1280	80	5
6	24576	1536	96	6
7	28672	1792	112	7
8	32768	2048	128	8
9	36864	2304	144	9
A	40960	2560	160	10
B	45056	2816	176	11
C	49152	3072	192	12
D	53248	3328	208	13
E	57344	3584	224	14
F	61440	3840	240	15

Decimal Value = IV + III + II + I

Appendix G

Answers to Exercises

Sample answer for EXERCISE 5-1:
```
50 PRINT D
```

Sample run for EXERCISE 5-1:
```
6000
```

Note: You may have used a different Line number in your answer but the way to get the answer printed on the screen is by using the PRINT statement. If you didn't get it right the first time don't be discouraged. Type in Line 50 above and RUN the program. Then return to Chapter 5 and continue.

Sample answer for EXERCISE 5-2:
```
10 REM *TIME SOLUTION*
20 D = 6000
30 R = 500
40 T = D / R
50 PRINT "IT TAKES";T;"HOURS."
```

Note: Remember to **ENTER** each Line.

Sample run for EXERCISE 5-2:
```
IT TAKES 12 HOURS.
```

Note: In order to arrive at the formula in Line 40 it is necessary to transpose D = R * T and express in terms of T.

Sample answer for EXERCISE 5-3:
```
10 REM *CIRCUMFERENCE SOLUTION*
20 D = 35
30 C = 3.14 * D
40 PRINT "CIRCUMFERENCE =";C;"FEET."
```

Sample run for EXERCISE 5-3:
```
CIRCUMFERENCE = 109.9 FEET.
```

Sample answer for EXERCISE 5-4:
```
10 REM *CIRCULAR AREA SOLUTION*
20 R = 5
30 A = 3.14 * R * R
40 PRINT "AREA =";A;"SQUARE INCHES."
```

Sample run for EXERCISE 5-4:
```
AREA = 78.5 SQUARE INCHES.
```

Sample answer for EXERCISE 5-5:
A bare-minimum effort might look like this: (C = checks, D = deposits, B = old balance, N = new balance.)
```
10 B = 225
20 C = 17 + 35 + 225
30 D = 40 + 200
40 N = B - C + D
50 PRINT "YOUR NEW BALANCE IS $";N
```

Sample run for EXERCISE 5-5:
```
YOUR NEW BALANCE IS $ 188
```

Sample answer for EXERCISE 6-1:
```
10 REM CAR MILES SOLUTION
20 N = 100000000
30 D = 1000000
40 T = N * D
50 PRINT "TOTAL MILES DRIVEN IS";T
```

Sample run for EXERCISE 6-1:
```
TOTAL MILES DRIVEN IS 1E+14
```

Note: As discussed earlier, this answer is the number 1 followed by 14 zeroes. 100,000,000,000,000. One hundred Trillion. The Computer will not print any numbers over 99,999,999,999,999 without converting them to exponential notation.

Sample answer for EXERCISE 6-2:
```
20 N = 1E+8
30 D = 1E+6
```

Sample run for EXERCISE 6-2:
```
TOTAL MILES DRIVEN IS 1E+14
```

Note: The answer came out exactly the same as before, meaning we not only receive answers in SSN, but can also use it in our programs.

Sample answer for EXERCISE 7-1:
```
10 REM *FAHRENHEIT TO CELSIUS CONV.*
20 F = 65
30 C = (F - 32) * (5 / 9)
40 PRINT F;"DEG. FAHR.=";C;"DEG. CEL."
```

Sample run for EXERCISE 7-1:
```
65 DEG. FAHR. = 18.333333333333 DEG. CEL.
```

Observe carefully how the parentheses were placed. As a general rule, when in doubt -- use parentheses. The worst they can do is slow down calculating the answer by a few millionths of a second.

Sample answer for EXERCISE 7-2:
```
30 C = F - 32 * (5/9)
```

Sample run for EXERCISE 7-2:
```
65 DEG. FAHR. = 47.222222 DEG. CEL.
```

Note how silently and dutifully the Computer came up with the *wrong* answer. It has done as we directed, and we directed it wrong.

A common phrase in Computer circles is GIGO (pronounced "gee-goe"). It stands for "Garbage In - Garbage Out". We have given the Computer garbage and it gave it back to us by way of a wrong answer.

Phrased another way, "Never in the history of mankind has there been a machine capable of making so many mistakes so rapidly and confidently." A Computer is worthless unless it is programmed correctly.

Sample answer for EXERCISE 7-3:
```
30 C = (F - 32) * 5/9
```

Sample run for EXERCISE 7-3:
```
65 DEG. FAHR. = 18.333333 DEG. CEL.
```

Sample answer for EXERCISE 7-4:
Two possible answers: 30 - (9 - 8) - (7 - 6) = 28
30 - (9 - (8 - (7 - 6))) = 28
Sample programs:
```
10 A = 30 - (9 - (8 - (7 - 6)))
20 PRINT A
```
Or Line 10 might be
```
10 A = 30 - (9 - 8)- (7 - 6)
```
Try a few on your own.

Sample answer for EXERCISE 8-1:
```
10 A = 5
20 IF A <> 5 THEN GOTO 50
30 PRINT "A EQUALS 5"
40 END
50 PRINT "A DOES NOT EQUAL 5"
```

Sample run for EXERCISE 8-1:
```
A EQUALS 5
```

Sample answer for EXERCISE 8-2:
```
10 A = 6
20 IF A <> 5 THEN GOTO 50
30 PRINT "A EQUALS 5"
40 END
50 PRINT "A DOES NOT EQUAL 5"
60 IF A < 5 THEN GOTO 90
70 PRINT "A IS LARGER THAN 5"
80 END
90 PRINT "A IS SMALLER THAN 5"
```

Sample run for EXERCISE 8-2:
```
A DOES NOT EQUAL 5
A IS LARGER THAN 5
```

Note: We had to put in another STOP statement (Line 80) to keep the program from running on to Line 90 after printing Line 70.

530   Appendix G

Sample answer for EXERCISE 13-1:
```
1 CLS
2 INPUT "HOW MANY SECONDS DELAY DO YOU WISH";S
3 P = 330
4 D = S * P
5 FOR X = 1 TO D
6 NEXT X
7 PRINT "DELAY IS OVER.  TOOK";S;"SECONDS."
```

Explanation:
  Line 1 CLearS the screen to get ready for Line 2.
  Line 2 uses INPUT to ask how many seconds you wish to delay.
  Line 3 defined P, the number of passes required for a one-second delay.
  Line 4 multiplied the delay for one second times number of seconds desired, and called that product D.
  Line 5 began the FOR-NEXT loop from 1 to whatever is required.
  Line 6 is the other half of the loop.
  Line 7 reports the delay is over, and prints S, the number of seconds. Obviously, S is only as accurate as the program itself since it merely copies the value of S you entered in Line 2.

Sample answer for EXERCISE 13-2:
```
10 PRINT "*** SALARY RATE CHART ***"
20 PRINT
30 PRINT "YEAR","MONTH"
40 PRINT
50 FOR Y = 5000 TO 20000 STEP 1000
60 REM *CONVERT YEARLY INCOME INTO MONTHLY*
70 M=Y/12
80 PRINT Y,M
90 NEXT Y
```

Sample run for EXERCISE 13-2:
```
*** SALARY RATE CHART ***

YEAR            MONTH

5000            416.6666666667
6000            500
7000            583.3333333333
                etc...
```

Sample answer for EXERCISE 13-3:
```
10 R = .01
20 D = 1
30 T = .01
35 CLS
40 PRINT "DAY","DAILY             TOTAL"
50 PRINT " # ","RATE              EARNED"
60 PRINT
70 PRINT D, R;"              ";T
80 IF R >= 1000000 THEN END
90 R = 2 * R
100 D = D + 1
110 T = T + R
120 GOTO 70
```

Sample run for EXERCISE 13-3:
```
DAY            DAILY          TOTAL
 #             RATE           EARNED

 1             .01            .01
 2             .02            .03
 3             .04            .07
                              etc...
```

Sample answer for EXERCISE 13-4:
```
5 CLS
10 PRINT "LENGTH","WIDTH             AREA"
20 FOR L = 0 TO 500 STEP 50
30 W = (1000 - 2 * L)/2
40 A = L * W
50 PRINT L, W;"             ";A
60 NEXT L
```

Sample run for EXERCISE 13-4:
```
LENGTH         WIDTH          AREA
 0             500            0
 50            450            22500
                              etc...
```

Sample answer for EXERCISE 14-1:
```
10 PRINT "THE         TOTAL       SPENT"
20 PRINT "BUDGET","YEAR'S        THIS"
30 PRINT "CATEGORY";TAB(14);"BUDGET";
TAB(24);"MONTH"
```

Sample answer for EXERCISE 14-2:
```
10 PRINT "*** SALARY RATE CHART ***"
20 PRINT
30 PRINT " YEAR";TAB(8);"MONTH";TAB(25);
"WEEKLY"
40 PRINT
50 FOR Y = 5000 TO 20000 STEP 1000
60 REM *CONVERT YEARLY INCOME INTO MONTHLY*
70 M=Y/12
80 W=M/4
90 PRINT Y;TAB(7);M;TAB(24);W
100 NEXT Y
```

Sample answer for EXERCISE 15-1:
```
10 FOR A=1 TO 2
20 PRINT "A LOOP"
30 FOR B=1 TO 2
40 PRINT "    B LOOP"
42 FOR C=1 TO 3
44 PRINT "       C LOOP"
48 NEXT C
50 NEXT B
60 NEXT A
```

Sample answer for EXERCISE 16-1:
Addition of the following single Line gives a nice clean printout with all values "rounded" to their integer value:

```
55 A = INT(A)
```

Worth all the effort to learn it, wasn't it?

Sample answer for EXERCISE 16-2:
```
55 A=INT (10*A)/10
```

When 3.1415927 was multiplied times 10 it became 31.415927. The INTeger value of 31.415927 is 31. 31 divided by 10 is 3.1. Etc...

Sample answer for EXERCISE 16-3:
This was almost too easy.
```
55  A=INT (100*A)/100
```

Sample answer for EXERCISE 16-4:
```
85 T = INT(10*T)/10
```

Sample answer for EXERCISE 17-1:
```
10 INPUT "TYPE ANY NUMBER";X
20 T = SGN(X)
30 ON T+2 GOTO 50,60,70
40 END
50 PRINT "THE NUMBER IS NEGATIVE."
55 END
60 PRINT "THE NUMBER IS ZERO."
65 END
70 PRINT "THE NUMBER IS POSITIVE."
```

Sample answer for EXERCISE 18-1:
See Appendix H -- user programs.

Sample answer for EXERCISE 18-2:
```
10 GOSUB 10000
10000 S=VAL(RIGHT$(TIME$,2))
10010 FOR N=1 TO S
10020 D=RND(1)
10030 NEXT N
10040 RETURN
```

Sample answer for EXERCISE 21-1:
```
10 PRINT CHR$(77);CHR$(79);CHR$(68);
20 PRINT CHR$(69);CHR$(76);CHR$(32);
30 PRINT CHR$(49);CHR$(48);CHR$(48)
```

Sample answer for EXERCISE 22-1:
```
10 CLS
20 INPUT "FIRST STRING"; A$
30 INPUT "SECOND STRING"; B$
40 PRINT : PRINT "ALPHABETICAL ORDER:"
50 IF A$<B$ THEN PRINT A$,B$ : END
60 PRINT B$,A$
```

Appendix G

Sample answer for EXERCISE 23-1:
```
10 PRINT "INPUT STRING"
20 INPUT A$
30 IF LEN (A$)>10 THEN GOTO 50
40 STOP
50 PRINT "10 CHARACTER LIMIT WAS EXCEEDED."
```

Sample answer for EXERCISE 23-2
```
10 CLS
20 INPUT "ENTER PASSWORD"; A$
30 FOR X=1 TO 11
40 READ N
50 P$ = P$ + CHR$(N)
60 NEXT X
70 IF A$ = P$ THEN 100
80 PRINT "WRONG PASSWORD - GET LOST"
90 END
100 PRINT "CORRECT PASSWORD - ENTER"
110 DATA 79,80,69,78,32,83,69,83,65,77,69
```

Sample answer for EXERCISE 24-1
```
10 CLS
20 INPUT "INPUT YOUR STREET ADDRESS";A$
30 A = VAL(A$): PRINT
40 PRINT "YOUR NEIGHBOR'S STREET NUMBER IS"; A+4
```

Sample answer for EXERCISE 24-2
```
10 CLS
20 FOR X = 101 TO 120
30 A$ = STR$(X)
40 PRINT A$+"WT",
50 NEXT X
```

Sample run for EXERCISE 24-2
```
101WT          102WT
103WT          104WT
105WT          106WT
107WT          108WT
109WT          110WT
111WT          112WT
113WT          114WT
```

Sample answer for EXERCISE 25-1:
```
10 CLS
20 INPUT "ISN'T THIS A SMART COMPUTER";A$
30 B$ = LEFT$(A$,1)
40 IF B$ = "Y" THEN PRINT "AFFIRMATIVE": END
50 IF B$ = "N" THEN PRINT "NEGATIVE": END
60 PRINT "THIS IS A YES OR NO QUESTION"
70 GOTO 20
```

Sample answer for EXERCISE 25-2:
```
10 CLS: MAX$=""
20 FOR I = 1 TO 3
30 READ A$
40 N$ = MID$(A$,2,3)
50 IF N$>MAX$ THEN MAX$=N$ : P$=A$
60 NEXT I
70 PRINT "THE PART NUMBER WITH THE LARGEST"
80 PRINT "NUMERIC PORTION IS ";P$
90 PRINT: LIST
100 DATA N106WT,A208FM,Z154DX
```

Sample answer for EXERCISE 25-3:
Choice C: P-

Sample answer for EXERCISE 25-4:
```
1 CLS
10 A$ = STRING$(20,42)
20 PRINT TAB(20-LEN(A$)/2);A$
30 PRINT : LIST
```

Sample answer for EXERCISE 27-1:
```
10 A = 5
20 B = 12
30 C = SQR (A 2+B 2)
40 PRINT "THE SQUARE ROOT OF ";A;" SQUARED"
50 PRINT "PLUS ";B;" SQUARED IS ";C
```

Sample answer for EXERCISE 27-2:
```
10 PRINT "ENTER A NUMBER"; N
20 PRINT "LOG (EXP ";N;") = "; LOG
(EXP(N))
30 PRINT "EXP (LOG ";N;") = "; EXP
(LOG(N))
40 PRINT
50 GOTO 10
```

Sample answer for EXERCISE 29-1:
```
10 PRINT "START HORIZ. BLOCK (0-239)"; H
30 PRINT "END HORIZ. BLOCK (0-239)"; I
50 PRINT "START VERT. BLOCK (0-63)"; V
70 PRINT "END VERT. BLOCK (0-63)"; W
90 CLS
100 FOR X = H TO I
110 FOR Y = V TO W
120 PSET X,Y
130 NEXT Y
140 NEXT X
```

Sample answer for EXERCISE 29-2:
Delete Lines 40 and 60 and change Lines 30 and 50 to:
```
30 FOR H = 0 TO 318
50   PRINT CHR$(239);
```

Sample answer for EXERCISE 30-1:
A. MOVE THE DOT DOWN
```
10 PRINT "HORIZ. START (0-63)"
20 INPUT H
30 PRINT "VERT. START (0-42)"
40 INPUT V
50 CLS
60 PRESET (H,V+1)
70 PSET (H,V)
80 V=V-1
90 IF V>0 THEN GOTO 60
```

B. MOVE THE DOT TO THE LEFT
```
10 PRINT "HORIZ. START (1-62)"
20 INPUT H
30 PRINT "VERT. START (0-43)"
40 INPUT V
50 CLS
60 PRESET (H+1,V)
70 PSET (H,V)
80 H=H-1
90 IF H>0 THEN GOTO 60
```

Sample answer for EXERCISE 30-2:
```
60 LINE (145,40)-(145,60)
70 LINE -(195,60): LINE -(195,40)
```

Sample answer for EXERCISE 31-1:
Insert the following Lines:
```
144 P = ABS(55+(315*(V>50)))
145 PRINT @P,"PING!": BEEP
155 PRINT @P,"     "
```
Note that PRINT@ both prints the "PING" and makes it disappear by printing blanks in its place.

Sample answer for EXERCISE 35-1:
```
10 CLS: PRINT TAB(17) "CREDITS   TAX    TOTAL"
20 FOR I = 1 TO 3
30 READ A$,X,Y,Z
39 REM    1234567890123456789012345678901 23
40 U$="\               \   ##.#      .#    ##.#"
50 PRINT USING U$;A$,X,Y,Z
60 NEXT I
70 READ A$,N
80 V$="\    \  ###.##"
90 PRINT TAB(29);: PRINT USING V$;A$,N;
100 DATA ASTRAL COMPUTER, 18.3,,7,19.0
110 DATA BIOFEEDBACK ADAPTER, 1.8,0,1.8
120 DATA PERSONALITY MODULE, 7.2,,3,7.5
130 DATA "DUE:", 28.3
```

Sample answer for EXERCISE 37-1:
Add or change the following lines:
```
5 DIM A(210)
10 INPUT "WHICH CAR TO EXAMINE";W
130 FOR B = 201 TO 210
135 READ A(B)
140 NEXT B
180 PRINT "LIC. #";TAB(10);"ENG. SIZE";
185 PRINT TAB(24);"COLOR";TAB(33);"STYLE"
210 PRINT W;TAB(10);A(W);TAB(24);A(W+100);
215 PRINT TAB(33);A(W+200)
400 DATA 20,20,10,20,30,20,30,10,20,20
```

Sample answer for EXERCISE 37-2:
DELETE Lines 50,55, and 60, and change Line 30 to:
```
30 DIM A(52) : FOR C=1 TO 52: A(C)=C: NEXT C
```

Sample answer for EXERCISE 38-1:
Change Line 50 to:
```
50 IF A$(F) >= A$(S) THEN 90
```

An alternate approach is to reverse the order of printing:

```
110 FOR D=N TO 1 STEP -1: PRINT A$(D): NEXT D
```

Sample answer for EXERCISE 39-1:
```
10 CLS
20 FOR E=1 TO 4
30 FOR D=1 TO 4
40 REM ENTRY DATA : NAME, NUMBER, $$$
50 READ R$(E,D)
60 PRINT R$(E,D),
70 NEXT D: PRINT
80 NEXT E: PRINT
1000 REM * DATA FILE *
1010 DATA "JONES, C.","10439        100.00"
1020 DATA "ROTH, J.","10023         87.24"
1030 DATA "BAKER, H.","12936        398.34"
1040 DATA "HARMON, D.","10422        23.17"
```

Sample answer for EXERCISE 39-2:
Add:

```
100 REM * SORT *
110 FOR F=1 TO 3
120   FOR S=F+1 TO 4
130     IF R$(F,1) <= R$(S,1) THEN 190
140       FOR J=1 TO 3
150         T$ = R$(F,J)
160         R$(F,J) = R$(S,J)
170         R$(S,J) = T$
180       NEXT J
190   NEXT S
200 NEXT F
210 PRINT : PRINT "ALPHA SORT" : PRINT
220 FOR E=1 TO 4
230   FOR D=1 TO 3
240     PRINT R$(E,D),
250   NEXT D: PRINT
260 NEXT E
```

Sample answer for EXERCISE 39-3:
Change these lines:
```
130 IF VAL(R$(F,3)) <= VAL(R$(S,3))
    THEN 190
210 PRINT : PRINT "NUMERIC SORT": PRINT
```

Sample answer for EXERCISE 40-1:
Change Line 20 to:
```
20 FOR P=1 TO 320
```

Sample answer for EXERCISE 40-2:
Graphic codes for the "snail":
```
228,233,230,239,229,224
224,231,231,231,231,231
```

Appendix G

Sample answer for EXERCISE 44-1:
```
10 PRINT "IS GATE 'X' OPEN?"
20 INPUT A$
30 PRINT "IS GATE 'Y' OPEN?"
40 INPUT B$
50 PRINT "IS GATE 'Z' OPEN?"
60 INPUT C$
70 PRINT
80 IF A$="Y" OR B$="Y" OR C$="Y" THEN 110
90 PRINT "OLD BESS IS SECURE."
100 END
110 PRINT "A GATE IS OPEN."
120 PRINT "OLD BESS CAN GRAZE."
```

Sample answer for EXERCISE 48-1:
```
10 REM *TEST GRADER*
20 PRINT "ENTER FIVE ANSWERS"
30 N=0 : CLS
40 DIM B(5)
50 FOR J=1 TO 5: READ B(J): NEXT
100 FOR I=1 TO 5
110 PRINT "ANSWER NUMBER";I;":";
120 INPUT A
130 PRINT A,B(I)
140 IF A=B(I) THEN GOTO 170
150 PRINT "WRONG"
160 GOTO 190
170 PRINT "CORRECT"
180 N=N+1
190 PRINT
200 NEXT I
210 PRINT N;" RIGHT OUT OF 5 IS ";
220 PRINT N/5*100;" PERCENT."
230 DATA 12,45,38,26,39
```

Sample answer for EXERCISE 48-2:
```
100 CLS
110 PRINT "SELECT ONE OF THE FOLLOWING INVESTMENTS"
120 PRINT "  1 - CERTIFICATE OF DEPOSIT"
130 PRINT "  2 - BANK SAVINGS ACCOUNT"
140 PRINT "  3 - CREDIT UNION"
150 PRINT "  4 - MORTGAGE LOAN"
160 INPUT "INVESTMENT (1-4):";F
170 ON F GOTO 1000, 2000, 3000, 4000
180 GOTO 100 : REM F NOT BETWEEN 1 AND 4
1000 REM * CERTIFICATE OF DEPOSIT *
1010 PRINT "THE C.D. PROGRAM IS NOT YET WRITTEN."
1020 GOSUB 10000: GOTO 100
2000 REM * SAVINGS ACCOUNT PROGRAM *
2010 CLS: PRINT "THE ROUTINE CALCULATES SIMPLE"
2020 PRINT "INTEREST ON DOLLARS HELD IN DEPOSIT"
2030 PRINT "FOR A SPECIFIED PERIOD USING"
2040 PRINT "A SPECIFIED % OF INTEREST."
2050 INPUT "AMOUNT OF DEPOSIT (DOLLARS): ";P
2060 INPUT "HELD FOR HOW MANY DAYS:";D
2070 CLS: PRINT "FOR A STARTING PRINCIPAL OF"
2080 PRINT "$";P;"AT A RATE OF";R;"%
2090 PRINT "FOR";D;"DAYS.  THE INTEREST AMOUNTS"
2100 PRINT "TO $";R/100/365 * D * P
2110 END
3000 REM * CREDIT UNION PROG. *
3010 PRINT "THE C.U. PROGRAM NOT YET WRITTEN."
3020 GOSUB 10000 : GOTO 100
4000 REM * MORTGAGE LOAN PROG. *
4010 PRINT "THE M.L. PROGRAM NOT YET WRITTEN."
4020 GOSUB 10000 : GOTO 100
10000 FOR I=1 = 1 TO 1000 : NEXT : RETURN
```

Sample answer for EXERCISE 50-1:

```
10 ON ERROR GOTO 100
20 CLS
30 FOR I = 1 TO 10
40 X = RND(21)-1 : F = X-10/X
50 PRINT I, "X=";X,"F(X)=";F;
60 IF F<0 THEN PUNT ELSE PRINT
70 NEXT I
80 INPUT "PRESS ENTER TO CONTINUE";Z: GOTO 20
100 IF ERR = 2 THEN 140
110 IF ERR = 11 THEN 130
120 PRINT "ERROR";ERR: END
130 PRINT "ATTEMPT TO DIVIDE BY ZERO IN ";ERL
135 RESUME NEXT
140 PRINT "SYNTAX ERROR IN LINE ";ERL
150 RESUME NEXT
```

Appendix H

User Programs

12-Hour Clock

```
1 REM *COPYRIGHT 1983 D.A. LIEN*
3 REM <<<12-HOUR CLOCK>>>
10 PRINT "THE HOUR IS"
20 INPUT E
30 LET F=INT (E/10)
40 LET E=E-(F*10)
50 PRINT "THE MINUTES ARE"
60 INPUT C
70 LET D=INT (C/10)
80 LET C=C-(D*10)
90 PRINT "THE SECONDS ARE"
100 INPUT A
110 CLS
120 LET B=INT (A/10)
130 LET A=A-(B*10)
140 FOR N=1 TO 90
150 NEXT N
160 LET A=A+5
170 IF A>9 THEN GOTO 190
180 GOTO 380
190 LET A=0
200 LET B=B+1
210 IF B>5 THEN GOTO 230
220 GOTO 380
230 LET B=0
240 LET C=C+1
250 IF C>9 THEN GOTO 270
260 GOTO 380
270 LET C=0
280 LET D=D+1
290 IF D>5 THEN GOTO 310
300 GOTO 380
310 LET D=0
```

```
320 LET E=E+1
330 IF E>9 THEN GOTO 350
340 GOTO 370
350 LET E=0
360 LET F=F+1
370 IF (F=1) AND (E=3) THEN GOSUB 400
380 PRINT AT 8,22,F;E;":";D;C;":";B;A
390 GOTO 140
400 LET A=0
410 LET B=0
420 LET C=0
430 LET D=0
440 LET E=1
450 LET F=0
460 RETURN
```

Checksum For Business

For those responsible for inventory numbers or check clearing and balancing in business, a checksum is a most useful testing "code". This simple program calculates error-free checksums almost instantly. It is designed for 6-digit numbers and so can be used for stock number verification or other applications.

```
1 REM *COPYRIGHT (C) 1983 BY
2 REM *COMPUSOFT PUBLISHING*
3 REM <<< CHECKSUM >>>
10 PRINT "FIRST DIGIT IS ";
20 INPUT A
30 PRINT A
40 PRINT "SECOND DIGIT IS ";
50 INPUT B
60 PRINT B
70 PRINT  "THIRD DIGIT IS ";
80 INPUT C
90 PRINT C
100 PRINT  "FOURTH DIGIT IS ";
110 INPUT D
120 PRINT D
130 PRINT "FIFTH DIGIT IS ";
140 INPUT E
```

```
150 PRINT E
160 PRINT "SIXTH DIGIT IS ";
170 INPUT F
180 PRINT F
190 PRINT
200 PRINT "THE NUMBER IS
";A;B;C;D;E;F
210 LET S=A+2*B+C+2*D+E+2*F
220 LET T=INT (S/10)
230 LET U=S-T*10
240 LET S=T+U
250 IF S>9 THEN GOTO 220
260 PRINT "CHECKDIGIT IS ";S
```

Craps

The game is as old as history. A testimonial to the intelligence and ingenuity of our ancient ancestors. An excellent way to demonstrate the running of twin Random Number Generators.

You don't need to know how to play the game -- the Computer will quickly teach you.....There's one born every minute...)

```
1 REM *COPYRIGHT (C) 1983 D.A. LIEN*
3 REM <<<CRAPS>>>
10 RAND 0
20 PRINT "PRESS <ENTER>";
30 PRINT " TO CONTINUE"
40 INPUT A$
50 CLS
60 GOSUB 300
70 LET P=N
80 PRINT
90 PRINT "YOU ROLLED ";P,
100 IF P=1 THEN GOTO 140
110 IF P<4 OR P=12 THEN GOTO 200
120 IF P<>7 AND P<11 THEN GOTO 150
130 IF P=7 OR P=11 THEN GOTO 170
140 REM *P CAN NOT EQUAL 1*
150 PRINT "YOUR POINT IS ";N
160 GOTO 230
170 PRINT "YOU WIN."
180 PRINT
```

```
190 GOTO 20
200 PRINT "YOU LOSE."
210 PRINT
220 GOTO 20
230 GOSUB 300
240 LET M=N
250 PRINT
260 PRINT "YOU ROLLED ";M,
270 IF P=M THEN GOTO 170
280 IF M=7 THEN GOTO 200
290 GOTO 230
300 LET A=INT (RND*6+1)
310 LET B=INT (RND*6+1)
320 LET N=A+B
330 RETURN
```

Automatic Ticket Number Drawer

Like to make a big splash at the next Rotary Club, Country Fair, or other ticket drawing giveaway? This program uses the random number generator to pick the lucky number(s) and eliminate charges of stuffing the ticket box, besides giving the whole affair some pizzazz. If your own number comes up and you are charged with rigging the computer, you're on your own.

```
1 REM *COPYRIGHT(C) 1983 D.A. LIEN*
3 REM <<<TICKET NO. DRAWER>>>
10 RAND 0
20 REM *PICKS WINNER TICKET*
30 PRINT
40 PRINT "LOWEST TICKET NO. IS"
50 INPUT B
60 PRINT
70 PRINT "HIGHEST TICKET NO. IS"
80 INPUT H
90 PRINT
100 LET E=H-B+1
110 PRINT "NO. OF WINNERS"
120 INPUT W
130 CLS
140 PRINT
150 PRINT
```

```
160 PRINT
170 PRINT "AND THE WINNING";
180 IF W>1 THEN GOTO 210
190 PRINT " TICKET IS"
200 GOTO 220
210 PRINT " TICKETS ARE"
220 PRINT
230 FOR N=1 TO W
240 LET Z = RND*E
250 PRINT
260 PRINT TAB 12; ">----->>>   " ; INT (Z+B-1)
270 NEXT N
```

Index

INDEX

A

ABS 294
ADDRSS 51
AND 442
Animation 410
APPEND 463
Arrays 375
    Multi-Dimension 395
    Vector Arrays 395
    Numeric 376
    String 385
    String Matrices 399
ANSwer 95
ARCCOS 304
ARCSIN 304
ASCII 246
ASC 248
ASCII format 453
Assembly Language Call 467
ATN 303
Auto Log-On 84

B

Batteries 1, 15
BEEP 402, 425
BREAK 170
Buffer 459
Byte 5, 160

C

CALL 467
Calling a subroutine 214

Cassette
    connection 31
    operation 166
    interface 166
CHR$ 247
CDBL 289
CINT 289
CLEAR 258, 277
CLOAD 168
CLOSE 461
Clock 3
CLS 178
COM 457, 477
Communications Parameters 91
Concatenate (+) 260
Conditional branching statements 148
Conditional tests (IF, THEN) 148
CONT 184
COPY 30
COS 301, 337
CSAVE 166
CSAVEM 468
CSNG 289
CSRLIN 473
CTRL-C 107
Cursor 25
CUT 37

D

DATA 226
DATE$ 3
DAY$ 5
Debugging 210, 489
Decrement 176

DEFDBL 286
DEFINT 288
DEFSNG 284
DEFSTR 257
DEL 9
Deleting 25
DIM 380
Downloading 77, 94
Dumping 166
Duplex (Half/Full) 92

E

Endless Loop 171
E-notation 138
EDIT 116
EDIT. 120
ELSE 244
END 113
ENTER 103, 242
EOF 464
EQV 449
ERL 504
ERR 504
ERROR 500
Error Codes and Messages 501
ESC 8
EXP 298

F

Files
    MAXFILES 459
    OPEN 459
    CLOSE 461
    OUTPUT 459
    APPEND 463
    PRINT# 461
    INPUT$ 465
    LINE INPUT 465
    INPUT# 463
FIND 29
FIX(N) 292
Flags (Debugging) 206, 497

Flowcharting 483
FOR (Files) 459
FOR - NEXT 171, 193
FRE(0) 160
Function Keys 13, 122, 475
Functions
    arithmetic 157
    integer 199
    intrinsic 292
    string 268

G

GOSUB 214
GOTO 148
Graphics 309, 405
Graphing with PRINT AT 335

H

HIMEM 474

I

IF - THEN 147
Image Line -- see Print Using
Immediate Mode 157
IMP 450
Increment 176
INKEY$ 340
INKEY$ Buffer 341
INKEY$ Graphics 416
INP 470
INPUT 152, 242
    Real Time Input 416
INPUT# 463
INPUT$ 465
Inserting 25
INSTR 273
INT 199, 292
Inverse trigonometry 303
IPL 478

Index 553

K

Keyboard 6
KEY LIST 122
KEY ON, OFF, STOP 475, 476
KILL 169

L

LABEL 13
LCOPY 368
LEFT$ 268
LEN 256
LET (optional) 132
LINE 326
Line editor 116
LINE INPUT 465, 474
Line Numbers 108
Line Printer 365
LIST 112, 183
LIST ### 183
LLIST 366
LOAD 164
LOADM 470
LOG 295
LPOS 473
LPRINT 365
LPRINT TAB 366
LPRINT USING 368, 473

(margin note: LINE FEED p 96 ← pointing to Line editor)
(margin note: SEE SAVE p 458 next to LLIST)

M

Math Operators 129
Matrix 379
MAXFILES 459
MAXRAM 474
MDM 457, 477
Memory 5, 160
Memory Address 435
Memory Map 436
MERGE 453
MID$ 269
Modem 60, 457

Modular Programming 483
Module 483
MOTOR ON, OFF 478
Multi-Dimension arrays 395
Multiple Statement Lines 235

N

Nested FOR-NEXT loops 194
NEW 106
NEXT, optional 244
NOT 447
Null Modem Adapter 91

O

ON ERROR GOTO/GOSUB 502
ON - GOTO/GOSUB 210, 476
OPEN 459
Operators
   arithmetic 129
   Logical 442
   Relational 146
OR 447, 449
ORIGinate 95
Order of Operations 141, 448
OUT 470
OUTPUT 459

P

Parentheses 141
PAUSE 177
PEEK 435
Pixel 309
POKE 438
Power (Electrical) 15
POWER (Run time) 479
POS(N) 244
PRESET 309
PRINT 104, 108
PRINT AT 330
PRINT# 461

PRINT TAB   188
PRINT USING   347, 356
Print Zones   135, 179, 189
Program   — PRINTERS 28
   listing   112
   resident   131
Protective ENDs   181, 197
PSET   309

Q

Quotation marks   104

R

Radians   301
RAM   43, 452
READ   226
REM   112
RESERVE WORDS 521
Reset Button   6, 107
Resident Program   131
RESTORE   230
RESUME   503
RETURN   214
RIGHT$ 269
RND(X)   218
ROM   435
RS-232C Port   94, 457
RUN   106, 183
RUN ###   183
RUNM   470

S

SAVE   163, 455, 457-458
SAVEM   468
Saving on Cassette 166, 457
SCHEDL   43
Scientific notation   138
SCREEN   473
Search   387

SELect   37
SGN   213
SIN   300, 335
Soft Keys   13, 122
Sorting   387
SOUND, ON, OFF   431
Special graphic characters   11
Speed Dialing   84
SQR   293
STEP   173
STOP   184
STRING$ 276
Strings
   arrays   385
   comparisons   251
   length   256
   manipulation   260
   packed   409
   variables   238
STR$ 267
Subroutine   214
Syntax Error   109

T

TAB   188
TAN   301, 337
TELCOM   59, 68
TEXT   7, 24
THEN   147
TIME$ 5
Timer loop   181
TO   171
Travel Kit   63
Trigonometric Functions   300
Troubleshooting   158, 500

U

Unconditional branching   148
Uploading   82, 93

V

VAL 264
Variables
    names   137, 237
    numeric   132
    string   238
VARPTR   470
Video Display Worksheet   310

W

Word Processing   23
    Cursor Speed   25
    Inserting   25
    Deleting   25
    Print Outs   27
    FIND   29
    COPY   30
    PASTE   30
    CUT   37
    Cassette Storage   31
    SELect   37

XYZ

XOR   450

\+   129
−   129
*   129
^   293
/   129
,   120
;   153, 188
( )   141
=   129
\>   146
<   146
<>   146
<=   146
\>=   146
◀ Left arrow   7, 418
▶ Right arrow   7, 418
▲ Up arrow   7, 418
▼ Down arrow   7, 418

COMPUSOFT® PUBLISHING

A DIVISION OF COMPUSOFT, INC., SAN DIEGO

Customer Service Dept. 100a
P.O. Box 19669
San Diego, CA 92119

Thank you for purchasing *The TRS-80 Model 100 Portable Computer*.

Every book that deals with the rapidly changing field of personal computers requires updating. *The TRS-80 Model 100 Portable Computer* is no exception.

We at CompuSoft Publishing want to be certain that you are informed of any changes, updates or errors. If you fill out this page and return it to us we will send you the latest UPDATE MEMORANDUM without charge.

Name _____

Street _____

City _____ State _____ Zip _____

For Additional Copies

of

The TRS-80 Model 100 Portable Computer
A Complete Step-by-Step Learner's Manual

Contact your local Computer, Electronics or Book Store

or

Send $19.95 each + $2.00 Postage & Handling
(California addresses add 6% sales tax)

Foreign Orders
Payable in U.S. funds on a U.S. bank
Surface: Send $19.95 + $3.00
Allow 6 to 8 weeks for delivery
Air: Send $19.95 + $10.00

TO

COMPUSOFT® PUBLISHING
P.O. Box 19669, Dept. 100a
San Diego, CA 92119

Dealer inquiries welcomed

Educational Discounts available for quantity purchases.

Write for details.

ISBN #0-932760-17-1

Library of Congress #83-72487

Also Available From CompuSoft Publishing:

The BASIC Handbook *Encyclopedia of the BASIC language*
ISBN 0-932760-05-8 $19.95

Learning TRS-80 BASIC *for Models I, II/16 and III*
ISBN 0-932760-08-2 $19.95

Learning IBM BASIC *for the Personal Computer*
ISBN 0-932760-13-9 $19.95

Learning TIMEX/Sinclair BASIC
ISBN 0-932760-15-5 $14.95

Learning TRS-80 Model 4 BASIC
ISBN 0-932760-19-8 $19.95

plus $2.00 Postage and Handling — $3.00 foreign orders

(California addresses add 6% sales tax)

COMPUSOFT® PUBLISHING
P.O. Box 19669, Dept. 100a
San Diego, CA 92119